Deadly Imbalances

*Tripolarity and Hitler's Strategy
of World Conquest*

Randall L. Schweller

Columbia University Press New York

Columbia University Press
Publishers Since 1893
New York   Chichester, West Sussex
Copyright © 1998 Columbia University Press
All rights reserved

Library of Congress Cataloging-in-Publication Data
Schweller, Randall L.
    Deadly imbalances : tripolarity and Hitler's strategy of world
conquest / Randall L. Schweller.
        p.   cm.
    Includes bibliographical references and index.
    ISBN 0–231–11072–3 (cloth : alk. paper). — ISBN 0–231–11073–1
(pbk. : alk. paper)
    1. International relations.   2. Balance of power.   3. Polarity.
I. Title.
JZ1305.S39   1997
327.1'01–dc21   97–22406
                                                                  CIP

Casebound editions of Columbia University Press books are printed on
permanent and durable acid-free paper.
Printed in the United States of America
c 10 9 8 7 6 5 4 3 2 1
p 10 9 8 7 6 5 4 3 2 1

For my parents and for Leah

Contents

Acknowledgments

The theme of this book popped into my head sometime in early 1989, though I cannot remember exactly how or why. Back then, I did not expect that it would take three years longer to complete the book than it took the combatants to fight World War II. As is true of most protracted wars, the original reasons for fighting have long since been forgotten or abandoned by war's end. Through it all, however, my one constant purpose has been to explain the Second World War, to understand what happened and why.

It is a pleasure to acknowledge here the debt I owe to Robert Jervis and Jack Snyder, my Columbia tutors, who communicated to me a lasting interest in the study of international relations. They have been a constant source of insight, good counsel, and encouragement. I am also deeply grateful to Robert G. Kaufman and Glenn H. Snyder, who read the entire manuscript with exceptional care and thoughtfulness; their wide erudition and keenness of mind greatly improved the book.

I owe the most to those persons whose works are cited in the text. The depth and scope of that debt will be apparent to the reader. I only hope that in standing on their shoulders, I have complied with the Chinese direction, and not spat on their heads.

I had a wonderful experience as a graduate student at Columbia University. In particular, I developed cherished friendships with my "comps buddies," Tom Christensen and Jon Mercer, who taught me so much about the field and, more important, about good fellowship. I must note my gratitude to Deborah Welch Larson, who, when I was her research assistant, taught me by example how to research and write scholarly work; and to Edward Mansfield, now my colleague at Ohio State, for his patience and comments early on, when I was attempting to formulate the inchoate ideas that motivated this study. From 1993 to 1994, I had the great fortune to be a National Security Fellow at the Olin Institute for Strategic Studies at Harvard University's Center for International Affairs. In particular, I should like to express my deep gratitude to Professors Samuel Huntington, Stephen Rosen, and Michael Desch for their generosity and friendship. During its crucial phases, the study was sustained by grants from the Mershon Center at The Ohio State University. I especially thank the Directors of the Mershon Center, Richard K. Herrmann and Richard Ned Lebow, for their help in this regard.

I am grateful to Kate Wittenberg at Columbia University Press for believing in the manuscript and for encouraging me to improve it. Leslie Bialler provided expert editorial advice. Alex Coolman assisted in the production of the book. My twin brother, Russell Schweller, offered brilliant editorial suggestions (most of which I took) to strengthen the prose of the introductory chapter. The research assistance of Matthew Diascro and Calvin "Pete" Peterson is much appreciated. Vaughn Shannon prepared the index.

I thank the editors of *International Security* and *International Studies Quarterly* for permission to use a few passages from my articles in those journals in 1993 and 1994.

Above all I am indebted to Catherine Romano for her love and support and for being everything that she is and always will be to me. The book is dedicated to my father, David Schweller, who encouraged me in all I have tried to do, and to the memory of my mother, Linda Schweller, who struggled with great courage against mental and physical illnesses before succumbing to them.

Randall L. Schweller
Columbus, Ohio
June 1997

Deadly Imbalances

Introduction

At the height of its power in the summer of 1942, Hitlerite Germany had enslaved four hundred million people; its empire stretched from the Mediterranean to the Arctic, from the English Channel to the Black Sea and almost to the Caspian. Between the Ukrainian steppes and the Pyrenees only Switzerland remained free. Even Mussolini, whom Hitler once called "the leading statesman in the world,"[1] had been reduced to a pathetic pawn. Far from the turmoil in Europe, Hitler's U-boats were carrying the Nazi offensive to the New World, engaging enemy forces off the Atlantic coast of North America and in the Caribbean Sea.

The enormity of Hitler's ambitions and Nazi brutality had by this time provoked the formation of a global counter-coalition solely aimed at defeating Germany and its Axis partners. All that was asked of any available ally was that it should share faithfully this one major purpose. Among the members of the Allied coalition, however, only the Soviet Union, which had already suffered serious losses the year before, was actively fighting German land forces in Europe. And unlike in 1941, when the *Wehrmacht* had stalled in the snow outside Moscow and Leningrad, the renewed German offensive of 1942 had carried the spearheads of Hitler's panzer armies to Stalingrad and deep into the Caucasus, where they threatened Russia's richest oil fields and, by extension, the Red Army's ability to continue the struggle against Germany.[2]

In short, by mid-1942, Nazi Germany not only threatened to take control of the European Continent but actually appeared on the verge of accomplishing that goal. Had the *Wehrmacht* defeated the Soviet Union before the United States mobilized its awesome war potential, Germany would soon have been in position, after several years of reconfiguring its forces, to wage a truly hegemonic war against the North American Continent. As Gerhard Weinberg observes: "A total reordering of the globe was at stake from the very beginning, and the leadership on both sides recognized this."[3] How have historians and political scientists explained this unprecedented systemic disequilibrium?

Though it is widely believed that structural constraints and pressures played an important role in the origins of the First World War, scholars do not typically associate systemic factors with the outbreak of the Second World War. Hence, while the statesmen of World War I are traditionally imagined as gored on the horns of a structural dilemma, unable to avoid a war that none of them wanted,[4] such a story of external compulsion is rarely told about the leaders of World War II, which evokes not Greek tragedy but an epic morality play driven by a unique cast of "larger than life" characters. The problem with this standard historical account, according to Reinhard Meyers, is that

> the actors in the drama appear only as personified images, no longer as real persons. Those men with the stiff collars appear as the embodiment of character-types reflected in a momentous spectacle—the man of Munich, who confronts the armed might of Germany with an umbrella, draws back in terror and gives way, because he lacks courage and determination. . . . The drama has a villain (Hitler) and a sinner (Chamberlain)—what more does one need to explain the outbreak of war in 1939, especially when the supporting roles are played by lesser villains such as Mussolini and Stalin, and lesser sinners like Beck and Daladier.[5]

Most international relations theorists have similarly adopted this villain/sinner image to explain the origins of World War II. The father of structural realism himself, Kenneth Waltz, at least partially endorses it: "A small-number system can always be disrupted by the actions of a Hitler and the reactions of a Chamberlain. . . . One may lament Churchill's failure to gain control of the British government in the 1930s, for he knew what actions were required to maintain a balance of power."[6] Likewise, prominent game theorists, such as Emerson Niou and Peter Ordeshook, "sympathize . . . with the analyses that interpret Hitler's personality . . . as critical to the outbreak of World War II rather than some breakdown in traditional balance-of-power forces."[7] While John Mueller argues that Hitler alone caused World War II, since "it almost seems that after World War I the only person left in Europe who was willing to risk another total war was Adolf Hitler."[8]

Yet, "to say that the second World War occurred because Hitler wanted war," declares E. H. Carr, "is true enough but explains nothing."[9] At best, it is a flimsy explanation that borders on tautology and, just as important, ignores situational factors that were crucial antecedent causes of the war. Thus, seeking to shed new light on an important case that scholars have come to think of as familiar, this study considers the role of structural causes in the outbreak of World War II. I argue that the structure of the international system prior to the Second World War was tripolar—not multipolar, as commonly believed—and that this needs to be taken into account in explaining the alliance patterns and foreign-policy strategies of the major powers prior to and during the war.[10]

To restrict the analysis to structural elements alone, however, would be just as wrongheaded as the prior pattern of focusing entirely on individual personalities or other unit-level factors. Structural conditions are merely permissive or "profound" causes of specific actions: they allow certain things to happen by providing opportunities for and constraints on actors' behavior.[11] In Waltz's phrase, structure can "tell us a small number of big and important things";[12] it is particularly useful for explaining behavioral regularities and enduring features of international politics; why certain policies succeed or fail; when war will be more or less likely.

But system structure neither determines specific outcomes nor dictates actions, and so it cannot tell us why a particular event occurred at a particular time. In history, the external environment has rarely (if ever) left policymakers with no other choice but to act the way they did. Political leaders in control of significant human and material resources can shape events and change the course of history, though often in directions not foreseen or intended. Sometimes their (in)actions have precipitated war or made it more likely; at other times they have prevented war under conditions favorable to its outbreak. As A. J. P. Taylor puts it: "International anarchy makes war possible; it does not make war certain."[13]

Complex historical events, like the Second World War, cannot be predicted or wholly explained by general causes. As historians are quick to point out, specific events have specific causes. Any interpretation of the origins of the war must therefore include the particular interests and goals of the major actors as specific causes that supplement the more general causes and thereby provide greater determinateness to the explanation. Most historians agree that both objective situations and human agents (their intelligence, heroism, wickedness, and blunders) make history; the two causal levels complement, rather than compete with, each other. Causal disputes, when they are not the result of conflicting appeals to evidence or of basic interpretations of the facts, often turn on the relative weight assigned to the two levels of causation. The "relationship between the given conditions and the policy of statesman," observes F. H. Hinsley, "is not a constant and mechanical relationship. . . . One war may be almost entirely due to the given conditions and hardly at all the consequence of the conduct of the men involved. Another war may be almost entirely due to that conduct."[14] Establishing a hierarchy of causes, the relative significance of one cause or set of causes or of another, which fixes their relation to one another, is the essence of historical interpretation. Different causal judgments tend to reflect, therefore, competing assessments of the interplay among unit- and structural-level factors and the relative weight assigned to each level.

The Causal Role of Hitler?

Let us return to the question of Hitler's role and significance as a cause of World War II. Historians have conventionally viewed the emergence of Hitler as a necessary and sufficient condition for the war. His revisionist aims, they contend, far exceeded those of traditional German statesmen.[15] Thus, while Stresemann and Brüning would have been more than satisfied with the frontiers of 1914, Hitler consistently repudiated them and made it clear that a restoration of the huge gains Germany had made by the Treaty of Brest-Litovsk (1917) would not satisfy him. Furthermore, Hitler's ideas on race and space were not shared by his Weimar predecessors;[16] and his barbaric policies of exterminating and enslaving Jews and the inhabitants of those territories he mapped out for future German "living space" would have been unthinkable to any prior German leader.

Revisionists counter that Hitler did not invent the doctrines of race and space and that he was not the only German of his day who believed in them. Indeed, these were relatively old ideas. Hitler's call for German "living-space" was inspired by nineteenth-century German geopolitics; his vulgarized, racist version of Social Darwinism had, by 1900, gained wide acceptance in Germany, both in academic circles and among the masses; and his claim that Germany had not been defeated in World War I but instead stabbed in the back by Jews or those inspired by Jews was also commonly believed in Germany after Versailles.

Yet, even if we concede that Hitler's ideas distinguished him from prior German leaders (and I believe that they did), the question remains: Was Hitler's ideology or one similar to it necessary for the outbreak of the Second World War? The diversity of interests and ideological concerns that have motivated revolutionary states throughout history suggests that Naziism was not a necessary cause of the war. "Napoleonic France and Hitlerite Germany," notes Gilpin, "gave very different governances to the Europe each united."[17] It is not a specific set of interests or particular ideology that unites and defines all revolutionary states, but rather a shared belief that the status-quo order, which neither serves their interests nor reflects their enhanced power, is illegitimate and must be overturned by force of arms.[18] All German parties and statesmen, for instance, took it for granted that the Treaty of Versailles required drastic revision. Nazi ideology was just one of many possible expressions, albeit an especially vicious anti-Semitic one, of the average German's hostility toward what was perceived as an unduly harsh settlement.

In this regard, the legacy of Versailles was a dangerous imbalance of power that placed Germany in an unnatural position of "artificial inferiority": though denied its "natural weight" by the terms of the treaty, Germany was left intact at the insistence of the Anglo-Saxon powers and remained potentially the strongest power in Europe. Since "Powers will be Powers," Taylor argues, it "was perfectly obvious that Germany would seek to become a Great Power again."[19] Germany, in his view, was a "normal" state: it acted as any other state would have behaved under similar objective conditions.[20] Moreover, Taylor's Hitler was an ordinary, traditional German leader, "no more wicked and unscrupulous than many other contemporary statesmen."[21] He was not a conspirator who planned the war far in advance but rather a "sleepwalker," whose thoughts of becoming master of the world were simply "daydreams."[22] At worst, Taylor's Hitler was a daring improviser, ingeniously exploiting the mistakes and foibles of his feckless opponents. In the end, Hitler stumbled into a world war that he neither intended nor wanted.

We may reject entirely (as most historians have done) Taylor's charitable characterization of Hitler, and yet still agree with his basic argument that "acute structural imbalance" was a sufficient cause of the Second World War. That is, we may concede that Hitler was not a "normal" German statesman, that he intended the Second World War, sought world conquest, and planned for it long in advance, and still conclude that these factors were not necessary causes but rather irrelevant or epiphenomenal to the outcome; at best, they made a highly probable event more likely to occur.

According to this interpretation, an underlying "geopolitical reality" operates in accordance with objective laws such that the outcome (in this case, World War II) could not "logically" have been any different from what it was, regardless of the policies and decisions of human agents. There is some evidence to support this position. For instance, in 1925, long before Hitler arrived on the scene, Sir James Headlam-Morley predicted "a new alliance between Germany and Russia . . . which would no doubt be cemented by an attack on Poland." Remarkably, he goes on to divine the very scenario that led to the outbreak of war: "Austria rejoined Germany; that Germany, using the discontented minority in Bohemia, demanded a frontier far over the mountains, including Carlsbad and Pilsen, and at the same time, in alliance with Germany, the Hungarians recovered the southern slopes of the Carpathians."[23]

Adherents of "geopolitical determinism" claim that structural imbalances made violent change inevitable. The main thrust of their argument is that, unless post-Versailles Germany proved to be an extremely "abnormal" state in an altruistic, self-abnegating sense, it was destined to become a rising, dissatisfied power; and when such states have gained sufficient strength to wage hegemonic wars against the established order, they have done so more often than not. At a minimum, they have threatened or risked war in an attempt to get others to redress their grievances. Given that wars are often not intended but only risked at the time, World War II was an accident waiting to happen. It was only a matter of time before the tension between Germany and its neighbors boiled over; the established powers could do little or nothing to keep the lid on the kettle.

In contrast with this deterministic notion of structure, the conceptual approach taken in this book posits structure as a permissive cause of action, providing the conditions that "let" rather than "make" things happen. According to this view, Hitler, while not a unique figure in history, was hardly a streetcar that arrives at regular intervals. (The same can be said of Stalin, Chamberlain, Churchill, Roosevelt, Mussolini, and Daladier.) The goals and policy decisions of statesmen, sometimes even those of extraordinarily unremarkable ones, can (and often do) exert a profound effect on the course of history, and so human agency must be taken into account. But structure matters too. If Hitler had been the leader of Equador rather than Germany, he could not have started the Second World War. If the United States had not disengaged from Europe and demobilized its armed forces, Hitler would have been denied his "window of opportunity" to grab the Continent. In short, while Hitler may have been a necessary cause of World War II, he was certainly not an altogether sufficient one.

This theoretical approach departs from the conventional international-relations wisdom that cautions against integrating variables at different levels of analysis.[24] It is my belief that if international relations theory continues to be restricted to either structural or unit-level theories, opportunities for further advances in knowledge will be missed. The objective of this book is to break out of these strictures and develop a theoretical framework that recognizes "the necessity of both certain predisposing conditions and the actions of certain individuals"[25]—that is, the complex interrelations between structure and agency. Systems theory is a holistic approach specifically designed to uncover these unit-structure interactions.

Systems Theory and Structure

A system refers to a set of elements interacting to form a whole. "Systemness," as J. David Singer describes it, "is largely in the eye of the beholder; one can look at or imagine an extraordinary diverse range of social, biological, or physical entities and assign them to a system."[26] All that is required of a system is that the component entities be so interrelated as "to make reciprocal impact feasible, if not unavoidable."[27] To say that something is a system is to imply that the whole is different from the sum of the parts. Complex systems, such as the international system, are composed of many parts interacting in a nonsimple way.[28] Four remarks are important in this respect.

First, the behavior and outcomes of such systems are determined by the interplay among the units and the structural environment within which they are embedded; therefore, the dynamics of complex systems cannot be inferred through study of unit or structural attributes alone. Second, straightforward purposive action within a complex system often produces unintended consequences. This is true regardless of whether the initial intention underlying the action is fulfilled or frustrated by the system.[29] Third, consequential transformations in system dynamics do not occur in a linear manner, that is, the effect of variable A on B is not in direct proportion to the magnitude of A. An example of a nonlinear causal relationship would be one in which an initial increase in variable A increases the value of B, but a further increase in the value of A results in either a decrease or no change in the value of B. Fourth, relationships are nonadditive and noncommutative. By "nonadditive" I mean that the combined effect of the system's variables cannot be known by summing the singular effect of each variable.[30] "Noncommutative" refers to the order in which the elements are taken and how that order affects what they combine to produce.

The concept of structure refers to the arrangement or relationship of a set of interrelated elements in a definite pattern of organization within a substance, body, or system. A structural account of international politics should specify (1) the various parts of the system, (2) the relative spatial arrangements of these parts with respect to each other and, sometimes, (3) to other related systems, together with (4) the properties of each part.[31] Since there is some confusion about this last point, let me explain.

Ever since Waltz made the partially correct but misleading statement, "With a reductionist approach, the whole is understood by knowing the attributes and the interactions of its parts,"[32] many students of international politics have mistakenly come to believe that references to the properties and interactions of the units of a system are reductionist and thus do not belong in the definition of structure. While it is true that the whole cannot be known through the study of its parts, neither can the characteristics of a system be known without reference to the properties of its units and how they interact. Suppose we want to know the degree of flexibility of various necklaces.[33] Reductionist analysis, because it derives the characteristics of the whole from those of its parts, would conclude that a pearl necklace will be rigid because pearls are rigid. This type of reductionist argument is clearly false. But it does not follow, as Waltz's definition of structure suggests, that necklaces can be ranked in order of increasing flexibility solely according to the length of the bands and the number of elements without reference to the physical properties of the units. Because the elements must have some degree of rigidity if the band is to be flexible, it matters indeed whether the necklace is composed of pearls, metallic tubes, soft or hard plastic, glass beads, paper, or some combination thereof. One would find that, all other things being equal, a necklace made of pearls will be more flexible than one made of paper.

Applied to international politics, this logic suggests that systems of like structure will behave differently depending on the attributes of the constitutive states. For example, the "post-World War II" bipolar system might not have been characterized by a prolonged Cold War had Britain and the United States—or Germany and the Soviet Union—emerged as the two poles after the war. In all likelihood, an Anglo-American bipolarity would have been relatively peaceful, perhaps even cooperative; whereas a Nazi-Soviet bipolar rivalry might not have remained cold. As should be clear, system dynamics are related to, though not solely determined by, the properties of the constitutive units; they are the product of the interaction of unit-level and structural causes.

A New Balance-of-Power Theory

One reason why unit-level explanations have dominated the literature on World War II is that the predictions of balance-of-power theory—the most widely accepted systems theory of international relations and the cornerstone of realism—are often indeterminate and thus not very useful.[34] In *Theory of International Politics*, Waltz attempts to solve this problem by recasting balance of power in a more rigorous and deductive mold. Operating at a high level of abstraction, Waltz's systems theory addresses broad questions: why balances recurrently form after their disruption; what degree of stability is to be expected of international systems of varying structures; how the constraining effects of structure reduce the variety of behaviors and outcomes, so that balancing behavior results even when no state seeks balance as an end.

Employing an explicit economic analogy, Waltz deduces that anarchic systems, like free markets, form spontaneously and function according to their own internal logic. Unrestrained competition among actors generates benefits unintended by the participants. Most important, self-help systems create dynamic equilibria (i.e., perpetual balances of power in world politics) and are governed by a competitive selection process, similar to natural selection in the theory of evolution. By rewarding and punishing units according to their actions, the system perpetuates successful behavior: actors seeking to survive and thrive imitate the behavior of other successful actors, while those who resist fall by the wayside. Fear of being selected out by the competitive system drives a socialization process that reduces variety (unsuccessful or irrational behavior) by establishing norms and encouraging conformity.[35]

The central hypothesis of the theory concerns the effect of polarity on the stability of the system. Waltz maintains that multipolar systems are inherently unstable because "uncertainties about who threatens whom, about who will oppose whom, about who will gain or lose from the actions of other states accelerate as the number of states increase."[36] Accordingly, bipolarity is the most stable system, since it contains the fewest number of actors required by a balance-of-power system.[37]

Waltz's ideas have been both the intellectual springboard for important research within the structural-realist paradigm[38] and the main target for detractors of neorealism.[39] Some critics of Waltz's theory charge that, in its sacrifice of richness for rigor, structural realism caricatures rather than models classical realism.[40] Others admire the power and elegance of Waltz's theory but complain that, as a systemic-level theory, it is too abstract to generate useful hypotheses about specific foreign-policy behavior, as Waltz readily admits.[41] By sacrificing some of Waltz's parsimony, however, it is possible to turn his theory of international politics into one of foreign policy.

Following Waltz's lead, several recent studies of the Second World War have focused on systemic-level, rather than unit-level, variables.[42] The problem with these studies is that they simply posit a multipolar interwar system containing five or more poles (their causal variable) without first establishing specific criteria for distinguishing polar from nonpolar powers and then measuring the distribution of capabilities to reveal the actual polarity of the system. When these tasks are performed, as in the present study, the international system in 1938 is shown to be a tripolar (not multipolar) system revolving around Germany, the Soviet Union, and the United States.

The goal of this book is twofold: to offer a new, structurally informed interpretation of the origins of World War II and to devise a systems theory that yields determinate balance-of-power predictions. To accomplish these tasks, Waltz's systems theory is modified in two ways. First, the distribution of capabilities is measured not only by the number of Great Powers but also by their relative size. Second, states are identified as either (1) unlimited-aims revisionists, (2) limited-aims revisionists, (3) indifferent toward the status quo, (4) status quo but willing to accept peaceful and limited change, and (5) staunchly status quo and unwilling to accept change of any kind. These two elements, the capabilities and interests of the major powers, are the pillars of traditional realist theory and the basis of my model of international politics, which will be outlined in the following chapters.

Methodology: Expanded Observable Implications

Needless to say, the Second World War was, like all complex and momentous world events, the product of its unique historical moment. As such, it "does not fall neatly into a class of events that could be studied in a systematic comparative fashion through the application of general laws in a straightforward way."[43] To be sure, unique events pose unique methodological and interpretive problems, problems not generally found in the analysis of simple phenomena or common events. Nevertheless, the scientific method can still be applied successfully to explain a singular case study, such as the Second World War. The key is to generate as many observable implications of the theory as possible. This task requires the researcher to ask, "If the world were as I describe it and it worked according to the theoretical principles I have deduced, what would be the observable implications of my theory?"

With regard to the present study, the logic of inference underlying this approach raises the question: "If the structure of the international system was tripolar and the interests of the states were as I claim prior to the Second World War, how should this have affected the behavior of the poles with each other and with the non-polar actors in the drama?" This question yields specific hypotheses, which are then used to direct the way data are collected, organized, and evaluated. The empirical fit of the researcher's paradigm is tested against alternative hypotheses and explanations about the event. The more predictions a theory generates, the more tests we can construct to evaluate it. On this point, King, Keohane, and Verba suggest that one can "disaggregate to shorter time periods or smaller geographic areas. One can also collect information on dependent variables of less direct interest; if the results are as the theory predicts, we will have more confidence in the theory."[44]

In the current study, World War II is disaggregated across space and time into several cases by examining the alliance strategies and foreign policies of all the major powers (Britain, France, Germany, Italy, Japan, the Soviet Union, and the United States) during the period 1934–45. Cutting the data into shorter time periods and smaller geographical areas offers numerous observations against which the implications of the theory can be tested. Specifically, shorter time periods are analyzed by precisely measuring changes in the system's structure that occurred between the years 1933 and 1940, and evaluating whether those structural changes affected the various foreign policies of the major powers in a manner consistent with the predictions of my theory or as predicted by alternative theories of the outbreak of the Second World War. With respect to smaller geographical areas, the system-wide effects predicted by my theory should also be felt within regional systems and specific sets of countries. The logic is straightforward: if the international system was tripolar this should have an observable effect not only on relations among the three poles but also on interactions between poles and second-tier Great Powers and among the lesser great powers (LGPs) themselves. Because the geographical location of states plays an important role in the nature and extent of their interactions with one another, my selection of particular sets of nations to investigate is partly, but not exclusively, guided by geographical considerations.

While disaggregating the tripolar system into its component parts or geographic networks permits more tests of the theory, it means that the data will not be all at the same level of analysis. This practice is conceptually sound, I believe, because the causes of global wars and major-power alliance choices are always a mixture of both regional and systemic motivations and conditions. The world has never simply exploded from peace to system-wide war—the transition always proceeds in stages, slowly diffusing conflict throughout the entire system. This is not to imply that systemic-level factors are unimportant in determining the causes of war and alliances. Rather, it is to suggest that collecting information at both the systemic and regional levels increases our understanding of the effects of structure on a specific country's foreign-policy decisions at any given time. Further, it is one of the few tools available to the researcher of unique events for verifying whether the proposed theory or an alternative one better explains the case.[45]

Goals and Outline of the Book

The story of World War II is not a mystery; there is no surprise ending. The purpose of this book is therefore not to uncover some new fact or set of facts that calls for a radical reinterpretation of the causes of the war. Instead, this study uses basic international relations theory to offer a new explanation for the pattern and sequence of events as we know them. It is my hope that this account is consistent with and complementary to the general historiography on the war. In the process of exploring the case, I have also looked for associations between variables that may be generalizable, with the ultimate goal of theory creation. The limits of my theory will be readily apparent to the reader; needless to say, the model does not explain everything. This is to be expected, for modern science will never devise a theoretical masterkey of history that, with a satisfying click, turns in every lock, opens all its dark chambers, and reveals all its secret workings.[46]

The book proceeds as follows. Chapter 1 lays out the basic variables of the model and operationalizes them for the interwar period. Chapters 2 and 3 develop the hypotheses on tripolar dynamics and alliance patterns respectively that will guide the rest of the study. Chapter 4 applies the theoretical discussion of tripolarity to explain Hitler's diplomatic and military strategy to achieve German world dominion. Chapters 5 and 6 test the various hypotheses generated in chapters 2 and 3 against the alliance behavior and foreign-policy strategies of all the Great Powers prior to and during the war. Chapter 7 summarizes the findings of the study and suggests how they might be relevant to our own increasingly tripolar world.

Chapter 1

The Capabilities and Interests
of the Major Powers

Classical realism centered on two core elements: the capabilities and interests of the great powers. With regard to capabilities, traditional realists did not treat all great powers as equals. Instead, they ranked the great powers as being of the first or second (and sometimes third) tiers. This was and remains an essential task because capability inequalities among the great powers are the very motivation for balance of power theory and practices: they determine whether a balance exists and, when the system is imbalanced, whom the "balance" favors and in what ways states should react. A second focus of attention was the interests (or intentions) of the great powers. The key distinction in this regard was between satisfied defenders of the status quo and dissatisfied revisionist powers bent on overthrowing the established order. Today we might refer to these two types of states as security-maximizers and power-maximizers.

   In contrast, Waltzian neorealism treats all great powers as "like units" in terms of their capabilities and interests. By eliminating this variation, Waltz constructs a new, more elegant and parsimonious version of realism that yields powerful insights about system dynamics and regularities in state behavior. The downside of greater parsimony and elegance, however, is that realism becomes a theory of international politics and not one of foreign policy. Furthermore, Waltz's focus on abstraction and aggregation often obscures both variations in the properties of systems of the same structure and the processes by which states respond to threats and opportunities presented by their external environment. In this chapter, I modify Waltz's theory to account for variations among the great powers. The revised theory more accurately models traditional realism than does neorealism. More important, by trading neorealism's parsimony and rigor for greater richness and more determinate hypotheses about system dynamics and specific state behavior, realist theory and its insights can be applied to a specific case, such as World War II.

Two Modifications of Waltz's Systems Theory

The Distribution of Capabilities

Waltz offers a tripartite theoretical definition of system structure: 1) the ordering principle, either anarchy or hierarchy; 2) the functional differentiation of units; and 3) the distribution of capabilities. He claims that because international politics take place within an anarchic realm and "as long as anarchy endures, states remain like units," international systems differ only along the third dimension, the distribution of capabilities.[1] Waltz operationalizes this dimension by simply counting the number of Great Powers in the system; the total number of Great Powers defines the polarity of the system.

Using this definition of polarity, Waltz distinguishes between only two types of international systems: bipolar and multipolar. Declares Waltz: "Until 1945 the nation-state system was multipolar, and always with five or more powers. In all of modern history the structure of international politics has changed but once. We have only two systems to observe."[2] Historically, however, the resources of the Great Powers have varied considerably and these imbalances often prove decisive in explaining their individual foreign-policy strategies.[3] The key question is, Does it matter that Waltz abstracts considerably from reality?

For Waltz, the answer is clearly no; his theory pertains to the properties of systems, not individual states. For those who would use his theory to explain foreign policy,[4] however, it does pose a problem, as Christensen and Snyder correctly point out.[5] To turn Waltz's ideas into a theory of foreign policy, the descriptive accuracy of the theory must be improved to account for power inequalities among the major actors.

Not surprisingly, recent attempts to apply Waltz's theory to analysis of the post-cold-war system have focused on power asymmetries among the Great Powers. For instance, Mearsheimer states: "Both [bipolar and multipolar] systems are more peaceful when equality is greatest among the poles."[6] Many analysts, however, strongly disagree with this proposition.[7] Niou and Ordeshook conclude that system stability does not require "either a uniform or a highly asymmetric resource distribution."[8] And Wagner and Niou, Ordeshook, and Rose maintain that the most "peaceful distribution" is one in which one actor is "near-predominant"—it controls exactly half of the system's resources.[9]

To specify more fully the distribution of capabilities, I employ a two-step process. First, each Great Power is weighted according to its relative share of the total resources of the major-power subsystem. This measure captures the relative power disparities among the Great Powers and it drives the analysis. By itself, however, it is too unwieldly to be useful as a way to classify different types of systems. To solve this problem, I further divide the Great Powers into two tiers: poles and Lesser Great Powers (hereafter LGPs). To qualify as a pole, a state must have greater than half the military capability of the most powerful state in the system; all other Great Powers are classed as LGPs. In simple terms, my definition of a pole means that the combined strength of any two poles must be enough to defeat a third pole. The further division among Great Powers into two tiers, poles and LGPs, also accords with the commonsense notion that poles must be Great Powers of the first rank. Diplomatic historians of the pre-1945 era frequently spoke of various tiers of Great Powers. Even during the bipolar Cold-War era, a two-tier distinction was intuitively, if not always explicitly, recognized: the fact that the United States and Soviet Union were the poles did not mean that Great Britain, France, Italy, West Germany, and Japan were not Great Powers—they were simply Great Powers of the second rank.

Compared with most states in the system, LGPs possess a considerable amount of military strength. Thus, unlike small states and middle powers, LGPs exert significant influence on the global and regional balances of power by either: (1) stabilizing the system when it is in disequilibrium or (2) when a polar balance exists, playing the role of kingmaker by tipping the scales in favor of one of the poles or coalitions. Yet, as second-ranking Great Powers, they cannot sustain themselves against threatening polar powers exclusively by their own resources of military personnel and material. Consequently, they must choose between either dependence upon the sufferance of a more powerful polar neighbor or reliance upon their own allies. Bondage of some sort is the unavoidable price LGPs have to pay for security. Like all nonpolar powers, LGPs seek external means (allies and/or foreign military and economic aid) to maintain themselves in the face of more powerful neighbors.

Because LGPs often do not possess sufficient resources to provide for their own security, they are typically in a position vis-à-vis potential allies of demanding more assistance than they can provide in return. For this reason, they may be perceived as unattractive alliance partners, unless their geographic position is of such extreme strategic significance that potential allies cannot afford for them to be overrun and controlled by the enemy. Polar powers, by contrast, usually have the option of supporting themselves by either external or internal means or some combination thereof. And because the security of lesser powers generally requires at least one polar ally, poles are well-placed within the system to receive aid.

More precise specification of the distribution of capabilities in the system is better descriptive theory. This is not unimportant, for if Waltz and other theorists have misspecified the distribution of capabilities for certain historical periods their analyses may be flawed. Indeed, because Waltz states that both the 1914 and 1939 systems are multipolar, his analyses of the origins of the First and Second World Wars are contradictory. As Christensen and Snyder correctly point out, under multipolarity "states are said [by Waltz] to be structurally prone to either of two opposite errors that destabilize the balancing system."[10] They go on to show how perceived offensive/defensive advantage under multipolarity explains why states unconditionally balanced in 1914 (as if chained together, once one state went to war, its allies had to follow), while they attempted to ride free on the balancing efforts of others in 1939 (they passed the buck). Christensen and Snyder, however, fall into the same trap as Waltz: They assume that the systems of 1914 and 1939 are structurally comparable (if not entirely the same).

I will argue, instead, that the system changed during the 1930s, moving from multipolarity to tripolarity, and that this partly explains the origins and alliance dynamics of the Second World War. According to data generated by the Correlates of War (COW) project, by 1938 the combined capabilities of the United States, the Soviet Union, and Germany accounted for more than 70 percent of the total power capabilities held by the Great Powers, and this 70 percent share was evenly distributed among the three powers.[11] And yet, while there has been a fair amount of scholarly discussion acknowledging the volatility of the triangular "political" nature of the interwar period—

namely, the ideological battle between fascism, liberal democracy, and communism—the interwar system's tripolar power configuration has gone largely unnoticed. Consequently, structural theories of international politics have ignored the properties of tripolarity,[12] focusing instead on unipolar, bipolar, and multipolar (four-or-more-actor) systems.[13] The general point is that changes of the system, such as the one that occurred between the two world wars, often go undetected when cruder measures of the distribution of capabilities are used.

An important caveat must be made here: statesmen act on their subjective understanding of the distribution of power, and this sometimes diverges from the objective situation. Consequently, as William Wohlforth points out: "If 'power' influences international relations, it must do so through the perceptions of those who act on behalf of the state. The quantitative measures of power used in the literature to test various power theories are thus estimators of perceived power."[14] To the extent that the success of their policies depends on correctly assessing the distribution of power, statesmen will be highly motivated to try to get it right. Of course, some actors will do the job better than others, and occasionally an actor will wildly misperceive the structure. Prior to an actual test of strength, all actors are essentially making informed guesses about each other's relative power; only war can truly clarify the situation.

When perceptions markedly differ from the objective reality, theories based on the objective structure of the system will fail to predict the behavior of those actors that hold these misperceptions. But this fact does not invalidate the usefulness of structural theory, nor does it greatly complicate the analysis. Structural theories can still explain why, given the actor's subjective understanding of the structure, it behaved as it did and why the policy failed. This is because the objective structure inevitably affects the actors whether they perceive it correctly or not. Usually, but by no means in every instance, structure rewards those who pursue policies in accordance with its dictates and punishes (by thwarting their policy aims) those who do not.

The Character of the Units: State Interest

Waltz describes the units as "unitary rational actors, who, at a minimum, seek their own preservation and, at a maximum, drive for universal domination."[15] He further asserts that, for his theory to work, it need not be assumed that "all of the competing states are striving relentlessly to increase

their power," only that some states continue to maintain an interest in preserving themselves.[16] While acknowledging that states do not always seek to
maximize their power, Waltz does not incorporate this variance as a model-
based feature; it simply washes out of the analysis. States are described
instead as like units. This is important for two reasons.

First, the characteristic balancing behavior of Waltz's self-help system is
triggered precisely by states that wish not simply to survive but also to weaken
and destroy other states and, at a maximum, to achieve universal supremacy.[17]
Since Waltz makes no attempt to determine the extent of a state's goals from
its structural position in the system, the catalyst driving his balance-of-power
theory must come from outside the boundaries of his system.[18] Second,
Waltz's theory assumes that systems of the same polarity behave similarly
despite differences in the power-seeking interests of the units. Indeed, the separate effect of structure on the behavior of the system—that is, the effect of
structure apart from unit-level causes and attributes—is the very essence of
his theory. Yet, Stephen Walt convincingly shows that states balance against
threats rather than imbalances of power.[19] This means that changes in unit
interests alone can drastically alter system dynamics and stability.

At bottom, Waltzian neorealism suffers from a status-quo bias: that is,
it views the world solely through the lens of a satisfied established state.[20]
In contrast, traditional realists invariably distinguished between two types
of states: Morgenthau called them imperialistic and status-quo powers;
Schuman employed the terms satiated and unsatiated powers; Kissinger
referred to revolutionary and status-quo states; Carr distinguished satisfied from dissatisfied Powers; Johannes Mattern, among other geopoliticians, divided the world into "have" and "have-nots," Wolfers referred to
status quo and revisionist states; and Aron saw eternal opposition between
the forces of revision and conservation.

Unlike traditional realists, who recognized that the primary goal of some
states is aggrandizement rather than security, contemporary realists typically assume that states are willing to pay high costs and take great risks to
protect the values they possess but will only pay a small price and take low
risks to improve their position in the system.[21] Thus, Joseph Grieco declares
that "states, according to realist theory, are profoundly *defensive* actors."[22]
Similarly, Waltz writes:

> In anarchy, security is the highest end. Only if survival is assured can
> states safely seek such other goals as tranquility, profit, and power.

Because power is a means and not an end, states prefer to join the weaker of two coalitions. . . . If states wished to maximize power, they would join the stronger side. . . . [t]his does not happen because balancing, not bandwagoning, is the behavior induced by the system. The first concern of states is not to maximize power but to maintain their positions in the system.[23]

Waltz is right to say that states seeking to maximize their power will bandwagon, not balance. But it is simply not true that the first concern of *all* states is security.[24] Here, he takes a distinctly status-quo perspective.[25] Only in reference to satisfied countries can it be said that the primary goal is "to maintain their positions in the system."[26] In contrast, classical Realists described the "true interests" of states as "a continuous striving for greater power and expansion." For them, the goal of diplomacy was "to evaluate correctly the interplay of opposing forces and interests and to create a constellation favorable to conquest and expansion."[27]

Preventing relative losses in power and prestige is sound advice for satisfied states that seek, above all, to keep what they have. But staying in place is not the primary goal of revisionist states. They want to increase their values and to improve their position in the system. These goals cannot be achieved simply by ensuring that everyone else does not gain relative to them. They must gain relative to others; and throughout history states striving for greater relative power, often driven by prestige demands for their rightful "place at the table" or "place in the sun," have routinely sacrificed their security in such a quest.[28] As Raymond Aron points out: "All great states have jeopardized their survival to gain ulterior objectives. Hitler preferred, for himself and for Germany, the possibility of empire to the security of survival. Nor did he want empire—or an accumulation of power—as a means to security."[29]

Calling for a New Order, dissatisfied states are attracted to expanding revisionist powers. Waltz overlooks such states when he asserts: "Secondary states, if they are free to choose, flock to the weaker side; for it is the stronger side that threatens them. On the weaker side they are both more appreciated and safer[.]"[30] States are safer on the weaker side? This is a curious claim. Are they also more appreciated by the weaker side?

Consider, for instance, the case of Italy in 1936. Mussolini believed that he would be more appreciated and politically autonomous as Hitler's satellite than as a member of the weaker Anglo-French coalition. Unlike Britain and France, Nazi Germany supported Mussolini's goal of turning the Mediterranean into an "Italian Lake."[31] Moreover, Mussolini's decision to hitch Italy's wagon to the rising Nazi star was motivated by his raw Social-Darwinist predilections. As Alan Cassels asserts, "Fascists worshipped strength, and what Mussolini called a fascist foreign policy meant in effect siding with the strongest power."[32]

In the end, Italy paid a high price for siding with Germany. It did not prove to be the safer choice, but not because Italy joined the stronger coalition, as Waltz's logic would have us believe. To the contrary, Italy was crushed because, after the U.S. actively entered the war, it was on the weaker side.

The general point is that most states, even of the Great-Power variety, must ultimately serve someone: only "top dogs" can expect otherwise. And because members of military alliances always sacrifice some foreign-policy autonomy, the most important determinant of alignment decisions is the compatibility of political goals, not imbalances of power or threat.[33] Satisfied powers join the status-quo coalition, even when it is the stronger side; dissatisfied powers, motivated by profit more than security, bandwagon with an ascending revisionist state.

For these reasons, I treat the power preferences of the actors as a model-based feature that both differentiates the units of the system and, as a result, systems of the same structure. By relaxing neorealism's assumption that states value what they possess more than what they covet, the full range of state interest emerges: some states value what they covet more than what they have; others are entirely satisfied with their possessions; still others value what they have only slightly more than what they covet, and vice versa; and some states consider their possessions to be meager but are not envious of others.

We may conceptualize this range of state interest in the following way. Let x be the costs a given state is willing to pay to defend the status quo; and y be the costs the same state is willing to pay to revise it;[34] and let x and y range from 0 to n. The state's interest can then be represented as $x - y$ and will fall somewhere on the horizontal axis in Figure 1.1 (below). In this formulation, the concept of state interest is treated as a continuous variable that, in theory, can take on all possible numerical values in a given interval. For the purpose of analysis, however, it is useful to simplify somewhat by viewing the concept as an orderable discrete variable in which (in this case) five categories are arranged from smallest to largest.

States residing at the extreme positive end of the scale are staunchly in support of the status quo and will resist, with all of their resources, any modification of it for fear that even a small change will cause the whole existing

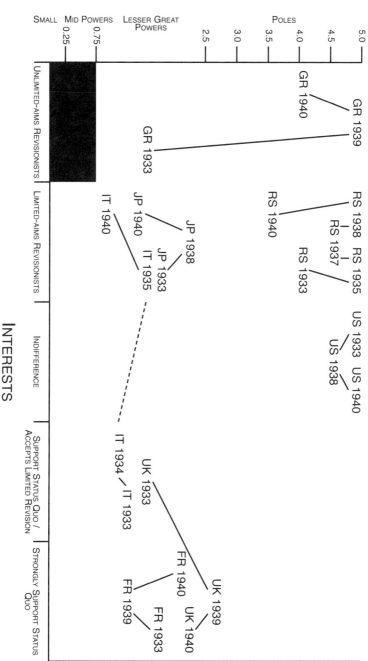

CAPABILITY

RELATIVE POWER: TOP SCORE=5

FIGURE 1.1

order to unravel. These are usually states that won the last major-power war and created a new world order in accordance with their interests by redistributing territory and prestige.[35] As satiated powers, these staunchly status-quo powers seek to protect the established order and to maintain their relative position; for them, the costs of nonsecurity expansion exceed the gains.

Immediately to the left of this category are satisfied states that support limited and peaceful revision of the status quo in order to satisfy the legitimate claims of unsatisfied states and thereby preserve the essential characteristics of the existing international order. States that fall in the middle of the scale are indifferent toward the status quo and generally seek to avoid the costs of either maintaining or modifying it. To the left of these states are what I call "limited-aims" revisionist states. These states either do not have the capabilities to aspire to anything more than limited revision and/or value some aspects of the existing order but want to modify it to their advantage. Though generally complaining about their treatment by the established powers, these states will, under certain circumstances, support the status quo. At the extreme end of the scale are "unlimited-aims" revisionists, which aspire to conquer the world (or a large portion of it) and so must be great powers of the first rank.

By dividing states into five distinct categories, this scheme takes into account the very real and important difference between a state that is somewhat revisionist and one that is truly **revisionist**; and between status-quo and doggedly **status-quo** states. It is worth pointing out, however, that the scheme is still based on the traditional realist classification of states as either satisfied or dissatisfied. Status-quo states are security maximizers (as opposed to power-maximizers), whose goal is to preserve the resources they already control. The statement by Britain's First Lord of the Admiralty in June 1934, for instance, precisely captures the interests of a status-quo power: "We are in the remarkable position of not wanting to quarrel with anybody because we have got most of the world already or the best parts of it and we only want to keep what we have got and prevent others from taking it away from us."[36] Revisionist states, by contrast, seek to undermine the established order for the purpose of increasing their power and prestige in the system; that is, they seek to increase, not just to maintain, their resources. For these states, the gains from nonsecurity expansion exceed the costs of war.[37] Revisionist states are often those states that have increased their power "after the existing international order was fully established and the benefits were already allocated."[38] Thus, they often share a common desire to overturn the status quo order—the prestige, resources, and principles of the system.

Revisionist states are not always actively engaged in overturning the status quo; they may be temporarily passive because they lack the relative economic, military, and/or political capabilities needed to challenge the protector(s) of the status quo (examples of revisionist states are the Soviet Union, 1919–39; Germany, 1919–36; and Japan, 1919–31). Buzan points out, "even the most rabid revisionist state cannot pursue its larger objectives if it cannot secure its home base."[39] It should also be noted that revisionist states need not be predatory powers; they may oppose the status quo for defensive reasons. As Schuman comments, revisionist states typically "feel humiliated, hampered, and oppressed by the *status quo*" and thus "demand changes, rectifications of frontiers, a revision of treaties, a redistribution of territory and power" to modify it.[40]

To some readers, it may appear that the pairing between security-maximizing and power-maximizing is illogical, for power is a *means* to security and other goals; so-called power-maximizers are really maximizers of prestige, economic wealth, and other values parallel to security. Further, as realists correctly point out, the logic of anarchy means that power is the fundamental feature of international politics; it is the ultimate basis for any state aim, whether it seeks world mastery or simply to be left alone. I fully concur with the notion that power and security are often complementary goals; but sometimes they are not. Excessive accumulations of power can make a state less secure, and too much emphasis on security can weaken a state's overall power. The distinction I am trying to make between power-maximizing and security-maximizing is a traditional and commonsense one; it is the difference between the goal of making gains and that of avoiding losses.

By elevating the concept of state interest to an equally prominent position as that occupied by the distribution of capabilities, the model more accurately reflects the twin-pillared aspect of traditional realist theory—its equal focus on both the power and interests of states. Unlike Waltz's theory, which is all structure and no units, the revised theory contains complex unit-structure interactions, such that predictions are codetermined by the power and interests of the units and the structures within which they are embedded. Because neither level is "ontologically primitive," the theory offers a partial solution to the agent-structure problem raised by Wendt.[41]

Other factors, such as geography, military technology, and misperception of structure, might be added to the theory.[42] While these elements will be mentioned when necessary, I do not fully incorporate them within the model. To do otherwise, I believe, would be to unnecessarily complicate the theory, since it is my contention that these factors are generally less important than the power and interests of the units—without which geography and military technology provide only partial answers. Supporting this view, Posen has tested hypotheses on geography and military technology against the military doctrines of interwar France, Britain, and Germany, and he concluded that these factors alone are indeterminate.[43]

To this point, I have defined the two essential elements of a systems theory of international politics as the structure of the system and the power-seeking interests of the units. The relative sizes of the Great Powers determine the structure of the system. At the unit level, states are identified according to their level of support for or dissatisfaction with the status quo. By including both unit and structural attributes in the definition of the international system, what emerges is both a positional and ideational model of system structure. That is, the theory derives hypotheses about system stability and state behavior based on the arrangement of the units and their interests or identities.

Operationalizing the Variables for the Case:

1. Capabilities of the Major-Powers Between the Wars

Data from the Correlates of War (COW) project is used to measure the relative capabilities of the major powers. I have chosen the COW Capability data set for two reasons. First, the present study is concerned with the relative "fighting capabilities" of states. The COW measures stress is on military forces-in-being, which is appropriate for the present analysis. It will be shown that statesmen, in choosing their course of action, responded to the current balance of power: e.g., by 1937, Hitler saw Germany's military advantage as a wasting asset and so decided to wage a series of offensive wars before his window of opportunity closed; that the United States could have extracted far more resources from its economy than it had by 1938 provided little comfort to Britain and France in 1940 and the Soviet Union in 1941.

Though it will remain a debatable point, I believe that the measures comprising the COW index provide a reasonably accurate picture of the power bases held by the major actors with respect to their relative fighting capabilities. Originally a skeptic myself, I arrived at this view after having constructed my own "capability-index formula" (see the appendix to the book) to test the validity and reliability of the COW numbers for the period 1938–40. My formula consists of ten separate power indices—eight of which are not used in the COW capability index—that attempt to measure the critical mass (population and territory), economic war potential, and military capabilities of the Great Powers. The result of this mini-experiment was that the Great-Power capability shares yielded by my index are virtually identical to those given by the COW index.

Second, because the COW index is the most widely used and available data set, skeptics should have no difficulty in checking my results. By using the COW capability index, I have attempted to minimize criticism of my study on the basis of measurement alone. That said, I am under no illusion that one can entirely eliminate criticism along these lines, regardless of what measures are chosen. Nevertheless, structural-realist studies demand specification in one way or another of the relative capabilities of the major actors, and for this task there are simply too many disadvantages in relying solely on my own or some other, more obscure index. I am confident in the descriptive accuracy of my own power index, however, and the reader may, if s/he so chooses, substitute it for the COW index.

COW capability scores reflect three distinct measures of national power: 1) military (forces in-being), 2) industrial (war potential), and 3) demographic (staying power and war-augmenting capability). Each component is divided into two subcomponents. The military dimension consists of the number of military personnel and military expenditures; the industrial component is measured by production of pig iron (pre-1900) or ingot steel (post-1900) and fuel consumption; and the demographic component is divided into urban and total population. The composite power index is the sum of each state's mean score for the six measures as a percentage of all scores within the Great-Power subset.

Table 1.1 provides the following data for all seven major powers for the years 1930 through 1940: (1) their percentage shares for each of the six components; (2) their overall strength as a percentage share of total major-power capabilities; and (3) their relative strengths represented as a power ratio with 5 as the top score.

Table 1.2 shows the relative strengths of the major powers from 1933 to 1940. As the data indicate, prior to 1935, the international system was bipolar, with the United States and the Soviet Union as the two poles. The remaining major powers were LGPs, but Germany was on the verge of attaining polar status. Britain and France, which possessed far less than half the capabilities

TABLE 1.1
Percentage Distribution of the COW Index Among the Major Powers, 1930-1940

		Military Strength		Economic Strength		Population		Overall Strength[1]	Relative Strength[2]
		Personnel	Expendit	Energy Consump	Iron & Steel Prod	Urban Pop	Total Pop		
USA	1930	11.19%	11.90%	55.77%	56.21%	32.41%	23.08%	31.76%	5.00
	1931	11.02%	11.93%	53.51%	60.37%	31.64%	22.95%	31.90%	5.00
	1932	10.28%	14.68%	51.24%	45.76%	30.80%	22.79%	29.26%	5.00
	1933	8.89%	11.85%	51.65%	55.16%	29.94%	22.64%	30.02%	5.00
	1934	8.13%	11.52%	50.31%	50.98%	29.05%	22.54%	28.76%	5.00
	1935	5.39%	7.86%	50.13%	40.81%	28.17%	22.46%	25.81%	4.95
	1936	7.52%	9.80%	51.58%	44.10%	27.23%	22.37%	27.10%	5.00
	1937	7.48%	8.54%	50.80%	43.57%	26.26%	22.30%	26.49%	5.00
	1938	7.20%	5.89%	46.23%	30.32%	25.40%	22.25%	22.88%	4.58
	1939	4.52%	3.24%	50.23%	39.80%	25.17%	22.35%	24.22%	5.00
	1940	2.76%	3.52%	52.88%	49.77%	25.09%	22.31%	26.06%	5.00
UK	1930	13.90%	8.71%	13.47%	0.60%	16.37%	8.65%	10.28%	1.60
	1931	13.90%	8.35%	14.18%	0.65%	15.94%	8.55%	10.26%	1.60
	1932	13.30%	7.47%	14.98%	1.14%	15.46%	8.49%	10.14%	1.70
	1933	11.51%	6.92%	14.10%	0.32%	14.97%	8.41%	9.37%	1.56
	1934	10.46%	7.74%	14.09%	1.91%	14.46%	8.35%	9.50%	1.65
	1935	6.87%	6.30%	13.61%	11.80%	13.92%	8.30%	10.13%	1.94
	1936	8.68%	9.38%	13.10%	10.88%	13.35%	8.25%	10.61%	1.96
	1937	8.39%	10.30%	12.69%	11.19%	12.90%	8.21%	10.61%	2.00
	1938	8.39%	9.71%	13.05%	11.12%	12.44%	8.17%	10.48%	2.10
	1939	5.33%	26.10%	13.37%	11.16%	12.28%	8.17%	12.74%	2.60
	1940	6.16%	21.11%	12.72%	10.80%	12.22%	8.09%	11.85%	2.27
FR	1930	17.97%	8.48%	7.14%	12.84%	5.75%	7.82%	10.00%	1.57
	1931	19.22%	8.45%	7.31%	17.90%	5.65%	7.74%	11.05%	1.72
	1932	17.70%	12.43%	7.19%	18.57%	5.47%	7.64%	11.50%	1.96

TABLE 1.1 (CONTINUED)

		Military Strength		Economic Strength		Population		Overall Strength[1]	Relative Strength[2]
		Personnel	Expendit	Energy Consump	Iron & Steel Prod	Urban Pop	Total Pop		
	1933	16.35%	10.89%	7.09%	15.37%	5.29%	7.55%	10.42%	1.73
	1934	15.07%	10.15%	6.47%	11.85%	5.10%	7.48%	9.35%	1.62
	1935	11.73%	8.46%	5.92%	7.37%	4.90%	7.40%	7.63%	1.46
	1936	15.19%	10.46%	5.49%	6.08%	4.70%	7.32%	8.21%	1.51
	1937	14.70%	7.36%	5.62%	6.69%	4.49%	7.26%	7.69%	1.45
	1938	12.96%	4.79%	5.60%	6.46%	4.31%	7.18%	6.88%	1.37
	1939	7.87%	3.38%	5.13%	6.61%	4.26%	7.14%	5.73%	1.18
	1940	30.18%	12.11%	4.58%	0.34%	4.24%	7.03%	9.75%	1.80
GR	1930	4.98%	2.77%	13.01%	17.04%	17.34%	11.12%	11.04%	1.73
	1931	4.97%	2.51%	12.23%	0.67%	17.05%	11.31%	8.12%	1.27
	1932	4.78%	3.42%	12.21%	2.54%	16.71%	11.53%	8.53%	1.45
	1933	4.30%	9.39%	12.05%	1.44%	16.34%	11.76%	9.21%	1.53
	1934	10.37%	10.17%	12.45%	22.96%	15.94%	11.76%	13.94%	2.42
	1935	9.87%	15.68%	12.58%	19.38%	15.50%	11.76%	14.13%	2.71
	1936	15.40%	24.51%	12.65%	17.45%	15.05%	11.77%	16.14%	2.97
	1937	14.46%	27.28%	13.22%	16.83%	14.54%	11.74%	16.35%	3.08
	1938	17.44%	38.61%	15.11%	23.84%	14.10%	11.76%	20.14%	4.03
	1939	37.23%	39.67%	17.31%	20.37%	15.74%	13.55%	23.98%	4.95
	1940	19.92%	44.98%	16.50%	18.27%	16.66%	14.32%	21.77%	4.17
IT	1930	14.56%	4.53%	1.77%	2.37%	6.19%	7.72%	6.19%	0.97
	1931	13.68%	5.09%	1.79%	3.23%	6.24%	7.66%	6.28%	0.98
	1932	14.85%	6.47%	1.76%	4.60%	6.16%	7.62%	6.91%	1.18
	1933	13.22%	7.30%	1.82%	4.14%	6.07%	7.59%	6.69%	1.11
	1934	11.91%	6.54%	1.98%	3.56%	5.97%	7.57%	6.25%	1.08
	1935	29.54%	5.01%	2.08%	0.25%	5.85%	7.56%	8.38%	1.60
	1936	8.86%	12.08%	1.55%	1.84%	5.73%	7.54%	6.27%	1.15
	1937	11.18%	10.22%	1.78%	1.77%	5.58%	7.53%	6.34%	1.20

TABLE 1.1 (CONTINUED)

		Military Strength		Economic Strength		Population			
		Personnel	Expendit	Energy Consump	Iron & Steel Prod	Urban Pop	Total Pop	Overall Strength[1]	Relative Strength[2]
	1938	10.84%	3.88%	1.84%	2.44%	5.45%	7.52%	5.33%	1.06
	1939	7.87%	2.21%	1.77%	1.90%	5.46%	7.51%	4.45%	0.92
	1940	9.86%	1.29%	1.63%	0.21%	5.49%	7.42%	4.32%	0.83
USSR	1930	24.57%	59.88%	4.76%	7.83%	12.24%	29.51%	23.13%	3.64
	1931	24.49%	59.88%	6.58%	12.87%	13.49%	29.68%	24.50%	3.84
	1932	23.57%	50.97%	7.76%	19.51%	14.82%	29.79%	24.40%	4.07
	1933	32.23%	49.08%	8.37%	16.10%	16.24%	29.90%	25.32%	4.22
	1934	30.93%	49.90%	9.50%	1.33%	17.75%	30.11%	23.25%	4.04
	1935	27.83%	53.81%	10.28%	14.85%	19.35%	30.30%	26.07%	5.00
	1936	33.59%	30.83%	10.77%	14.90%	21.05%	30.50%	23.61%	4.35
	1937	34.36%	28.50%	10.46%	15.03%	22.79%	30.74%	23.65%	4.46
	1938	34.92%	28.27%	11.77%	19.00%	24.77%	30.95%	24.95%	5.00
	1939	24.22%	19.78%	12.19%	14.60%	23.40%	29.10%	20.55%	4.24
	1940	25.35%	13.04%	11.69%	15.00%	22.44%	28.70%	19.37%	3.71
JP	1930	12.81%	3.72%	4.08%	3.11%	9.70%	12.11%	7.59%	1.19
	1931	12.72%	3.79%	4.39%	4.31%	9.99%	12.11%	7.89%	1.23
	1932	15.52%	4.56%	4.86%	7.89%	10.57%	12.13%	9.25%	1.58
	1933	13.51%	4.57%	4.93%	7.47%	11.15%	12.16%	8.96%	1.49
	1934	13.13%	3.99%	5.19%	7.40%	11.73%	12.19%	8.94%	1.55
	1935	8.78%	2.88%	5.39%	5.54%	12.31%	12.22%	7.85%	1.50
	1936	10.75%	2.94%	4.85%	4.75%	12.89%	12.25%	8.07%	1.48
	1937	9.42%	7.79%	5.43%	4.92%	13.44%	12.23%	8.87%	1.67
	1938	8.25%	8.85%	6.40%	6.81%	13.52%	12.17%	9.33%	1.86
	1939	12.96%	5.62%	0.00%	5.56%	13.69%	12.19%	8.34%	1.72
	1940	5.78%	3.95%	0.00%	5.62%	13.86%	12.12%	6.89%	1.32

1. Percent Share of Major Power Subset.
2. Top Score = 5.

TABLE 1.2
The Relative Strengths of the Major Powers
(with Percentage Share of the Major Power Capabilities).

Year	US	USSR	Germany	UK	France	Italy	Japan
1933	5.00	4.22	1.53	1.56	1.73	1.11	1.49
	(30.02)	(25.32)	(9.21)	(9.37)	(10.42)	(6.69)	(8.96)
1934	5.00	4.04	2.42	1.65	1.62	1.08	1.55
	(28.76)	(23.25)	(13.94)	(9.50)	(9.35)	(6.25)	(8.94)
1935	4.95	5.00	2.71	1.94	1.46	1.60	1.50
	(25.81)	(26.07)	(14.13)	(10.13)	(7.63)	(8.38)	(7.85)
1936	5.00	4.35	2.97	1.96	1.51	1.15	1.48
	(27.10)	(23.61)	(16.14)	(10.61)	(8.21)	(6.27)	(8.07)
1937	5.00	4.46	3.08	2.00	1.45	1.20	1.67
	(26.49)	(23.65)	(16.35)	(10.61)	(7.69)	(6.34)	(8.87)
1938	4.58	5.00	4.03	2.10	1.37	1.06	1.86
	(22.48)	(24.95)	(20.14)	(10.48)	(6.88)	(5.33)	(9.33)
1939	5.00	4.24	4.95	2.60	1.18	.92	1.72
	(24.22)	(20.55)	(23.98)	(12.74)	(5.73)	(4.45)	(8.34)
1940	5.00	3.71	4.17	2.27	1.80	.83	1.32
	(26.06)	(19.37)	(21.77)	(11.85)	(9.75)	(4.32)	(6.89)

SOURCES: I have compiled the data using the "Correlates of War Capability Data Set Printout" from July 1990.

of the most powerful state in the system (the U.S.), had fallen from the first to the second tier of Great Powers, which also included Japan and Italy.

By 1935, the bipolar system evolved into a tripolar system, as Germany attained weak third-pole status. During this early stage of rearmament, Germany would require allies to counterbalance either of the other two poles. By 1938, German strength had substantially increased, creating a virtual equilateral tripolar system, in which all three poles possessed roughly equal shares of between 20 and 25 percent of total Great-Power capabilities and were far stronger than any of the other major powers.

2. Interests of the Major Powers Between the Wars

The Revisionist Powers

Germany

The Treaty of Versailles cut back Germany's frontiers in the east, forbade its union with Austria in the south, and demilitarized a large industrial area in the west. It imposed severe limits on the size of Germany's armed forces and prohibited certain weapons and activities entirely. It imposed on Germany what were called economic "reparations" (rather than "indemnities"), which covered all the war costs of Belgium, the future costs of the other allies for reconstruction, and payments to survivors of those killed in battle. Lastly, it stripped Germany of all its colonies, which were placed into a newly devised category of "mandates" under the control of Britain, France, Japan, South Africa, New Zealand, and Australia.[44]

The French demand for permanent military control of the Rhineland, however, was denied by the British and Americans. Instead, the treaty provided only for the temporary military occupation of the Rhineland by allied troops and for its permanent demilitarization. To this, the Anglo-Saxon countries added a guarantee to assist the French in the event of an unprovoked German attack. These treaties, however, never became effective, leaving France without even its second-best solution to its security problem.

From the start, Germany was determined to overthrow the established order of Versailles. Unlike Nazi Germany, however, Weimar Germany was a limited-aims revisionist power, seeking only to free Germany from the "shackles of Versailles." Even Gustav Stresemann, who inaugurated the policy of *rapprochement* with France and at Locarno waived German claims to Alsace and Lorraine, agreed to the permanent demilitarization of the Rhineland. He promised that Germany would not use force to change its boundaries in the east, but was determined to revise the most unjust and untenable provisions of the Versailles settlement. Stresemann believed that evidence of Germany's "good behavior" would gradually allay France's fears and pave the way toward substantial concessions.[45]

When Hitler arrived on the scene, Germany became an unlimited-aims revisionist power: it set out to conquer the world or, at a minimum, a large portion of it. Hitler's actions were designed not to enhance Germany's security but rather to increase its power; he viewed the Reich's possessions as meager, and so would risk very little to protect them. Consider, for instance, the logic of the Nazi-Soviet nonaggression pact from Germany's perspective. Esmonde M. Robertson writes:

> Virtually all of Lithuania, previously a vital German interest, was to pass to the Soviet sphere of influence. The two remaining Baltic states, and even Finland, were to be included in the Soviet sphere. Bialystok in northern Poland, which was valued for its timber as well as the oil wells east of the San in the south, together with the town of Lemberg, which had a strong Germany minority, were to be handed over to the

Russians. . . . That the Soviet Union should have a free gift of territory conquered for it by the German army and in which Germany had either cultural or economic interests, was regarded as preposterous by the opponents of the regime. . . . There can be little doubt that for the immediate future Stalin seemed to have gained more from the treaty than Hitler. He could now strengthen the Soviet Union's military economy and raise the striking power of the Red Army. The additional territories in the west moreover made it possible for him . . . to adopt a strategy of defense in depth.[46]

The far-reaching concessions made by Hitler in the Nazi-Soviet pact are inconsistent with neorealism's central claim that states are security-maximizers that seek relative, not absolute, gains. If ever there was an "easy case" for confirming the hypothesis that concern for relative gains inhibits cooperation, this was it: two powerful, greedy, untrustworthy states, in close geographic proximity to one another, whose regimes had recently pilloried each other as the negation of everything for which the other stood. For these reasons, even if the agreement had not contained relative gains for the Soviet Union, most realists would not have predicted cooperation between these two states.

By allowing the Soviets to make relative gains *vis-à-vis* Germany, Hitler defied neorealist logic: he decreased Germany's security, at least over the short run. This is not surprising, however, since Hitler's foreign policy was driven not by security but instead by his obsession to become master of Europe and then the world. To change the status quo for Germany, Hitler was willing to pay high costs and take great risks. If this meant that deals had to be struck by which Germany gained relatively less than its partners in crime, so be it. Of course, Hitler understood that these gaps in gains benefiting Germany's partners carried the risk of decreasing the Reich's security. But then, states do not wage apocalyptic wars if they are unwilling to put their security—indeed, their survival—at risk. As Hillgruber put it, "the sentence printed in bold-face letters in *Mein Kampf*, 'Germany will either be a world power or there will be no Germany,' was, quite literally, the crux of Hitler's program."[47]

The Soviet Union

One of the original allies in the war against Germany, Russia was not even invited to the Versailles Peace Conference. The Bolsheviks, who had gained power in November 1917, pulled Russia out of the war on March 1918, when they signed a peace treaty dictated by Germany. Russia's withdrawal from the war facilitated Germany's final bid for total victory. The Western allies would never forgive the Bolsheviks, whom they despised anyway, for this treachery.

Driven by a universalistic ideology of revision, the Soviet Union struggled for many years after the peace to gain influence on the Continent, to undermine the social order of Western Europe, and to promote world revolution. It should not be surprising, therefore, that the victors would treat Soviet Russia as a "pariah state" and cast it along with Germany out of the society of Europe. The weakness of the new Bolshevik regime, however, dictated a defensive posture in foreign affairs that was obscured by the workings of the Comintern. Revision remained a long-term Soviet goal; but over the short term, Russia was in no position to attempt any provocative moves. Indeed, Soviet foreign policy throughout the interwar period was characterized by extreme caution lest the capitalist powers gang up on the Bolsheviks rather than fighting each other. The most the Soviets could hope for was low risk, limited revision for essentially defensive purposes. Stalin planned to accomplish this by making sure that the Soviet Union sat out the next capitalist war, and that one side paid heavily for Russia's benevolent neutrality.

The defensive nature of Soviet foreign policy was particularly evident during the period 1933–35, when world events and a pervasive sense of insecurity combined to force the Soviet Union into championing the themes of collective security, universal disarmament, and cooperation with the democratic West. Specifically, Soviet foreign policy was driven by two events: (1) the deterioration in Japanese-Soviet relations following Japan's invasion of Manchuria in 1931, which escalated into a quasi-war along the Soviet Union's relatively undefended Far East borders[48] and (2) the ten-year nonaggression pact between Poland and Germany concluded in January 1934, and ostensibly directed against the USSR.[49]

Isolated and alarmed by the possibility of a two-front war against Japan in the East and a German-Polish combination in the West, the Soviets cynically declared their support for the status quo and their desire for cooperation with the Western democracies. This policy partially bore fruit on May 2, 1935, when the Soviet Government concluded a mutual assistance pact with France. The pact was rendered virtually meaningless, however, by an accompanying protocol that protected France from any commitment that might bring it into conflict with Britain. For France, the real obstacle to an alliance (or any cooperation) with the Soviets was the aversion of both Britain, upon whom France was absolutely dependent and whose relations with Russia were dominated by the widespread hostility of the Conservatives to Bolshevism, and of the members of the Little Entente (particularly Romania) and Poland, who feared the Soviet Union more than Germany. The half-hearted French policy toward the Soviet Union and continued distrust of the Soviets among the rest of the major powers was clearly demonstrated by the exclusion of the Soviet Union, an ally of both France and Czechoslovakia, from the Munich Conference in 1938.

Japan and Italy

Both of these lesser great powers were limited-aims revisionist states. Though technically victors in the First World War, Rome and Tokyo left Versailles feeling so betrayed that they could not be relied upon to defend the new order. Soon after the settlement both states began undertaking military preparations for naked revisionist assaults against it. At Versailles, the Italians resented the way the allies had concluded the Sykes-Picot Agreement behind their backs; they were further annoyed when Yugoslavia, largely comprised of Croats and Slovenes from the former enemy, the Austro-Hungarian empire, was accorded preferential treatment (Fiume was assigned to Croatia) over Italy. On May 25, 1919, the Italian Prime Minister told the British:

> I cannot look forward without grave apprehensions to the future of continental Europe; the German longing for revenge must be considered in conjunction with the Russian position. We can thus see even now that the settlement to be arrived at will lack the assent of more than half the population of the European continent. If we detach from the block on which the new European system will have to rely for support forty million Italians, and force them into the ranks of the malcontents, do you think that the new order will rest on a firm basis?[50]

The danger of which the Italian Prime Minister warned eventually came to pass. By the 1930s, both Italy and Japan had substantially increased their military power and both sought to expand beyond their present territorial borders. It was Japan that unleashed the initial blow against the established order in 1931; Italy followed with its attack against Abyssinia in 1935.[51] Imperial Japan strove for regional hegemony over East Asia, announcing the so-called "New Order" in 1938; while Mussolini tried to create a second Roman Empire by securing limited aims in the Mediterranean, the Balkans, and Africa.

The Status-Quo Powers

France and Britain

The Versailles settlement represented a compromise between the divergent views held by Britain and France regarding how best to preserve the newly established and fragile peace. The French staunchly supported the status quo, believing that only a clear preponderance of power on the side of the status-quo defenders and a firm, demonstrated resolve to use that power to enforce strictly the terms of the Treaty in its entirety would prevent a revolt by the dissatisfied powers. Most important, the French strategy called for containment and deterrence of Germany by ensuring that France maintained superior power over its potentially stronger and inherently aggressive neighbor.

In contrast, British policy attempted to eliminate the danger of a new European explosion by removing the causes of revolt. "This meant," as Arnold Wolfers describes, "taking the new order merely as a starting point in a process of continuous adjustment, intended eventually to produce a new and more generally satisfactory settlement."[52] In adopting a benevolent "engagement" strategy toward the revisionist powers, Britain hoped to moderate the course of change and render it less provocative. Peaceful and limited revision, the British believed, would reconcile the dissatisfied states with the essential framework of the established order and convert them into status-quo powers.

For Britain, the legacy of Versailles was a sense of guilt. Many Englishmen shared John Maynard Keynes's fear that the Treaty's harsh terms "might impoverish Germany now or obstruct her development in the future."[53] "Ashamed at what they had done," Gilbert and Gott suggest, the British "looked for scapegoats, and for amendment. The scapegoat was France; the amendment was appeasement. . . . France was blamed for having encouraged Britain in an excess of punishment. Justice could only be done by helping Germany to take her rightful place in Europe as a Great Power."[54]

In the eyes of British appeasers,[55] a stable and constructive peace required "a large part of 'Eastern Europe' proper should be reconstructed under German leadership;" the states of Eastern Europe "ought to be as efficiently connected with Germany along the whole course of the Danube as are the American States along that other 'ole man river,' the Mississippi."[56] They welcomed German revision in the east because it would satisfy Germany's legitimate prestige demands and appetite for expansion; divert German attention away from the West; prevent the danger that Germany and the Soviet

Union might draw together; and replace the chaos and weakness of Central Europe with a strong and coherent German bloc—one that would effectively buffer the West from the poison of Russian communism. This logic proved expedient, if short-sighted, in 1938, when the British realized that war could only be avoided not by stabilizing the status quo in Central Europe but rather by actively promoting its change, at Czechoslovakia's expense, in the hope of satisfying the revisionist powers.

In contrast, the French, convinced that they had already "lost the peace" at Versailles, violently opposed German expansion in the East for several reasons.[57] First, they feared that any change in the territorial status quo in Europe would set a dangerous precedent that might unleash a general assault on the Versailles order. "*Une fois le premier détail de l'architecture tombé,*" Herriot warned, "*tout l'édifice tomberait lui-même.*"[58] [Once the keystone falls, the edifice will fall of its own weight]. Second, French security now relied on the assistance of precisely those countries in Eastern Europe, particularly Poland and Czechoslovakia, which it considered substitutes for its traditional ally, Czarist Russia. Lastly, the French feared that Germany, if it expanded in the East, would become so powerful that it could turn around and defeat France. German expansion of any kind contradicted the main goal of French policy, which was to prevent Germany from actualizing its potential power; to keep it in a permanent state of "artificial weakness." The French could hardly be expected to sanction an increase in Germany's relative power through the absorption of its allies. As it was, the "German menace" already possessed natural advantages over France and posed, in the minds of the French, a very real and most dangerous threat to their country's survival.

The United States

Refusing even to ratify the Versailles Treaty, the United States turned its back on Europe and tried to insulate itself against war by neutrality legislation. Most Americans came to believe that U.S. entry into the war had been a terrible mistake. Reflecting this view, Congress objected to Articles 10 and 16 of the Covenant, which were regarded as requiring the United States to guarantee by sanctions and military force the territorial integrity of all League members against any act of "aggression." In a narrow sense, the U.S. was a status-quo power in that it was a satisfied state, for whom the costs of war outweighed the potential gains of nonsecurity expansion. With regard to the status quo in Europe, however, the United States was indifferent and determined not to expend any American blood or treasure in support of it. Thus, the Neutrality Acts of August 31, 1935 and February 29, 1936, inspired by the Nye Committee's thesis that munition makers and bankers had conspired to force the United States into the European war in 1917, embargoed "arms, ammunition, and implements of war" and prohibited the extension of loans and credits to all belligerents.[59] By these Acts, the United States showed that, prior to 1937, it had no immediate concern either with the maintenance of the status quo or with its revision in any specific direction. In 1937, the U.S. adopted a policy of permitting belligerent trade on a cash-and-carry basis; and when the war commenced in 1939, it repealed the arms embargo. Both policies benefited sea powers and so were more favorable to Britain than Germany. But it was not until the passage of the Lend-Lease Act in March of 1941, which discriminated against Germany, that the United States became an active supporter of the status-quo in Europe.

The next step is to link unit-structure interactions to expected outcomes, i.e., system stability, alliance patterns, individual foreign policies. The theory's two independent variables combine to produce many permutations, each of which must be analyzed according to its own systemic properties. For this reason, it is not possible to make quick deductions for all types of systems, let alone tests for all classes of cases. The discussion will therefore be limited to tripolarity and the Second World War, arguably the two most misunderstood cases.

Chapter 2

A Study of Tripolar Systems

Discussions of polarity in international relations theory generally focus on the distinction between bipolar and multipolar systems. Tripolar systems are either ignored or lumped under the broader rubric of multipolarity. This chapter asks the question, Does tripolarity merit study apart from other systems of greater and lesser numbers of poles? To answer this question, we must first determine what distinguishes one type of international system from another.

Why Study Tripolarity?

Typically, but by no means exclusively, international systems have been demarcated by their differing polarities.[1] The term polarity usually refers to the number of Great Powers in the system. Given the sloppy state of the conceptual analysis in the field of international relations, however, polarity is frequently (mis)used in a behavioral rather than a purely structural sense to connote the number of antagonistic blocs in the system.[2] The problem with the latter definition is that it conflates the distinct concepts of polarity (the number of poles) and polarization (the number of alignments in the system).

In terms of the properties exhibited by the system, however, the addition of one Great Power, or pole, to any given power distribution does not always represent a meaningful change in system polarity. For instance, it is generally agreed that a new system occurs when moving from one to two poles or from two to three poles but not when moving from, for example, seven to eight poles or fifty to fifty-one poles. This means that in addition to knowing how systems are classified (i.e., what elements define the system under observation), we need to know what kinds of change constitute system transformation (a change in its dynamics) as opposed to changes within the system.

The key issue is whether a change in the defining properties (i.e., in structural realist theory, an additional pole) alters the *dynamics* of the system. In reference to the prior examples, we distinguish between systems of two and three poles because two is postulated to be a *threshold* for the specific characteristics exhibited by that system; while in the latter two examples, seven and fifty are not generally considered thresholds for their respective system dynamics.

Returning to our initial question, Is three a threshold number of poles? Since there is no debate that bipolar systems behave differently than systems of greater than two actors, it is a question of whether to distinguish between systems of three poles and those of four or more poles. Most theorists agree that three is indeed a threshold number. Robert Gilpin says, "Although students of international relations disagree on the relative stability of bipolar systems versus multipolar systems, almost all agree that a tripolar system is the most unstable configuration."[3] Likewise, Morton Kaplan and Kenneth Waltz associate tripolarity with extreme systemic instability. Kaplan asserts, "If there are only three essential national actors and if they are relatively equal in capability, the probability that two will combine to eliminate the third is relatively great."[4] Likewise, Waltz argues that "systems of three have distinctive and unfortunate characteristics. Two of the powers can easily gang up on the third, divide the spoils, and drive the system back to bipolarity. In multipolar systems four is then the lowest acceptable number [for balancing to occur], for it permits external alignment and promises considerable stability."[5]

Conversely, some theorists claim that tripolarity is the most stable system. In their study of system polarity and the frequency of major wars, Charles Ostrom and John Aldrich find tripolarity to be the *most* peaceful power configuration.[6] Likewise, David Garnham posits "a curvilinear relationship between the number of poles in the interstate system and the probability of major power war. The likelihood of war is lowest for a tripolar system, higher for a bipolar system, highest in a system with five poles, and less likely in larger systems.[7]

Much of the confusion about the stability of tripolar systems arises because some analysts (e.g., Waltz and Kaplan) define tripolarity as a system composed of three actors of roughly *equal* size, while others (e.g., Ostrom and Aldrich) identify tripolarity with any triadic configuration, regardless of the size disparities among the three units. Additional confusion arises because, as previously mentioned, some analysts use a behavioral definition (polarization) rather than a structural definition of system polarity. For such analysts, any conflict between two sides is bipolar, between three sides, tripolar, etc., no matter how many individual members are involved.

In addition, the two contradictory views of tripolarity can be partially explained by the unique ambiguity of coalitions in triads. Sometimes, the third member can act as a mediator or balancer; other times as an instigator or kingmaker. In the following passage, Georg Simmel notes this peculiar property:

> Where three elements, **A**, **B**, **C**, constitute a community, there is added to the immediate relationship which exists, for example, between **A** and **B**, the immediate relationship which they gain by their common relation to **C**. . . . Separations which the parties could not of themselves reconcile are accommodated by the third, or by their being included in a comprehensive whole. On the other hand, the direct union is not merely strengthened by the indirect, but it may also be destroyed. There is no relationship so complete between three that each individual may not, under certain circumstances, be regarded by the other two as an intruder. . . .[8]

As Simmel suggests, within a given tripolar system, the types of coalitions that form and the degree of stability exhibited is a function not only of the distribution of capabilities within the triad but also of the identity and interests of the units, that is, the relationships that form among the three members.

Tripolarity and System Stability

Why are tripolar configurations believed to be so unstable? Consider the effect of polarity on balance-of-power systems composed of all equally sized units (a simplifying assumption that will be relaxed in the later discussion of tripolar dynamics). In addition, assume that all states must choose one side or the other—none can be neutral. For descriptive purposes, I will invoke the well-worn "image of two scales suspended upon a fulcrum, balancing only when equal weights are placed upon the two scales."[9] It is immediately obvious that all even-numbered systems are capable of balance, while all odd-numbered systems are not. This alone distinguishes a tripolar from a quadrapolar system. But how does this distinguish tripolarity from other odd-numbered systems? Coalition formation in the tripolar system will tilt the scale far more out of balance than it would any other odd-numbered system. In other words, when an odd-numbered system devolves into two opposing alliances, the inequality between the larger and smaller coalitions is greatest in a tripolar system, where one side is twice as strong as the other.

The equation to reflect the amount of inequality in the resources held by the stronger and weaker coalitions is: $I = ([a - b]/b) \times 100$, where $a =$ the resources of the larger coalition, $b =$ the resources of the smaller coalition, $p =$ the polarity of the system. The difference between the two coalitions is treated as a percentage of the amount held by the weaker coalition. Thus for $p = 3$: $I = ([66 - 33]/33) \times 100 = 1 \times 100$, or there is a 100 percent difference in strength between the stronger and weaker coalitions in a tripolar system. For $p = 5$: $I = ([60 - 40]/40) \times 100 = .5 \times 100$, or 50 percent. For $p = 7$: $I = ([57 - 43]/43) \times 100 = .33 \times 100$, or 33 percent. Thus, when there are seven poles in the system, the difference in strength between the two opposing coalitions is one third as great as in a tripolar system. This means that, assuming units of equal size, alliance formation for offensive purposes is extremely destabilizing in a tripolar system, much less destabilizing in a quintipolar system, and still less destabilizing for a system of seven or more actors. (I define stability as the preservation of all actors in the system).[10]

Tripolar systems are also particularly prone to indirect effects—systemic outcomes that do not correspond to the intentions of the actors.[11] For instance, given a tripolar system composed of three equally sized units, an increase in either hostility or cooperation between any two poles will, *ceteris paribus*, heighten the motivation to gang up against one of the poles. Why increased hostility between two poles should result in instability requires no explanation. Some readers, however, are wondering how increased cooperation between two poles likewise causes instability. The connection is not an obvious one because the outcome (system instability) is typically an indirect effect.

To illustrate, suppose each pole earmarks half of its unreserved forces against each of the other two poles. Now, imagine that poles *A* and *B* reciprocally reserve or demobilize all or some substantial part of the forces that each has been deploying against the other. They now have more forces and/or resources to target against *C*. Consequently, *C*'s defense has been made less secure with respect to both *A* and *B*, whether or not the action was designed to have this effect.[12] Arthur Lee Burns states the axiom this way: "The closer the alliance between any two or more Powers, the greater the increase of opposition or 'pressure' (other things being equal) between any one of the two and any third Power or group of Powers."[13]

In general terms, this means that an equilateral tripolar system has a greater chance of maintaining stability when bilateral contacts between the poles are of low frequency and intensity. This conclusion is similar to that reached by Deutsch and Singer, who, noting that an increase in the number of poles leads to an increase in their opportunities to interact, posited that systems of five or more actors are more stable than lesser number systems. The logic is straightforward: the large number of dyadic pairs divides the actors' attention, producing bilateral relations of low intensity and high flexibility.[14]

The problem is that low-level contact among the poles—the hypothesized condition that produces stability in systems of more than two actors—is extremely unlikely in a tripolar system: the small number of actors enables and encourages each member of the triad to focus its energies on the activities of the others. Ironically, the same logic that underpins Waltz's argument about the stability of bipolar systems—the higher attention, greater flexibility, and reduced uncertainty of two-actor systems compared with that of larger-numbered systems—leads to the opposite conclusion under tripolarity. The additional pole, while only slightly diminishing each actor's ability to concentrate on the others, means that no pole can rely solely on its own internal means to balance the other two. To survive, each pole must ensure that a hostile coalition does not form against it, and so each strives for a coalition with one of the other two members. But any coalition throws the system wildly out of balance, gravely endangering the isolated third.

In sum, the perverse effects of tripolar dynamics turn the logic of bipolar stability on its head: increased attention, certainty, and flexibility yields extreme instability. The difference is that in a bipolar system each pole is certain that it can rely on its own resources to balance the other, while in a tripolar system each member is certain that it cannot balance the other two solely by internal means and, more important, that any alliance forms a winning coalition. For this reason, if we consider only systems composed of all power-maximizing actors (an assumption that will be relaxed when I discuss tripolar dynamics in greater depth), tripolar systems are the most unstable.

As shown in figure 2.1, one may conceptualize the relationship between polarity and stability as curvilinear, not monotonic, as is commonly assumed within the literature. Uni- and bipolar distributions are generally acknowledged to be the most stable systems because balancing is accomplished by internal rather than external means. By contrast, balancing in multipolar systems requires coalition formation. As a result, the stability of multipolar systems is low to moderately stable, depending on the number of poles: even-numbered systems are more stable than odd-numbered ones. Under multipolarity, however, stability increases as the number of poles grows because there will be more blocking coalitions, greater interaction opportunities, and greater alliance flexibility. In addition, as the number of poles increases, so too does the chance of maintaining a divisible peace, that is, local conflicts are less likely to explode into system-wide war.

Aside from their unique structural properties, tripolar systems should be studied because they have existed and will continue to exist in the real world. In fact, many current observers believe that, with the demise of the Soviet Union, the post-Cold-War system is rapidly becoming a tripolar one composed of the United States, Japan, and Germany. (I discuss the emerging tripolar world in the concluding chapter.)

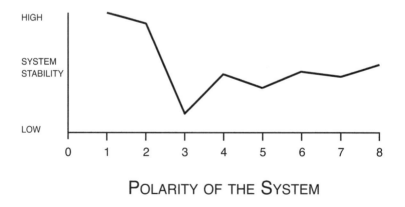

POLARITY OF THE SYSTEM

FIGURE 2.1

Analysis of Five Types of Tripolar Systems

To analyze the properties of tripolarity, I have borrowed hypotheses from sociological theories of coalition formation in triads.[15] In particular, the present study has been influenced by the work of the sociologist Theodore Caplow.[16] Citing six basic power configurations of the triad, Caplow suggests that "under certain conditions the formation of particular coalitions depends upon the initial distribution of power in the triad and may be predicted to some extent when the initial distribution of power is known."[17] Regarding the "certain conditions," Caplow assumes that: (1) a stronger member always defeats a weaker member and will seek to do so, (2) strength is additive, (3) each member seeks to defeat the others, preferring the defeat of two others to the defeat of one (4) all states prefer more territory to what they currently possess.[18]

Caplow's analysis of alliance formation takes place in a Hobbesian, all-against-all world. The triad exists unwillingly: it comprises three hostile states, each seeking the destruction of the others. Members seek coalitions for both defensive and offensive motives, for protection and aggrandizement. The security objective of the alliance is to defeat a potential hegemon and/or to prevent the formation of a threatening two-against-one coalition. The offensive incentive for alignment is the added strength gained by the defeat and partition of the isolated third member.

Building on Caplow's analysis, my theoretical framework adds the concept of state interest, that is, the mix of revisionist and status-quo states. As Simmel's work suggests, the identities of the units play an important role in determining the stability of coalition behavior within a given triad. Unlike Caplow, therefore, I do not interpret anarchy to mean that all units are mutually hostile and/or power-maximizers; interests as well as the distribution of power affect coalition behavior in the triad. For the purpose of simplifying the analysis, however, state interest is treated as a dichotomous variable: states are either revisionist or status quo.

Configurations of Tripolar Systems

Given the definitional requirement that the weakest pole must have half the resources of the strongest pole, there are five possible tripolar power configurations:

1. $A = B = C$
2. $A > B = C, A < B + C$
3. $A < B = C$
4. $A = B + C, B = C$
5. $A > B > C, A < B + C$

Definitions

1. *Revisionist powers*: states that seek to increase their resources and for whom the gains from nonsecurity expansion exceed the costs of war.
2. *Status-quo powers*: states that seek only to keep their resources and for whom the costs of war exceed the gains from nonsecurity expansion.
3. To qualify as a *pole*, a state must possess at least half of the resources of the most powerful state in the system.
4. Resources = military power potential
5. System stability means that no actor in the system is eliminated.

Assumptions

1. Wars are costly.
2. The alternatives among which the members of the triad may choose are: do nothing; align with another member to block an attack; align with another member to eliminate the third member; wage a lone attack to eliminate one or both members of the triad.
3. A stronger member or coalition defeats a weaker member or coalition.
4. The strength of a coalition equals the combined total resources of its members: If $A = 3$ and $B = 2$, then $AB = 5$.
5. In a coalition attack, the resources of the victim are divided proportionately among the winning coalition members. In a lone attack, they are absorbed in total by the victor.
6. Resources are increased only by eliminating a member of the triad. States do not voluntarily cede resources.

Among other things, this last assumption and the inclusion of status-quo states distinguishes the present analysis from that of Niou, Ordeshook, and Rose.[19] Glenn Snyder notes in his critique of Niou, et al. that their assumption of infinitely divisible and freely transferable resources[20] allows the authors to assert

> that states will voluntarily cede resources to a stronger challenger or attacker if necessary to avoid elimination and that, in turn, the challenger will accept the resource transfers in preference to gaining the same amount by war. . . . Hence, the device of peaceful ceding of resources was introduced to permit the third party to save itself . . . by buying off a member of the threatening coalition at a price short of suicide. The logical fit between bargaining-set theory and a desired theoretical outcome—stability—was improved, but at considerable cost to empirical realism.[21]

Thus, Niou et al. find, but I do not, that "the key feature of a three-country system is that no nation will be eliminated."[22]

Conversely, Wagner's analysis of three-actor systems assumes, as I do, that "the power of states can only be increased by conquest."[23] But in contrast to my assumption that the spoils are divided proportionately among the victors, Wagner assumes that states can only absorb the victim's "resources at a maximum rate of r units per 'day' " and "if two states are at war with a third, the rates at which they can each absorb the third's resources are determined . . . by how the victim targets its resources at the two opposing states."[24] Given the rules of Wagner's game, it follows that the victim must target its resources unequally, thereby forcing the more-opposed attacker to defect before the less (or un-) opposed attacker gains more than half the resources of the system. Thus, Wagner concludes, while I do not, that no actor is ever eliminated in a three-actor system.

The usefulness of Wagner's extra assumptions is an empirical question. The events of World War II, however, provide no examples of a two-against-one attack in which one of the attackers defected to join the victim's side. There is evidence to the contrary, however: Germany and the Soviet Union eliminated Poland with neither attacker defecting against its partner; and, though Hitler tried to cope with Nazi Germany's imminent defeat by offering alliances to the Soviet Union and the United States, neither defected to Germany's side. I suspect that, in the real world, the importance of acquiring and keeping a reputation for alliance loyalty deters some states from double-crossing their partners by absorbing more than their fair share of the spoils or by defecting when the victim offers a better deal. Anarchy does not mean, as Wagner implies, that agreements between allies are unenforceable, but rather that they must be self-enforcing.[25] Because trust as well as power is an essential ingredient for present and future cooperation, allies rarely double-cross their partners, even though game-theoretic logic says otherwise.

Type 1. The Equilateral Tripolar System: A = B = C

This power configuration represents, *ceteris paribus*, the most unstable of all systems because a system of three equally powerful states cannot be balanced by alliance formation. While this is true of any odd-numbered system composed of equal units, the imbalance is proportionally greatest in this triad, where *A* and *B* combined possess 66 percent of the total resources, as against *C*'s 33 percent share.[26]

Stabilizing an equilateral tripolar system, therefore, requires each pole to prevent the formation of a hostile alliance of the other two poles against itself. Although the power configuration heightens the tendency to gang up, the specific mix of revisionist and status-quo poles greatly affects system stability.

a. One revisionist pole

Given only one revisionist pole, a stable system should result. Potential aggression will likely take the form of the lone revisionist pole attacking the nearest status-quo pole. But such an attack is improbable because individual aggression in tripolarity tends to be self-defeating. On the one hand, if a stalemate results (and this is most likely among equally powerful poles) both combatants are weakened in relation to the neutral third, who obviously has no incentive to join the fray. On the other, if the revisionist pole appears to be winning, the neutral third must join the status-quo pole to ensure its own survival. Consequently, war is unlikely because the revisionist attacker can expect only a war of attrition or certain defeat.

A geographically distanced pole may assume one of four roles: 1) *tertius gaudens*, 2) the abettor, 3) the eyewitness, or 4) the mediator. The first two are likely to be played by a revisionist pole, the latter two by a status-quo pole. As *tertius gaudens* (the enjoying third) the remote pole turns the dissension of the two geographically proximate poles to its own advantage by asking an exploitative price for its support. As the abettor, it instigates conflict between the other members of the triad for its own purposes. In the role of eyewitness, it does nothing and seeks nothing from the conflict. In the mediator role, it declares neutrality toward the conflict and works to stabilize the triad.[27]

b. Two revisionist poles

A tripolar system composed of two revisionist poles is typically unstable because both power-maximizers are highly motivated to augment their resources at the expense of the lone status-quo pole. As a result, the two revisionist poles can be expected to put aside their competition temporarily so as to make substantial gains. And because the winning coalition consists of two equally powerful partners, each member can expect to gain half the spoils, such that neither pole will be left vulnerable to the other after the war. Hence, there is little to prevent the partitioning of the isolated status-quo state. Eliminating a member of the triad transforms the system into a relatively stable but competitive bipolar system, as the two remaining poles (both power maximizers seeking gains at the other's expense) are expected to resume their rivalry.

A favorable geographic position may temporarily protect the lone status-quo pole, but it will not appreciably stabilize this type of tripolar system. Suppose that the two revisionist poles are in close geographical proximity and the status-quo pole is distanced from them. The triad contains, in effect, two subsystems: one bipolar, the other unipolar, wherein the rivalry between the two revisionist poles protects the remote status-quo pole by preventing them from ganging up against it. The status-quo power may assume the role of either "the enjoying third" or the "abettor." In either case, it remains on the sidelines, hoping that the two revisionist poles will bleed each other to death.

But this is a dangerous strategy for the status-quo power because one of the revisionist poles may be able to defeat the other by either forming a winning alliance with one or more revisionist powers or by devouring weaker states until enough additional resources are acquired to defeat the nearest pole. Once accomplished, the victorious revisionist pole would be in control of at least twice as many resources as the lone status-quo pole. (Hitler's use of this strategy and why it failed will be discussed in chapters 4–6.)

c. Three revisionist poles

In this case, in which all three members are of equal strength and are revisionist powers, any possible coalition—*AB*, *BC*, and *AC*—is equally likely, making it an extremely volatile situation. All three members seek coalition, since isolation means extinction. But the structure of this type of tripolar system prohibits external "balancing" behavior (alliances for the purpose of counterbalancing a stronger or more threatening power or alliance) because any coalition easily *defeats* the isolated third member. In addition, since all three members are revisionist powers, each pole must always be suspicious of the other two and none can enjoy true long-term security. Consequently, this system should exhibit the tendency to evolve into a stable bipolar system, as two poles will be tempted to destroy the isolated third to gain lasting security. Eliminating one pole through partitioning should not present major difficulties because each member of the winning coalition is of equal strength and is therefore entitled to an equal share of the spoils.

d. Three status-quo poles

This, of course, is the most stable tripolar system because all members share an interest in preserving the status quo. In this system, in which no pole seeks the elimination of any other, the continued integrity of the three actors is virtually assured. System stability simply requires the poles to make their intentions known, avoid provocative acts, and coordinate and consult with the others about their individual foreign policies. Their tacit agreement not to attack each other may be formalized by mutual nonaggression pacts between all dyads and/or a collective security arrangement, whereby each member pledges to come to the aid of the victim of an armed attack.

I should note that Glenn Snyder has portrayed the so-called "alliance dilemma" differently. Snyder assumes that, in a multipolar setting composed of equally strong actors, status-quo states will prefer the outcome of all-around abstention from alliances to a situation of two rival coalitions; but each state's first choice is to form its own alliance while others abstain from doing so. According to this preference ordering, what Snyder calls "the primary alliance game" (the initial decision to align or abstain from alignment) follows the logic of an N-person prisoner's dilemma (PD).[28] The problem with this argument, however, is that, in light of the significant costs of alliances in terms of treasure and political autonomy, why should states prefer a situation in which they alone form an alliance to one in which no alliances form in the first place? Given Snyder's first assumption that "no state is aggressive, but none can know the intentions of others,"[29] the aligned state simply winds up paying the costs of alignment while gaining no real security benefits, just peace of mind.

Rather, when all actors are satisfied with the status quo, the primary alliance game is not a PD but a coordination problem known as "stag hunt" that is easily resolved by communication. No actor has any incentive to misrepresent or withhold private information regarding its true intentions, military capabilities and doctrine, or resolve to uphold the status quo. To the contrary, every member has an incentive to announce its benign intentions, to make costly signals to confirm them, and to avoid miscalculation. It is illogical to think that a small number of rational actors would have trouble reaching the efficient solution of no alliances, if coordination were in fact the only problem here.[30]

Realists would no doubt counter that the condition of international anarchy (understood as the absence of a sovereign arbiter to make and enforce agreements among states) creates uncertainty, such that states can never know or entirely trust each others' stated intentions.[31] Indeed, even if all states are confident that none secretly harbors aggressive aims, intentions can change. Uncertainty about the future impels prudent states wishing to survive to fear the worst and assume the costs entailed therein. Realists would also invoke the related argument of the security dilemma, the fact that a state's efforts to make itself more secure often have the unintended but inescapable effect of making others less secure. The pernicious effects of anarchy and the security dilemma, they argue, mean that rival alliances may form even when all states prefer that no coalitions emerge.

The problem with these arguments is that they ignore the availability or feasibility of bargains that would avoid the costs of alliances. If no state seeks to revise the status quo by force of arms, there is no reason why signaling and bargaining cannot prevent the inefficient outcome of alliance formation—an outcome that would only create unwanted hostility within the triad and that could trigger the far higher costs and dangers of a war down the road. When offensive military postures are distinguishable from defense ones, there is no security dilemma, as Jervis himself acknowledges.[32] Moreover, costly signals are easiest to make (that is, most effective in communicating the state's intentions) when technology and geography favor offensive military strategies and force structures. As I have written elsewhere:

> Under such conditions, security-seeking states can easily signal their benign intentions by spending heavily on defense to compensate for the advantage of offense. Other states should have no trouble inferring the true intentions of a state willing to engage in this kind of costly signaling. It is thus precisely when offense has the advantage that security-seeking states must cooperate to achieve security, and can easily do so.[33]

When offense has the advantage but it is not distinct from defense, the security dilemma is most intense. In such a world, however, the high risks of war (especially unwanted, inadvertent war) provide status-quo states with great incentives to seek security through cooperative means. Even under these conditions, which are least favorable for security regime formation, it is not at all obvious that states will choose individualistic policies and alliances over reliance on joint measures.[34] For these reasons, when all members of a triad support the status quo, no alliances will form. This "no alliance" prediction holds not only for equilateral tripolar systems but also for any power configuration consisting of all status-quo actors.

Type 2. The Paradox of Power: $A > B = C$, $A < B + C$

a. Three revisionist poles

In this type of tripolar system, A is slightly stronger than B and C, which are equally sized; but A is weaker than the combined strength of B and C. All three members strive for a coalition, as any combination defeats the isolated member. Paradoxically, under such circumstances, A's strength proves to be a handicap, since both B and C find A less attractive as a coalition partner than each other. This is true because, in either an AB or AC alliance, A would be in control of its weaker partner. Consequently, A, in a coalition with either B or C, would be expected to gain at least an equal share of the rewards, and probably the lion's share—further disadvantaging the weaker ally, who must receive the bulk of the reward to gain security. Alternatively, a BC coalition (in which both B and C are of equal strength) secures an equal distribution of the reward and does not threaten either member.

This is the logic behind William Gamson's theory of the "cheapest winning coalition." Under the assumption that "any participant will expect others to demand from a coalition a share of the payoff proportional to the amount of resources which they contribute to a coalition,"[35] Gamson deduces the logic of the cheapest winning coalition:

When a player must choose among alternative coalition strategies where the total payoff to a winning coalition is constant, he will maximize his payoff by maximizing his share. The theory states that he will do this by maximizing the ratio of his resources of the total resources of the coalition. Since his resources will be the same regardless of which coalition he joins, the lower the total resources, the greater will be his share. Thus, where the total payoff is held constant, he will favor the cheapest winning coalition.[36]

Gamson's theory of the cheapest winning coalition predicts a *BC* pairing for this triad, as it maximizes *B* and *C*'s share of the benefits for the same amount of resources.

b. One or two status-quo poles

When there is a mix of status-quo and revisionist states, the alliance patterns within this system become considerably more complex. If *A* is a status-quo pole, for instance, either *B* or *C* may align with it against the isolated third. Such an alignment is especially likely if either *B* or *C* is also a status-quo state, in which case an overpowering status-quo coalition will form to oppose the lone revisionist member of the triad.

If *B* and *C* are mutually hostile, *A* is in the enviable position of holding the balance, and so it can play the role of either balancer or kingmaker. As balancer, it seeks to preserve a stalemate between the two rivals. As kingmaker, it sells its services to the highest bidder. The motto of the kingmaker is: "*Cui adhaereo prae est*," translated as "the one that I join is the one which will turn the scales" or "the party to which I adhere getteth the upper hand."[37] When *A* is a status-quo state, it will likely adopt the role of balancer working for system stability; as a revisionist state, *A* is most likely to be an opportunistic kingmaker.

Britain prior to the twentieth century, when it was still the most powerful European state and a defender of the status quo on the continent, is the prototypical example of the balancer. Pointing out that Britain might well have played the role of kingmaker, Churchill proudly proclaims:

> Faced by Philip II of Spain, against Louis XIV under William II and Marlborough, against Napoleon, against William II of Germany, it would have been easy and must have been very tempting to join with the stronger and share the fruits of his conquest. However, we always took the harder course, joined with the less strong Powers, made a combination among them, and thus defeated and frustrated the Continental military tyrant, whoever he was, whatever nation he led.[38]

Churchill correctly points out that Britain, had it been a greedy revisionist state, would have bandwagoned with the aggressor to share in the spoils of victory. Other opportunistic strategies would also have been available. As a kingmaker, Britain could have bribed the weaker side for its assistance. If it were particularly devious, Britain might have instigated conflict on the Continent and then worked for a stalemate in order to gain relative to all the beleaguered combatants.

Three status-quo poles

When all three poles are status-quo states, no coalition is predicted. For reasons outlined above, this "no coalition" prediction holds for any system composed of all status-quo units.

Type 3. The Partitioned Third: $A < B = C$

When both B and C are revisionist, A cannot align with either because once the coalition has partitioned the isolated member of the triad, A will be destroyed by its stronger ally. The only remaining alliance, therefore, is BC, which can safely partition A because its members are of equal strength. For security reasons, B and C should seek to partition A: B must block AC and C must prevent AB. Therefore, the most likely scenario is the formation of a BC coalition for the purpose of partitioning A and achieving an equal balance between B and C.

However, if B and C are mutually hostile, is not it clearly in A's interest to prolong their rivalry by acting as a balancer, gaining at the expense of the other two poles? In the short run, yes; but in the long run, no. This is because the role of balancer is a dangerous one for the weakest member of the triad. The balancer must guarantee through skillful diplomacy that the two warring poles do not temporarily set aside their differences to gang up against it. This is no easy task for A. By playing the role of balancer and continually frustrating the desires of B and C, A will engender hostility with both B and C. Given the animosity directed against the balancer, one would expect this role to be played by a state that was considerably stronger than the other two, not by the weakest triadic member.

Type 4. The Balanced Tripolar System: $A = B + C, B = C$

Although somewhat counterintuitive, a stable tripolar system is most likely to obtain (other things being equal) when at least some of the poles are of unequal weights. Consider, for instance, a system of three revisionists states, where $A = B + C$. Because A is "near-preponderant" (it possesses half of the power resources in the system) and it seeks to increase its power, B and C realize that to survive they must align to counterbalance A. This type of tripolar system is essentially a behavioral dyad, and so it exhibits the high stability associated with bipolarity.[39]

Conversely, when the near-preponderant member of the triad is a status-quo power, an alliance between B and C is not required for their survival. Indeed, if either B or C is a status-quo power, it may align with A against the isolated revisionist pole. Moreover, given my definition of a pole, B and C must be of equal strength whenever their combined resources equal those of A (since no pole can have less than half the resources of the most powerful pole). As a result, a hostile bipolar stalemate may exist between B and C, leaving A to play the role of mediator, abettor, eyewitness, or *tertius gaudens* (see discussion above.)

Type 5. The Unbalanced Tripolar System: A > B > C, A < B + C

Less obvious is the inherent stability of a tripolar system where all of the poles are of different strengths: $A > B > C$, and $A < B + C$. To illustrate the peculiar dynamics of this system, consider a tripolar system in which the power ratio among the three poles is $A = 4$, $B = 3$, $C = 2$. Let us further assume that all members of the system are revisionist powers. At first glance, this system appears to be extremely unstable (i.e., one of the actors will be eliminated) and warprone, since any contest between two actors is decisive and any coalition is a winning coalition. Yet, this type of triad proves to be one of the simplest and most stable forms of a balance of power.

First, consider an isolated attack within this triad. In such a situation, it is immediately obvious to the third power that it must block the efforts of the attacker by joining the weaker side, or else be dominated by the victor. The attacker not only knows that the third power must resist its efforts to destroy the initial victim, but also that it has no hope of prevailing against such a coalition. Hence, a stronger member of the triad will not be tempted to try to defeat a weaker member by means of an isolated attack; the dynamics of the system discourage offensive actions.

Now let us consider an attack by a coalition against an isolated third pole. Although every coalition is a winning coalition, all pairings in a *4–3–2* triad are unbalanced—they consist of a stronger and a weaker member. Thus, if any coalition formed, went to war, and won as expected, the system would be transformed into a dyad with the weaker member of the winning alliance at the mercy of its stronger partner. The weaker ally will be imperiled even if the spoils of victory are divided equally, rather than according to each member's proportionate resources.[40]

In summary, given the dynamics of this system, any pairing will inevitably result in only one remaining actor; because this is obvious to all three poles, no coalition will form in the first place. Hence, although all actors are power maximizers and every pairing forms a winning coalition, the perverse effects of the unbalanced triad virtually assure the continued integrity of all the actors and the absence of war among them. This is true for all mixes of revisionist and status-quo states except for the following case.

Two status-quo poles

Ironically, when there are two status-quo poles, the system is potentially unstable. In this situation, the status-quo poles may be motivated, for defensive purposes, to wage a preventive war to eliminate the revisionist pole, which poses a latent (if not immediate) threat to their individual security.

The Enhanced Role of LGPs and Other Nonpoles Under Tripolarity

To this point, the discussion has been limited to the behavior of only polar powers. While this analysis leads to broad expectations about the overall stability of the five types of tripolar systems, it will not take us very far in explaining the specific dynamics of a given historical case. For this we need to consider the behavior of lesser great powers as well as poles. Indeed, the behavior of LGPs plays an important role in determining the stability of tripolar systems—a subject to which we now turn.

Empirically, LGPs have had the greatest effect on the stability of tripolar and, to a lesser extent, quadrapolar systems. By contrast they have had only a moderate effect on the stability of unipolar systems, and hardly any effect on the stability of multipolar (5 or more poles) and bipolar systems. A look at the distribution of capabilities within the Major-Power subset for the past 100 years shows why this proposition has held and will continue to do so. (See Table 2.1, below.)

Under bipolarity, the system's capabilities tend to be highly concentrated in the two poles with only a small proportion left over to be divided among

TABLE 2.1

Percentage Distribution of the COW Index Among the Major Powers and the Polarity of the International System, 1890-1980.

Year	#poles	US	Jap	Ger	UK	Rus	Fr	It	A-H
1890	5	19.6*	3.4	15.9*	21.0*	15.0*	12.7*	5.3	7.1
1900	4	21.6*	3.8	16.7*	20.6*	16.1*	10.1	4.9	6.1
1913	4	25.0*	4.4	18.2*	14.1*	16.7*	10.4	5.0	6.1
1925	1	34.9*	7.8	11.6	15.4	13.1	10.8	6.3	—
1934	2	28.8*	8.9	13.9	9.5	23.2*	9.3	6.2	—
1938	3	22.5*	9.3	20.1*	10.5	24.9*	6.9	5.3	—
1950	2	38.0*	7.0	8.1	9.8	31.4*	5.7	—	—
1960	2	37.0*	8.7	7.5	7.9	32.3*	6.6	—	—
1970	2	34.7*	12.0	7.2	6.4	34.7*	5.0	—	—
1980	2	30.3*	13.0	7.7	5.5	38.1*	5.4	—	—

* = Polar Power

SOURCE: "Correlates of War Capability Data Set Printout," Inter-University Consortium for Political and Social Research at the University of Michigan, July 1990.

the many remaining states. The huge capability disparity between the two polar powers and the remaining states makes it highly unlikely that a significant amount of LGPs—whose total power could affect the stability of the system—will exist in a bipolar system. Bipolarity results instead in a two-level distribution of capabilities: polar powers and insignificant lesser states (sometimes referred to as inessential actors) of varying sizes.

Conversely, under multipolarity (five or more poles), the system's capabilities are widely dispersed among the many poles, such that most of the significant actors are of roughly equal strength (i.e., 1890). Because the number of Great Powers (that is, poles and LGPs) in the international system has never exceeded eight, only one or two, if any, LGPs will exist under multipolarity, and they will be too weak and few in number to affect the polar balance. There are two reasons for this.

First, increasing the number of poles in the system produces a leveling effect that results in rough equality among the major powers. As multipolarity is not characterized by wide disparities among the major actors, we should not expect to find many LGPs, since most of the system's capabilities reside in the many poles. Second, as the number of poles increases, the impact of each pole on the stability of the system decreases, resulting in a corresponding decrease in the importance of each individual LGP. Consequently, a large number of LGPs will be required to affect the polar balance of power in a multipolar system, and this is mathematically improbable, if not impossible.

By contrast, the distribution of capabilities in tripolar systems—and to a lesser degree in four-pole systems—is not as highly concentrated as in bipolarity or as diffuse as in multipolar systems of five or more actors. In tripolar systems, the poles do not dwarf the other states in the system as they do in bipolarity, and so the balance is more easily tipped by strong LGPs than in multipolar systems of five or more actors. As a result, we should expect to find influential nonpolar actors in tripolar (e.g., 1938) and quadrapolar systems (e.g., 1900–1913).

Lastly, by definition, a unipolar system means that every Great Power with the exception of the hegemon must be a nonpolar power. Sheer numbers alone suggest that LGPs will play a significant role in the stability of unipolar systems. Numbers alone, however, are somewhat misleading. Given its exalted power position, the hegemon should be both willing and able to maintain the stability of the system, which, after all, has obviously been working to its own advantage. Yet, as the United States proved in the 1920s, hegemons have not always been willing to assume the role of system manager. The U.S.'s refusal to assume hegemonic leadership during the unipolar period of the 1920s, however, was largely a consequence of its being an artificial hegemon (that is, unipolarity was, in this case, a temporary effect of the Great War, as was the bipolar system of 1934). But, even here, the absence of hegemonic leadership did not enhance the importance of nonpoles on the stability of the system. Instead, the system remained relatively peaceful until the mid-1930s, when Germany and the Soviet Union returned to polar strength. In other words, it was not the free reign of nonpolar powers under unipolarity that caused the instability leading up to the Second World War; rather system instability occurred when two additional poles emerged to create a tripolar system.

In sum, the high capability concentration in bipolarity and the low capability concentration in multipolarity suggest that it is *unlikely* that LGPs will appear in either system and/or, if they do exist, that they will have a significant effect on the stability of the system. Conversely, the moderate concentration of power in tripolar and quadrapolar systems (and to a far lesser extent, unipolar systems) is conducive to the existence of LGPs in sufficient numbers and strength to affect the power situation among the poles. The impact of LGPs on system stability and alliance patterns will be greatest, however, under tripolarity. The next chapter brings these nonpolar states back into the analysis; and unlike the preceding analysis of tripolar systems, the theoretical discussion and hypotheses in chapter 3 apply to all classes of balance-of-power systems, that is, bipolar, tripolar, and multipolar.

Chapter 3

State Responses to Threats and Opportunities

It is commonly accepted among international relations specialists that the study of alliances is one of the most basic and important subjects in the field. There is also widespread agreement regarding the identity of, though not the answers to, the key questions: Why do states form alliances and how do they make these decisions? Do states more often align with the underdog or jump on the bandwagon? What initial conditions favor these types of behaviors? In light of this overwhelming consensus rarely encountered in the social sciences, it is all the more surprising to find so few studies exclusively devoted to the subject.[1] Indeed, there is nothing even approaching a grand theory of alliance behavior, and only a handful of studies have even attempted to construct one.[2]

My guess is that the glacial pace of progress in this area stems from two basic failings endemic to the literature. First, virtually all work on alliance behavior assumes that states form coalitions solely to achieve greater security. This assumption, while not entirely unreasonable, comes at the price of ignoring the other half of the equation: alliance choices motivated by opportunities for gain rather than danger; appetite and not fear. Second, studies of alliances rarely acknowledge that, under certain circumstances, the benefits of additional security and profit can best be achieved by not entering into a coalition.

Yet, specification of the conditions under which no coalition is predicted is a crucial first step toward a more complete understanding of when and why states do, in fact, form alliances and how they choose sides. The remedy for both of these problems, I believe, is to examine alliance behavior within the broader context of how states respond to both threats and opportunities.

Consider, for instance, the variety of state responses throughout history to a rising, dissatisfied power, i.e., appeasement, bandwagoning, engagement, balancing, containment, and "roll back" to name a few. Some of these strategies involve alliances, others do not; some use alliances for capability-aggregation purposes, others for peaceful management of system change; some seek security from the rising power, others aim to profit by it.

The primary objectives of this chapter, then, are twofold: (1) to identify and provide conceptual clarity to the various strategies states have employed to deal with threats and opportunities, and (2) to link these strategies to differences in the power and interests of states.

The Goals of Alliances

The most significant but overlooked factor driving alliance behavior is that dissatisfied states form alliances for entirely different reasons from those motivating satisfied states to ally. The former seek to make gains; the latter, to prevent or minimize losses. For status-quo states, alliances are a response to threats, and so they are always undertaken in the expectation of costs; they are a necessary but unwanted burden. For revisionist states, alliances are primarily a response to a perceived opportunity for profit and aggrandizement. Hence, revisionist powers anticipate that the benefits of alliance will far outweigh the costs, which are not insignificant as will be discussed.

With this in mind, the motivating force that pushes all states into a coalition is a desire to gain the benefit of greater brute force, coercive power, and/or "voice opportunity" for the purpose of either effecting or preventing some international change.[3] How these benefits are used depends on whether the ultimate goal is to uphold or revise the status quo.

Greater brute force enables status-quo states to defend against and ultimately defeat an aggressor; revisionist states use it to take territory from others. Enhanced coercive power strengthens the ability of status-quo states to deter and contain aggressors; revisionist states use it to bully established states into making territorial and institutional adjustments. Moreover, since any form of territorial redistribution involves making another state worse off, some coercion is always required to make the injured state accept the new situation. Thus, the benefit of greater coercive power may also be used by status-quo states in an attempt to satisfy revisionist powers by means of peaceful revision. Finally, alliances offer all members, whether status-quo or revisionist, a voice in intra-alliance politics and therefore a greater chance to modify their partners' behavior. Thus, alliances can be used as tools for managing rivalries and the rise of a dissatisfied power and for gaining leverage in bargaining situations, especially for weaker states vis-à-vis stronger neighbors.

The Size of Alliances

William Riker's "size-principle" hypothesis posits that the coalition most likely to form is one that contains just enough strength to defeat the opposing players.[4] This so-called minimum winning coalition is attributed to the commonsense desire among the winners not to spread the spoils among superfluous partners. The greater the number of losers, the greater the sum of their losses and the greater the gains of the winners; and the fewer the winners, the greater the share of each winner. Thus, given three players of the following sizes, $A = 4$, $B = 3$, and $C = 2$, the size-principle hypothesis predicts a BC coalition.

The added complexity of more-than-three actor games, however, reduces the determinateness of Riker's theory. If A, B, C, D equal 4, 2, 2, 1 respectively, the minimum winning coalition or size principle predicts either an AD or BCD coalition. Experimental evidence has shown, however, that AD is more likely than BCD because AD is a one-step coalition, whereas BCD requires two steps. Hence, bargaining costs are cheaper and less complex for AD than BCD.[5]

In contrast with Riker, Caplow assumes that each player desires control over all others, including the members of its own coalition. Consequently, each actor prefers, *ceteris paribus*, to align with weaker coalition partners. Returning to the example where A, B, C, D equal 4, 2, 2, and 1, respectively, Caplow's theory predicts a BCD coalition instead of AD because, given the large power disparity between A and D, D would be extremely vulnerable to A after the defeat of B and C. Instead, D feels more secure with B and C, which are only twice as strong as D, than with A, which is four times as powerful.[6]

Broadly speaking, the anarchic international environment forces all states to consider seriously the possibility that today's ally will be tomorrow's enemy. A theory of coalition formation under anarchic conditions must therefore account for the possibility that "the weakest player, by joining a nearly predominant strong player, only creates a condition in which he will be the next victim."[7] Caplow's theory takes this into account; Riker's theory does not.

Riker's size-principle hypothesis clearly applies to revisionist coalitions. This is because the *raison d'être* of offensive alliances is to maximize one's share of the spoils of victory. Any additional member beyond what is needed for victory diminishes each member's share of the winnings. For revisionist alliance members, the optimum coalition size, as Riker argues, is one just strong enough to defeat the target and no stronger. Furthermore, because the goals of revisionist states are not always complimentary, the revisionist leader will not only seek to limit membership in the coalition to the minimum number required to defeat the opposing alliance, but it will also enlist only those members that do not hold conflicting territorial interests.

States excluded from the alliance will, of course, seek to join if the cost of membership is less than their expected gain. In theory, however, their applications should be denied, since the profit interests of the alliance's essential members, particularly its leader, are ill-served by admitting states too weak to affect the balance of power.

In contrast, status-quo powers, whose primary interest is self-preservation and system stability, form alliances to deter or defeat revisionist states or coalitions. It is reasonable to assume, therefore, that they desire not minimum winning coalitions but rather very large coalitions that better serve their defensive or deterrent aims. Indeed, the larger the coalition, the less cost to each member of balancing against the threat. This is not to imply that free-rider problems do not exist in large coalitions.[8] It is precisely because alliance members can be expected to do less than their fair share that it makes sense to form a coalition that is clearly overpowering, not slightly more powerful, than the aggressor(s). The notion that aggressive states are better deterred by the threat of a community of power rather than a balance of power is the basis of Wilsonian collective security. Unlike in collective defense arrangements, under a collective security regime the primary danger from the free-rider problem only arises if and when deterrence fails.

Moreover, when the expansionist threat is large, there is less of a temptation to ride free. This is because, as Jervis argues:

International coalitions are more readily held together by fear than hope of gain. . . . It is no accident that most of the major campaigns of expansion have been waged by one dominant nation (for example, Napoleon's France and Hitler's Germany), and that coalitions among relative equals are usually found defending the status quo. Most gains from conquest are too uncertain and raise too many questions of future squabbles among the victors to hold an alliance together for long. Although defensive coalitions are by no means easy to maintain . . . the common interest of seeing that no state dominates provides a strong incentive for solidarity.[9]

For these reasons, the concept of the minimum winning coalition, which derives its logic from expectations of dividing the spoils of victory, is not operative for status-quo alliances, whose *raison d'être* is defense and/or deterrence and not conquest. Note that this hypothesis—that status-quo states are attracted to coalitions larger than necessary to defeat or deter the opposing state or alliance—contradicts a central tenet of balance of power theory, namely, that states react to power imbalances by joining the weaker side.

Indeed, all states were welcomed to pool their resources to fight Napoleon, the Kaiser, Hitler, and most recently Saddam Hussein. Thus, by war's end the resources of the status-quo coalitions far exceeded those of the aggressors.[10] Because Riker assumes that all actors are power maximizers (none are status quo), he cannot explain why overlarge coalitions have repeatedly formed throughout history. Critics of Riker's analysis point out that his assumption of only maximizing units also leads him to conclude wrongly that balance of power systems should be in continual disequilibrium.[11]

Status-quo states are not afforded the luxury of the size principle; they must endure the annoyances of large alliances, for example, increased transaction costs, disagreements over rules, and decisionmaking procedures that have distributional consequences regarding the burdens and benefits within the alliance.[12]

Recognizing that status-quo powers desire large, not minimum-winning, coalitions, it is important to point out that, *in practice, such coalitions have not always formed*, particularly by the outset of war. The reason is straightforward: sometimes (e.g., Europe during the 1930s) the status-quo powers are far weaker than the revisionist side. Status-quo states can form an overlarge coalition only if there are enough of them to do so. Furthermore, threat perception varies among states. All other things being equal, geographically remote states will perceive less threat to their security than will states that are contiguous or relatively close to potential aggressors. If and when these potential aggressors become active ones, the threat perception of remote states may change, such that they abandon their prior neutrality and join the status-quo coalition against the revisionist state or coalition.

Composition of Alliances: Birds of a Feather

Alliances are rarely a mix of revisionist and status-quo states. This is because revisionist states will only join a defensive, status-quo coalition if their survival absolutely demands it; otherwise they will flock together to overturn the status quo and thereby improve their power positions. Such bandwagoning behavior, however, creates tension for the revisionist leader, who, seeking a minimum winning coalition, must guard against "predatory" buckpassing, that is, states seeking to gain unearned spoils by following the jackal principle. In lieu of this inherent tension between the revisionist leader and its followers, revisionist states will tend to flock together, but only to a limited extent. Rather than balancing against the dominant revisionist power, other revisionist states will support it and egg it on, hoping to attain their own irredentist aims or simply to profit from whatever crisis emerges. Such behavior is captured by Italian Foreign Minister Ciano's remark of September 25, 1938, that "the Duce and I, though we did not incite Germany to war, have done nothing to restrain her."[13] Indeed, on June 10, 1940, Italy donned its traditional jackal clothing by entering the war after France had already been defeated.[14]

For the same reason that revisionist states flock together, status-quo states cannot readily embrace a revisionist state: To do so would be to risk unraveling the status quo to which they are committed. Further, status-quo coalitions promise a smaller payoff to dissatisfied states than do revisionist coalitions, since the former cannot, in principle and for domestic political reasons, offer territorial incentives to wean the revisionist state away from a revisionist coalition.

Intra-Alliance Dynamics: Entrapment/Abandonment Fears

First posited by Michael Mandelbaum, the concepts of entrapment and abandonment were systematically explored using a Prisoner's Dilemma, game-theoretic framework by Glenn Snyder, and later by Thomas Christensen and Jack Snyder.[15] Since the interests of alliance members are rarely identical, their partnership in a fluid multipolar international system (as opposed to a tight bipolar bloc system) is never absolutely firm. This potential fluidity produces entrapment/abandonment risks and anxieties within the alliance. "Entrapment," Glenn Snyder explains, "means being dragged into a conflict over an ally's interests that one does not share, or shares only partially."[16] The opposite fear is abandonment by the alliance partner, which may occur in a variety of ways: the ally may realign, dealign, or simply fail to live up to its treaty commitments when it is called upon to do so.

The alliance "dilemma" arises because it is difficult for states to reduce simultaneously the twin risks of entrapment and abandonment: they tend to vary inversely. In addition, the alliance game is embedded within an adversary game, and so a single action has multiple targets and consequences that must be taken into account. Thus, on the one hand, if the state tries to decrease the ally's fears of abandonment by demonstrating a firm commitment to the alliance, it may increase both the risk of entrapment by its ally and, in the adversary game, the hostility of the enemy. If, on the other hand, it weakens its commitment to the alliance in order to avoid entrapment, it heightens the ally's abandonment fears and may encourage the adversary to stand firmer.[17] As will be shown in chapters 4, 5, and 6, entrapment/abandonment dynamics significantly affected the intra-alliance politics of both the Axis and Allied coalitions.

State Responses to Threats

For security specialists, the question of how states respond to threats has been associated with the familiar "b" words: balancing, bandwagoning, and buckpassing.[18] Unfortunately, familiarity and frequent usage have not bred conceptual clarity. Indeed, a good case can be made that these metaphors, while descriptively colorful, have become more of a barrier than an aid to thoughtful analysis. For example, the literature has incorrectly treated these concepts as if they are mutually exclusive: that is, a state can balance, bandwagon, or buckpass but it cannot simultaneously do all three. It is easily shown, however, that all three behaviors and their respective goals can be achieved in one strategic move.

Consider, for instance, the Nazi-Soviet Nonaggression Pact from the Soviets' perspective. It was bandwagoning because the Soviets joined the strongest and most threatening side to avoid a German attack and to gain essentially unearned spoils in Central Europe. It was buckpassing because the German attack was redirected westward, where, Stalin believed, the two sides would bleed each other white to the advantage of the Soviet Union. The pact was therefore a clear example of "free riding": by facilitating war among the Western capitalist states, the Soviet Union would gain the benefits of a greatly diminished German and world capitalist threat without incurring the costs of fighting. Finally, it was also balancing because, by delaying a German attack, the Soviets were both buying time to bolster their depleted military forces and gaining additional territory and resources to defend themselves against Germany if and when it returned east.

The reason why these strategies can be implemented simultaneously is that, as Waltz has pointed out, balancing can be accomplished by both internal and external means. A threatened state, therefore, can bandwagon by joining the stronger or more dangerous side in order to redirect the threat elsewhere (pass the balancing buck to others) and/or gain time, space, and resources in preparation for war (internal balancing purposes).

The question of mutual exclusivity aside, there are six main strategies that states can pursue in response to a threat. Three involve alliance formation: balancing, bandwagoning, and binding; three are an alternative to alignment: distancing, buckpassing, and engagement. All six will be discussed in turn.

1. Balancing

Balancing means opposing the stronger or more threatening side in a conflict. It may take the form of either individual attempts by the threatened states to mobilize their national resources to match those of the challenger(s) or the establishment of formal or informal alliances directed against the rising state or coalition. When they have the capacity to do so, threatened states will engage in both types of balancing, internal and external, to counteract the threat. This is because states that attempt to avoid the costs of internal balancing but want the security benefits that an alliance offers will appear as unattractive allies to potential partners.

Several conditions are required for the balance of power to work. First and most basic, there must be some powerful states that wish to survive as autonomous actors, whose combined strength at least equals that of the strongest state in the system. Second, states must be vigilant and sensitive to changes in the distribution of capabilities, such as their ally growing weaker or their enemy growing stronger. Third, states must possess some mobility of action, that is, they must be able to respond quickly and decisively to changes in the balance of power. Fourth, external balancing often relies on the ability to project military power; therefore, status-quo states must not adopt strictly defensive military postures. Fifth, states essential to the balance must accept war as a legitimate tool of statecraft, even if they consider it to be a last resort. Lastly, ideology, religious affiliation, and prior territorial disputes must not rule out alignments needed to maintain the balance; that is, alliance handicaps impede the necessary fluidity in alliance making for a properly functioning balance-of-power system.[19]

2. Bandwagoning[20]

The term "bandwagoning" as a description of international alliance behavior first appeared in Quincy Wright's *A Study of War* and later in Kenneth Waltz's *Theory of International Politics*.[21] Both Wright and Waltz employ the concept of "bandwagoning" to serve as the opposite of balancing (which Wright calls "the underdog policy"): bandwagoning refers to joining the stronger coalition, balancing means allying with the weaker side.[22] Unlike Waltz, Wright believed that, under certain circumstances, great powers may engage in bandwagoning to preserve the balance of power. This occurs when "the stronger in a given war is a relatively weak state whose strengthening is necessary to hold a more powerful neighbor in check."[23]

2A. Walt's Bandwagoning: Preventive Strategic Surrender

Stephen Walt would call the above behavior balancing rather than bandwagoning. In *The Origins of Alliances* and several other works,[24] Walt offers a refinement of balance of power theory, called balance of threat theory. Like the structural balance of power theorists, Walt concludes that states usually balance and rarely bandwagon; but he argues that states do not align solely or even primarily in response to the distribution of capabilities. Alliance choices are driven instead by imbalances of threat—when one state or coalition is especially dangerous.[25] The level of threat that a state poses to others is the product of its aggregate power, geographic proximity, offensive capability, and the perceived aggressiveness of its intentions.

Walt claims that his theory "improves on traditional balance of power theory by providing greater explanatory power with equal parsimony."[26] Because aggregate power is only one of several components defining a threat, Walt's theory explains, *inter alia*, the formation of overlarge winning coalitions in World Wars I and II and "alliance choices when a state's potential allies are roughly equal in power. In such circumstances, a state will ally with the side it believes is least dangerous."[27]

Walt redefines the terms balancing and bandwagoning to suit his balance of threat theory: "When confronted by a significant external threat, states may either balance or bandwagon. *Balancing* is defined as allying with others against the prevailing threat; *bandwagoning* refers to alignment with the source of danger."[28] By these definitions, Walt, like Wright and Waltz before him, intends to place the concepts of balancing and bandwagoning in binary opposition: bandwagoning is meant to serve as the opposite of balancing. Without exception, the literature on alliance behavior in international relations theory has accepted Walt's definition of bandwagoning as aligning with the most menacing threat to a state's independence.[29]

In a later work, Walt fleshes out his definition of bandwagoning:

> Bandwagoning involves *unequal exchange*; the vulnerable state makes asymmetrical concessions to the dominant power and accepts a subordinate role. . . . Bandwagoning is an accommodation to pressure (either latent or manifest). . . . Most important of all, bandwagoning suggests a willingness to support or tolerate illegitimate actions by the dominant ally.[30]

One of several criteria for selecting a taxonomy is the "avoidance of unnecessary departures from common usage."[31] In borrowing the terms "balancing" and "bandwagoning" from balance of power theory, Walt wants to retain the original idea that "bandwagoning" should serve as the opposite of "balancing." But in so doing, he violates the rule of common usage with respect to the concept of bandwagoning.[32]

Conventional usage defines a bandwagon as a candidate, side, or movement that attracts adherents or amasses power by its momentum. The phrase, "to climb aboard the bandwagon," implies following a current or fashionable trend or joining the side that appears likely to win. Bandwagoning may be freely chosen or it can be the result of resignation to an inexorable force. By this standard, balance of power's definition of bandwagoning as "joining the stronger coalition" is faithful to common usage. Balance of threat's definition as "aligning with the source of danger" or "giving in to threats" only encompasses the coercive or compulsory aspect of the concept, captured by the phrase: "If you can't beat 'em, join 'em."

In fact, the behavior Walt defines as bandwagoning comes perilously close to the concept of capitulation, defined as "the act of surrendering or of yielding (as to a dominant influence)."[33] More specifically, Walt's bandwagoning is a preventive form of strategic surrender, by which the prospective loser agrees not to initiate hostilities and to transfer its residual military capability to the prospective winner in exchange for immunity of life, the avoidance of losses it would incur in a certain military rout, and (if the loser retains some bargaining assets) the possibility of political concessions, e.g., the survival of the loser's authority structure. Sometimes, the weaker side capitulates rather than fights in order to conserve its strength for a future battle under more favorable conditions. By giving in without a fight, it gains a breathing spell, during which it expects the balance of power to shift against the more powerful aggressor.[34]

In keeping with ordinary language, bandwagoning should not assume involuntary support gained through coercion, which is instead capitulation. This distinction is not simply a matter of "semantic taste." To see why, we must examine the motives Walt ascribes to bandwagoning:

What is the logic behind the bandwagoning hypothesis? Two distinct motives can be identified. First, bandwagoning may be adopted as a form of appeasement. By aligning with the threatening state or coalition, the bandwagoner may hope to avoid an attack on himself by diverting it elsewhere. Second, a state may align with the dominant side in war in order to share the spoils of victory. Mussolini's declaration of war on France and Russia's entry into the war against Japan in 1945 illustrate this type of bandwagoning, as do Italian and Romanian alliance choices in World War I. By joining what they believed was the stronger side, each hoped to make territorial gains at the end of the fighting.[35]

Walt correctly points out that states bandwagon out of fear of being despoiled or the desire to despoil others. But both motives for bandwagoning may be present when there is no imbalance of threat, that is, when neither side is perceived as significantly more dangerous than the other.

Consider Walt's first motive for bandwagoning: to avoid attack. For him, this means appeasing the most dangerous side. This need not be the case, however. Suppose war is coming, and a state caught in the crossfire must choose sides, but there is no imbalance of threat. Seeking shelter from the storm, the state may align with the stronger coalition because there is safety in numbers and its survival depends on its being on the winning side. Here, the source of greatest danger to the state does not come from one side or the other but from the consequences of being on the losing side, whichever that may be.[36]

Walt's second motive for bandwagoning—to share the spoils of victory—is certainly correct, but it is not consistent with his claim that "balancing and bandwagoning are more accurately viewed as a response to threats" rather than power imbalances.[37] Security from Germany was not the primary motivation for Italy's declaration of war against France in 1940 or Japan's decision to bandwagon with the Axis later in the year. Similarly, Stalin's eagerness to fight Japan in 1945 was driven more by the prospect of gaining unearned spoils than a desire for greater security from the U.S. or Japan. The opportunistic aspect of bandwagoning is especially important for assessing the alliance choices of revisionist states as will be discussed below. Walt identifies this motive but then overlooks it because the logic of his theory forces him to conflate the various forms of bandwagoning into one category: giving in to threats.

3. Binding

As the historian Paul Schroeder has pointed out, sometimes the function of alliances is not capability-aggregation but rather restraint or control over the actions of the partners in the alliance themselves. In such cases, states forego a counteralliance against a threatening state, which they fear may provoke greater conflict and perhaps war, and instead ally with the rival for the purpose of managing the threat by means of a pact of restraint (*pacta de contrahendo*).[38]

The state seeking to "bind" the rival hopes that, by allying with the source of threat, it will be able to exert some measure of control over its policy. An alliance accomplishes this by increasing both the state's influence over its ally and the number of opportunities it gets to voice its concerns. Along these lines, Joseph Grieco posits his "voice opportunities" thesis, according to which "weaker but still influential partners will seek to ensure that the rules [of a collaborative arrangement] so constructed . . . provide sufficient opportunities for them to voice their concerns and interests and thereby prevent or at least ameliorate their domination by stronger partners."[39]

When available, multilateral alliances and arrangements, such as collective security systems, are often used as a complement to or in lieu of bilateral "binding" strategies.[40] There are several objectives in adopting a multilateral binding policy. First, by incorporating the rising power in existing institutional arrangements, giving it a "place at the table" so to speak, the established powers seek to satisfy the prestige demands of the rising power. Second, through its membership in global institutions, the rising state is afforded a greater opportunity to voice its concerns and to build, in conjunction with the other great powers, a new international order that better reflects its enhanced power and interests. The established powers hope that this cooperative approach to change based on consensus will foster a renewed sense of legitimacy in the international order among all the great powers, including the rising power. Finally, the established powers use multilateral arrangements for the purpose of entangling the rising power in a web of policies that makes exercise of its power too costly. This assumes that the gains derived by the rising power from membership in the existing institutions are substantial, and that "belonging confers additional benefits from which outsiders can be excluded."[41]

4. Distancing

This hypothesis posits that threatened status-quo states will not ally with each other when their combined strength is insufficient to deter or defeat the aggressor(s). Instead, less directly threatened states will try to distance themselves from more immediately threatened states by refusing to coordinate their diplomatic and military strategies with the latter.[42] Distancing is frequently combined with the more positive strategy of trying to engage the enemy.

Suppose revisionist state A threatens status-quo states B and C, and $A > B + C$. No coalition is predicted, since A's strength exceeds B and C combined (which means that either B or C is not a pole or both B and C are not poles). In these types of situations, in which A is the dictator, a BC coalition will not form because joining the weaker side not only fails to make the state safer, but is also dangerous: the alliance may provoke the enemy and/or embolden its ally. In either case, the state is more likely to be dragged into a war it cannot win. Associating with the weaker alliance also increases the likelihood that the state will be seen as a potential target, while at the same time it risks diverting precious resources needed for home defense to the defense of its allies.

Geography plays a significant role in determining which states among the status-quo powers will exhibit distancing behavior and which will be desperately trying, despite the odds, to forge a coalition. The surplus security afforded by geostrategic insularity, which is unavailable to land powers, makes insular states (e.g., Britain, the U.S.) the most likely candidates for a distancing strategy. Obviously, a state that is contiguous to the aggressor, such as France during the interwar period, cannot hope to gain security by distancing itself from other status-quo states. For such states, distancing is not a serious strategic option.

In adopting a policy of distancing, the state seeks the boon Odysseus sought so successfully from Cyclops: to be eaten last.[43] Buying time in this way affords several benefits. First, the distancing state may be able to mobilize its defenses and thereby remedy the imbalance of power or at least make itself a less inviting future target for the aggressor. Second, the state can hope and pray that, before its number comes up, the aggressor will exhaust itself or satisfy its appetite for expansion. As Winston Churchill remarked about the behavior of Europe's small powers: "Each one hopes that if he feeds the crocodile enough, the crocodile will eat him last. All of them hope that the storm will pass before their turn comes to be devoured."[44]

Third, as the predatory state or coalition gains in strength with each conquest, the threat to other powerful status-quo states that have hitherto remained on the sidelines grows. Consequently, they are more likely to unite against the aggressor, switching from neutrality or twilight belligerence to active balancing. Fourth, there is always the possibility that, as time goes by, the opposing revisionist coalition will fall apart because of disputes over the division of military burdens and/or of the spoils of victory. And finally, the state may seek to be eaten last because it believes that the expansionist policies of the predator state will prove too costly for the latter's own domestic public, which will rise up and replace the hostile and expansionist government with a more friendly one.

For these reasons, when the potential status-quo coalition is weak, status-quo states often seek to distance themselves from other more immediately threatened states, that is, they choose to remain isolated even though potential allies are available. This hypothesis, I argue, captures the essence of British foreign policy in the late 1930s. It also explains why, after the fall of France, the Soviet Union distanced itself further from Britain rather than attempting to align with the underdog as balance of power theory predicts and against the source of greatest danger as balance of threat theory predicts.

The logic of the distancing hypothesis yields the following corollary hypothesis: The stronger two or more status-quo states become in relation to a more powerful revisionist state(s), the more they will draw together to oppose it (e.g., Britain toward France in 1939); and the weaker two or more status-quo states become relative to the revisionist threat, the more likely they will draw apart, e.g., The Little Entente and Belgium toward France after the Abyssinian crisis in 1935 and the remilitarization of the Rhineland in 1936.

5. Buckpassing

Buckpassing occurs when a threatened state attempts to ride free on the balancing efforts of others. In terms of the state's behavior, buckpassing is indistinguishable from distancing. The crucial difference between the two behaviors is that, in a buckpassing situation, the potential balancing coalition must be as strong or stronger than the attacker(s): A and B or $A + B > C$; where AB are the status-quo defenders and C is the revisionist state or coalition. Buckpassing is a form of "free-riding" behavior, and therefore it requires that there be a collective good (effective balancing) among the defending states. When the potential or actual coalition is not strong enough to deter or defend against the attackers, there is no collective good. Under these circumstances, status-quo states that eschew potential status-quo partners are not buckpassing but rather distancing. In a buckpassing situation, effective balancing against the attacker will benefit all potential targets of aggression whether or not they have been involved in the defeat or substantial weakening of that aggressor. It is therefore to each state's advantage not to incur the costs of balancing (i.e. the dilemma of the "free-rider") by redirecting the threat elsewhere and remaining on the sidelines. In other words, the buckpasser assumes that it can safely "bystand" while the defending state or coalition absorbs the initial blow of the attacker and in the process critically weakens or destroys it. For this reason, buckpassing has been associated correctly with the perception of defense advantage and wars of attrition.[45] If the buckpassing state believed otherwise (*viz.*, that the attacker would quickly overrun the defenders), it would not be in its interest to remain on the sidelines, since it would then be confronted by a newly triumphant and thus stronger attacker with fewer or no allies.

To this point, I have assumed that the defenders are strong enough *without* the help of the buckpasser to put down the threat. Even if we relax this assumption, at the very least, the defenders must be potentially strong enough *with* the aid of the abstaining state (the buckpasser) to effectively balance the threatening power or coalition. Otherwise, there is no collective good, free-rider dilemma, and therefore no buckpassing behavior.

6. Engagement

The policy of engagement refers to peaceful revision undertaken by established powers in an effort to accommodate the legitimate interests of a rising, dissatisfied power, which often demands territorial compensation for alleged harm to its interests through a shifting of the balance of power.[46] The most common form of engagement is the policy of appeasement, which attempts to settle international quarrels "by admitting and satisfying grievances through rational negotiation and compromise, thereby avoiding the resort to an armed conflict which would be expensive, bloody, and possibly very dangerous."[47] Typically, this process requires adjustments in territory and "spheres of influence" and the reallocation of global responsibilities and other sources of prestige commensurate with the growth in power of the rising state. Engagement is more than appeasement, however. It encompasses any attempt to socialize the dissatisfied power into acceptance of the established order. Engagement in this sense, it is worth pointing out, is distinguished from other policies not so much by its goals but by its means: it relies on the promise of rewards rather than the threat of punishment to influence the target's behavior.

The primary objective of an engagement policy is to minimize conflict and avoid war without compromising the integrity of the existing international order. In essence, the established powers seek to restore system equilibrium by adjusting the international hierarchy of prestige and the division of territory in accordance with the new global balance of power, while at the same time maintaining the formal institutional arrangements and informal rules of the system, that is, its governance structures.[48] The policy succeeds if such concessions convert the revolutionary state into a status-quo power with a stake in the stability of the system.

Engagement also serves three other important goals. First, it enables the status-quo powers to gain a clearer picture of the real (as opposed to declared) intentions and ambitions of the rising, dissatisfied power. Only by "engaging" Hitler's legitimate, pan-German aspirations could Britain and France discover whether Germany truly sought limited revision, as Hitler had repeatedly stated, or Continental hegemony and ultimately world conquest. Second, it is a useful policy for buying time to rearm and gain allies in case the rising power cannot be satisfied and war becomes necessary. Third, it can be used to break up dangerous combinations or to prevent them from occurring in the first place. For these purposes, engagement may be seen as an alternative to the formation of a counterbalancing alliance that risks uniting the dissatisfied powers into a rival coalition. The British government, viewing tight alliances as a primary cause of World War I, applied this insight in 1935, when it attempted to keep Italy out of the German orbit by appeasing Mussolini at the expense of Ethiopia and Spain. Indeed, Chamberlain's engagement policy toward Germany sought to accomplish all of the various goals associated with engagement, *viz.*, to satisfy Germany without recourse to war and without destroying the existing order; to uncover Hitler's true intentions; to buy time for rearmament; and to prevent the formation of a German-Italian alliance.

Engagement, when successful, is the most efficient and sensible solution to the rise of a dissatisfied power. It is a very tricky and sometimes dangerous policy to implement, however. For the policy to succeed, the rising power must have only limited revisionist aims and there can be no irreconcilable conflicts of vital interests among the powers.[49] As Martin Wight points out: "It is no good a satisfied power (let us say, Philip II's Spain) telling a dissatisfied power (let us say, Elizabethan England) that its legitimate interests can be fully secured within the existing arrangement of power, for there will be no possibility of agreement between what Spain calls 'legitimate' and what England calls 'vital.'"[50]

Moreover, engagement is most likely to succeed when the established powers are strong enough to mix concessions with credible threats, to use sticks as well as carrots, in their attempts to satisfy the rising power. Otherwise, concessions will signal weakness that emboldens the aggressor to demand more. For this reason, engagement should not be viewed as an alternative to balancing but rather as a complement to it—one that seeks a peaceful end to the rivalry and the balancing costs that accompany it.

Responses to Opportunities

There will be attempts to revise the status quo by force if the expected net gains for some state or group of states exceed the expected costs. Only when this condition is met would we expect to find attempts to alter the existing structure of institutions (prestige) and territory (power) in the system. Opportunity for gain is, however, merely a necessary and not a sufficient condition for expansionist behavior. Satisfied states, for instance, often do not take advantage of opportunities to expand. The explanation for this seemingly anomalous behavior involves the question of actor designation, that is, what unit of analysis is being examined.

In the above proposition, the reference to expected gains and losses applies to the state as a whole and not to specific individuals or groups within society. Since the costs of war are unevenly distributed among society, war always makes some persons worse off even if the majority gains. If we assert that most persons are risk averse when potential losses are high and the outcome is uncertain, then we should not expect leaders of "satisfied" states to undertake costly opportunistic expansion regardless of the anticipated overall benefits. This should be particularly true for satisfied *democratic* states, since war risks not only a majority backlash but also the formation of a hostile (anti-war) "passionate minority," which wields more political leverage than the unorganized or disinterested majority.[51] Recognizing that the primary goal of elected officials is to remain in office, democratic leaders are compelled to take a comparatively short-term, parochial (their own political futures) view of the gains and losses from war. In consequence, it is expected that, for political elites of satisfied democracies, a decision to initiate war will require more than a good probability that future gains will accrue to the state as an aggregate unit.

Bandwagoning For Profit

As mentioned, Walt associates bandwagoning with giving in to threats, unequal exchange favoring the dominant power, acceptance of illegitimate actions by the stronger ally, and involuntary compliance. This view of the concept illustrates the tendency among political scientists to ignore the role of positive inducements in the exercise of power. Yet, positive sanctions are the most effective means to induce bandwagoning behavior. States, like delegates at party conventions, are lured to the winning side because of the promise of future rewards.[52] By contrast, relying on force to coerce states to involuntarily bandwagon often backfires for the dominant partner. Seeking revenge, the unwilling bandwagoner becomes a treacherous ally that will bolt from the alliance the first chance it gets.

Bandwagoning dynamics move the system in the direction of change. Like a ball rolling down an incline, initial success generates further success, not greater resistance. In the language of systems theory, bandwagoning is a form of positive feedback. By contrast, the purpose of balancing behavior is to prevent systemic disequilibrium or, when deterrence fails, to restore the balance. Balancing is a form of negative feedback.[53]

This is not to suggest that bandwagoning effects are always undesirable— it depends on the nature of the existing order. If it is characterized by conflict, bandwagoning behavior may enhance the prospects for a more durable peace. In this regard, the bandwagon's *raison d'être* also matters. Jackal bandwagoning with a rising expansionist state or coalition that seeks to overthrow the status quo obviously decreases system stability. Conversely, "piling on" bandwagoning with the stronger status-quo coalition enhances system stability. Other forms of bandwagoning have indeterminate effects on system stability, e.g., wave of the future, falling dominoes, and the contagion effect.

What all these forms of bandwagoning have in common is that they are motivated by the prospect of making gains. Herein lies the fundamental difference between bandwagoning and balancing. Balancing is an extremely costly activity that most states would rather not engage in but sometimes must to survive and protect their values. Bandwagoning rarely involves costs and is typically done in the expectation of gain. This is why bandwagoning is more common, I believe, than Walt and Waltz suggest.

1. Jackal Bandwagoning

The primary goal of jackal bandwagoning is profit. Specifically, revisionist states bandwagon to share in the spoils of victory.[54] Because unlimited-aims revisionist powers cannot bandwagon (they are the bandwagon), offensive bandwagoning is done exclusively by lesser aggressors, what I call limited-aims revisionist states. Typically, the lesser aggressor reaches an agreement with the unlimited-aims revisionist leader on spheres of influence, in exchange for which the junior partner supports the revisionist leader in its expansionist aims. Just as the lion attracts jackals, a powerful revisionist state or coalition attracts opportunistic revisionist powers.[55]

Aside from the pleasure of acquiring additional territory, the motivation for jackal bandwagoning may also be security from the lion itself. As Roy Douglas remarks, "Stalin merits Churchill's famous epithet, "Hitler's jackal" as richly as does Mussolini, to whom it was applied. Pickings from the lion's kill were succulent and satisfying for lesser beasts; but they also afforded these creatures strength to resist the greater predator should he later turn his attentions to them."[56]

Sometimes the revisionist leader (pole) is stronger than the opposing status-quo coalition. In such cases, the revisionist leader does not require the active assistance of the junior partner. Instead, it seeks to prevent or block the formation of a powerful status-quo coalition.[57] When blocking is the goal, the revisionist leader often allows the limited-aims revisionist state to gain unearned spoils in exchange for a pledge not to join the adversarial coalition. Because the jackal is a scavenger and not a true predator, this type of bandwagoning is a form of predatory buckpassing: the jackal seeks to ride free on the offensive efforts of others.

Exemplifying this strategy, Hitler encouraged Italy, the Soviet Union, Japan, Hungary, and Bulgaria to feed on the pickings of the Nazi lion's kill in order to block the formation of a dangerous rival coalition. Together, Mussolini and Hitler successfully played on Hungary's and Bulgaria's revisionist aspirations to lure these states into the Axis camp. As part of the Munich agreement of September 30, 1938, a German-Italian court of arbitration pressured the Czech government to grant a broad strip of southern Slovakia and Ruthenia to Hungary. Then, when the Germans carved up the rest of Czechoslovakia in March 1939, Hitler, in a deliberate attempt to gain further favor with the Hungarian government, ceded the remainder of Ruthenia (Carpatho-Ukraine) to Hungary. In exchange for these territorial rewards, Hungary pledged its unshakeable support for the Nazi cause and its "foreign policy was brought into line with that of the Reich. On February 24, 1939, Hungary joined the Anti-Comintern Pact, on April 11 it left the League of Nations."[58]

2. Piling On

Piling on bandwagoning occurs when the outcome of a war has already been determined. States typically bandwagon with the victor to claim an unearned share of the spoils. When this is the motive, piling on is simply jackal bandwagoning that takes place at the end of wars. Contrariwise, states may pile on because they fear the victors will punish them if they do not actively side against the losers. Whatever the motivation, either opportunity or fear, piling on is a form of predatory buckpassing with regard to the winning coalition.

Historically, most major wars have ended with piling on behavior. In the War of the Spanish Succession, for instance, Louis XIV watched his hopes for victory vanish when two of his staunchest allies, Portugal and the Duke of Savoy, deserted the Franco-Spanish coalition and bandwagoned with the Grand Alliance to make gains at Spain's expense.[59] The Napoleonic Wars ended when Sweden, Austria, Spain, and certain German and Italian states sided with Prussia, Britain, and Russia at the precise moment that Napoleon's defeat appeared certain.[60]

During the First World War, Japan bandwagoned with the Entente powers because it coveted German possessions in Asia, while China did so to gain Anglo-French protection from Japan and Imperial Russia. For its part, Italy, expecting to gain unearned spoils at Austria's expense, declared war against its former friends in May of 1915.[61] In 1916, Russia's decisive victory over Austria persuaded Romania to enter the war on the Allied side.

In World War II, the Soviets wanted a fight to the finish with Japan to get in on the kill and thereby share in Japan's occupation. The U.S. had lost interest in Soviet help, however, as American forces had already borne the brunt of the Pacific war. In contrast, Turkey wanted to remain neutral but was coerced by the Allies into declaring war against Germany and Japan on February 23, 1945. Ankara did so because of the Allied decision not to invite to the coming San Francisco Conference to organize the United Nations any country that had not entered the war against the Axis by March 1, 1945.

3. Wave of the Future

States may bandwagon with the stronger side because they believe it represents the "wave of the future." During the Cold-War era, for example, many less-developed countries viewed communism in this way. Consequently, they did not have to be coerced to join the Sino-Soviet bloc. Third World elites as well as the masses were attracted to communism for rational reasons: they thought they could profit by it, as had the Chinese and the Soviets. This type of bandwagoning most concerned George Kennan in 1947, for he understood "that a given proportion of the adherents to the [communist] movement are drawn to it . . . primarily by the belief that it is the coming thing, the movement of the future . . . and that those who hope to survive—let alone to thrive—in the coming days will be those who have the foresight to climb on the bandwagon when it was still the movement of the future."[62] And indeed, the success of Sputnik caused more dominoes to fall than Soviet military pressure ever could. Recently, states throughout the globe have abandoned communism in favor of the newest wave of the future, liberal democracy. Van Evera points out that "the chain of anti-communist upheavals in Eastern Europe during 1989" is "the only widespread domino effect on record."[63] Yet, the massive decolonization of the 1950s and 1960s exhibited a similar domino effect. Both trends are instances of benign positive feedback, that is, they altered the course of international politics in a more stabilizing direction.

Wave-of-the-future bandwagoning is typically induced by charismatic leaders and dynamic ideologies, especially when buoyed by massive propaganda campaigns and demonstrations of superiority on the battlefield. Here, the bandwagon becomes a "mass orgy feeling that sweeps with the fervor of a religious revival."[64] For example, Germany's stunning military victories in May of 1940 convinced Japan to reverse its neutralist policy and bandwagon with the Axis. Hosoya writes:

[T]he rising prestige of Germany in the eyes of the Japanese resulted in resurrecting pro-Nazi sentiment from its demise following the conclusion of the Nonaggression Pact. This change in public opinion naturally affected the balance of power between the Anglo-American and Axis factions in Japan. Second, the existence of the French and Dutch colonies in Indochina and the East Indies now swam into the ken of the Japanese people, and a mood to seize the opportunity to advance into Southeast Asia spread to all strata of society.[65]

In this case, the Japanese public's psychological desire to support a winner dovetailed with their more rational interest in jackal opportunism. Both goals were captured by Japan's catch-phrase of the day, "Don't miss the bus."[66]

In its rarest form, wave-of-the-future bandwagoning may be the result of leaders and their publics simply enjoying "the feeling of 'going with the winner'—even a winner about whose substantive qualities they have no illusions."[67] With this in mind, Machiavelli criticized the Venetians for foolishly inviting King Louis "to plant his foot in Italy."

The king, then, having acquired Lombardy, immediately won back the reputation lost by Charles. Genoa yielded, the Florentines became his friends, the Marquis of Mantua, the Dukes of Ferrara and Bentivogli, the Lady of Forli, the Lords of Faenza, Pesaro, Rimini, Camerino, and Piombino, the inhabitants of Lucca, of Pisa, and of Siena, all approached him with offers of friendship. The Venetians might then have seen the effects of their temerity, how to gain a few cities in Lombardy they had made the king ruler over two-thirds of Italy.[68]

Other examples of supporting-the-winner bandwagoning include the near-unanimous enthusiasm with which the southern German states joined Prussia after its defeat of France in 1871 and with which the Austrians embraced the *Anschluss* with Germany in 1938.

4. The Contagion or Domino Effect

Throughout the Cold War era, the metaphors of "spreading disease" and "falling dominoes" were used interchangeably by U.S. officials to support the policy of containing communism. The Truman administration employed the contagion metaphor to justify intervening in Greece in 1947: "Like apples in a barrel infected by one rotten one, the corruption of Greece would infect Iran and all to the East. It would also carry infection to Africa through Asia Minor and Egypt, to Europe and France . . ."[69] The same argument became known as the "domino theory" when President Eisenhower used the metaphor in reference to Southeast Asia: "You have a row of dominoes set up, you knock over the first one, and what will happen to the last one is the certainty that it will go over very quickly. So you could have a beginning of a disintegration that would have the most profound influences."[70] More recently, President Reagan argued that if we "ignore the malignancy in Managua," it will "spread and become a mortal threat to the entire New World."[71]

Whether the metaphor is infection or falling dominoes, the underlying dynamic is the same: the bandwagon is set in motion by an external force, which touches off a chain reaction, fueling the bandwagon at ever-greater speeds. This mechanistic version of the domino theory posits revolutions as "essentially external events" that spread quickly because countries within a region are tightly linked and "because revolutions actively seek to export themselves."[72] Similarly, the contagion effect proposes tight regional linkages and cascading alliances as explanations for the spread of war.[73] To be sure, these metaphors capture not reality but rather, in Douglas Macdonald's words, "a stereotypical oversimplification of the international system and how it works."[74] Macdonald argues persuasively for a more nuanced, "contingent version" of the domino theory, which "adds several important qualifications in its description of domino dynamics that deny the theory's mechanistic and deterministic properties: dominoes are *likely* to fall under *certain* conditions *if* no action is taken to interrupt or confound the process."[75]

Though associated with the spread of revolution and war, contagion-type bandwagoning can also exert a positive influence on the stability of the international system. Consider, for instance, the recent land-for-peace accord between the Palestine Liberation Organization and Israel. In response to the agreement, Jordan, Syria, and Lebanon are each reported to be seeking similar arrangements with Israel. In the words of Uri Savir, the Foreign Ministry's director general who led the Israeli team in the secret negotiations with the PLO in Norway, "With all the progress around, everybody in the region seems to make an effort to jump on this new bandwagon."[76] In what appears to be the latest aftershock of the historic earthquake that ended the Cold War, a peculiar domino effect is unfolding in the Middle East—peculiar in that it is being welcomed by most scholars and practitioners of international relations.

5. Holding the Balance

In addition to bandwagoning policies, a revisionist state can create opportunities to make gains by instigating conflict among other states and extorting payments from them. A state that holds the balance of power can engage in these policies because it alone can contribute decisive strength to one side or the other. As discussed in the prior chapter, it can play the role of balancer or kingmaker.

As balancer, it is not interested in victory, but (viewed in a most charitable light) in repose and the restoration of system equilibrium. Sometimes, this can be accomplished by its assuming the passive role of intermediary, carrying conditions of peace from one camp to the other; at other times it must exert its strength as an armed mediator, dictating the terms of peace.[77] Both roles require the balancer to detach itself from others' rivalries and retain its freedom of action as long as it is unnecessary to commit itself, that is, as long as a stalemate exists between the two warring parties or coalitions. If one side gains the upper hand, the balancer directs its strength to the weaker side to restore the balance of power.

This disinterested view of the balancer's motives, however, is more myth than reality. In fact, the balancer usually seeks to divide and conquer; to retain the illusion of managing the system for the benefit of all, while doing so for its own selfish interests. Making this point, Kissinger suggests that "an isolationist, suspicious Britain, eager to play its traditional role of balancer of the equilibrium, was more likely to encourage divisions on the Continent than to ameliorate them."[78]

As kingmaker, the holder of the balance sells its services to the highest bidder. Maintaining its neutrality until the last moment, the kingmaker extorts profit by ensuring that it is the last to declare its allegiance to one or the other side in a conflict, when the supply of available allies is low and the demand for them is high.

In both roles, the state takes advantage of its fortuitous position to create opportunities for gain. In this regard, geography plays an important role. Insular powers, such as Britain and the United States, have been able to remain neutral in the balance of power system and therefore to hold the balance. Only the masterful diplomatic dexterity of a Metternich can maneuver an exposed Continental power, such as Austria was in 1812, into the balancer role, and thereby "to create what geographic separation supplied to more favoured states."[79] Whether taking the characteristic American form of profiting by other people's wars, or the British one of divide (the continent of Europe) and rule (elsewhere), holding the balance allows the state to make gains by inciting, aiding, and abetting conflict among others or simply by lying low and profiting from their misfortunes.

Holding the balance is not a guarantee of success. Instigating conflict is always a risky business *unless the balancer is stronger than both sides combined.* When this is not the case, the balancer must make sure that the differences among the other powers are greater than their collective differences with it. Otherwise, the balancer role will backfire with disastrous results, especially if, instead of an exhausting war of attrition, one side decisively defeats the other, or if both sides decide to put aside their rivalry and gang up against it.

An Alternative Theory of Alliances: Balance of Interests

To this point, I have argued that states can choose among many different strategies in response to threats and opportunities. I have also argued that the goals of the state, whether revisionist or status quo, affect its choice of policy. It is now time to bring in the capabilities of states as well as their interests and link these two elements to policy decisions. To do this, I propose the theory of balance of interests. The concept of balance of interests has a dual meaning, one at the unit level, the other at the systemic level. At the unit level, it refers to the costs a state is willing to pay to defend the status quo relative to the costs it is willing to pay to modify it. At the systemic level, it refers to the relative strengths of status-quo and revisionist states.

a. Balance of Interests at the Unit Level

To many observers throughout history, international politics has resembled a jungle, in which strong beasts and frightened rabbits coexist in a realm wonderfully described by Shakespeare in *Timon of Athens*: "If you wert the lion, the fox would beguile thee; if you wert the lamb, the fox would eat thee; if you wert the fox, the lion would suspect thee; . . . if you wert the wolf thy greediness would afflict thee, and oft thou shouldst hazard thy life for thy dinner."[80]

The following typology based on state interests and capabilities is inspired by this passage and is largely consistent with the behaviors Shakespeare attributes to the various beasts.

Lions are states that will pay high costs to protect what they possess but only a small price to increase their values. The primary goal of these states is consistent with contemporary Realism's assumption of actors as defensive positionalists and security-maximizers. But lions seek more than mere self-preservation. They are willing to pay high costs to protect and defend the existing international order. As the "defenders" of the status quo, they must be great powers of the first rank.

The choice of the lion to represent these states is partly inspired by Machiavelli's famous discussion of the lion and the fox: "A prince being thus obliged to know well how to act as a beast must imitate the fox and the lion, for the lion cannot protect himself from traps, and the fox cannot defend himself from wolves. One must therefore be a fox to recognize traps, and a lion to frighten wolves."[81]

Just as lions are the king of the jungle, satisfied polar powers rule and manage the international system. After all, states that find the status quo most agreeable are usually the ones that created the existing order; as the principal beneficiaries of the status quo, they more than anyone else have a vested interest in preserving it.[82] And just as lions "frighten wolves," status-quo poles must deter powerful revisionist states from aggression or, if that fails, bear the brunt of the fighting in order to defeat them. They take on these responsibilities not primarily in the expectation of gain or for altruistic reasons but rather for self-preservation and to maintain their relative positions and prestige in the system.[83] Providing for the common defense is a "dirty job but someone has to do it," and only great powers of the first rank can.[84] As Walter

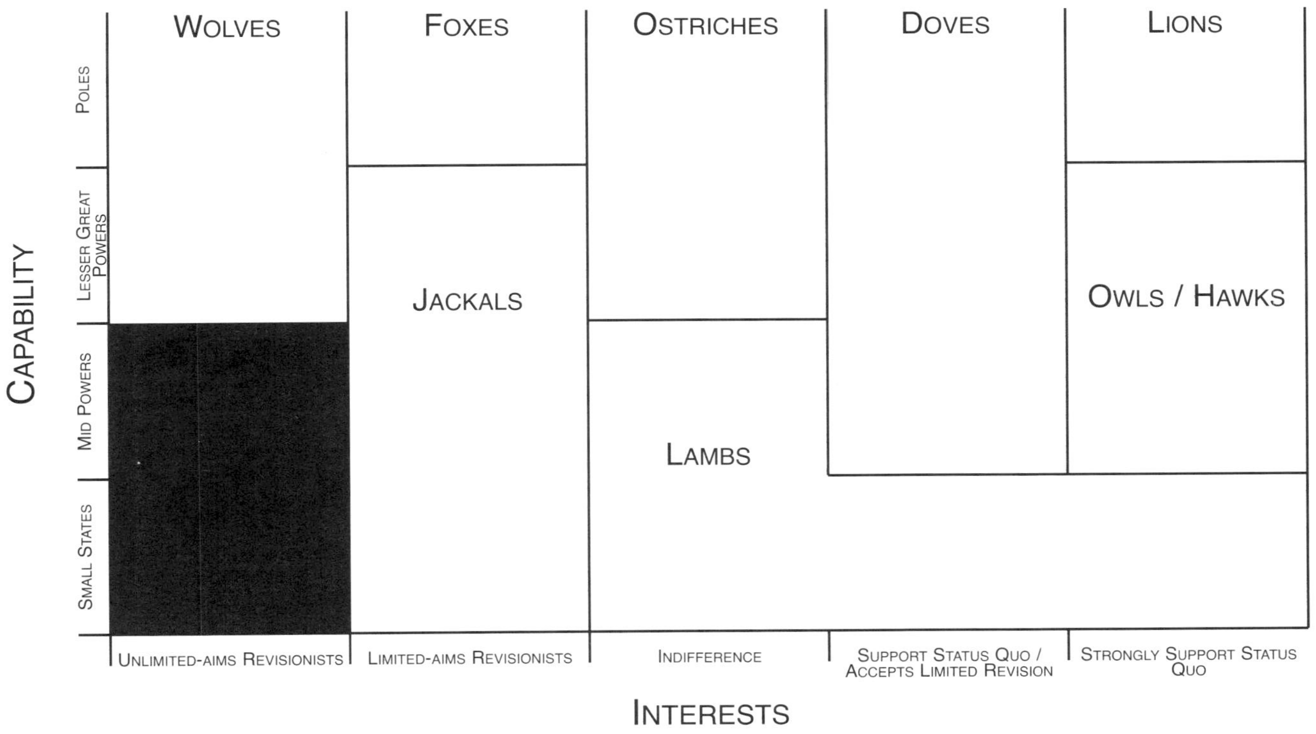

CAPABILITY

	SMALL STATES	MID POWERS	LESSER GREAT POWERS	POLES
UNLIMITED-AIMS REVISIONISTS				WOLVES
LIMITED-AIMS REVISIONISTS	JACKALS			FOXES
INDIFFERENCE	LAMBS			OSTRICHES
SUPPORT STATUS QUO / ACCEPTS LIMITED REVISION		OWLS / HAWKS		DOVES
STRONGLY SUPPORT STATUS QUO				LIONS

INTERESTS

FIGURE 3.1

Lippmann put it: "Only a great power can resist a great power. Only a great power can defeat a great power."[85] If they believe that others will provide these collective goods for them, however, they will be tempted to pass the buck.

Owls and Hawks are lesser great powers and middle powers that strongly support the status quo but do not possess enough military strength individually to defend it against challenges by strong revisionist states or coalitions. Their beliefs about the causes of conflict are consistent with the "deterrence model" view,[86] in that they perceive the rival to be a true aggressor that cannot be appeased but must instead be contained by superior force.

Whether they are classified as owls or hawks depends on whether the perceived threat to the existing international order is real or imagined. When the threat is real, as in the case of Hitler's Germany, they are owls, too wise to be fooled by a wolf in sheep's clothing. When the threat is imagined, they are hawks, whose aggressive behavior in support of the status quo provokes unnecessary conflict with essentially status-quo states that seek only limited and legitimate claims.

When a "lion" state exists, these states act as supporters, actively balancing (if they have the strength to do so) the revisionist power or coalition. In the absence of a lion, these states may still be able to contain or defeat the revisionist threat provided that there are a sufficient number of them to achieve the task and/or the revisionist threat is weaker than their individual strengths (that is, the aggressor is not a pole). In either case, however, they may still fail to balance the threat or they may do so in ragged fashion because of the "free-rider" problem. Specifically, less directly threatened states will be tempted to pass the balancing buck to more directly threatened ones. If a sufficient number of them engage in buckpassing behavior, the collective good of security will not be provided.

That said, a coalition among owls and hawks—true believers in the aggressive intentions and unlimited-aims of the enemy—is unlikely to be plagued by buckpassing behavior. Indeed, even when no lion exists and the combined strength of the status-quo supporters is weaker than that of the revisionist state(s), they will still form a coalition and, if pushed to do so, go to war in the belief that resistance is morally required regardless of whether the outcome has even a chance to succeed.

Ostriches are great powers (or potential ones) that behave instead like weak, insignificant states. They have the capacity (power potential) to impose their will on others, "to take the initiative, make alliances, stand at the head of coalitions,"[87] but choose not to exercise it (activate it). Instead, they will expend only those resources necessary to ensure that others cannot impose their will on them; to survive and safeguard their own autonomy. A state in this category, such as the United States in the 1930s, "makes use only of its 'defensive power,' adopts an attitude of 'isolationism,' it foregoes participating in competition, it refuses to enter the system, it desires to be left in peace."[88]

Doves are essentially status-quo states that hold a "spiral model"[89] view of the causes of conflict and war. Perceiving the demands of the opponent as basically defensive in nature, they are willing to accept some peaceful revision of the status quo for the purpose of appeasing the "legitimate" (in their eyes) grievances of dissatisfied powers.

Their main objective is to maintain the peace without sacrificing the essential characteristics of the status-quo order. For this purpose, they adopt engagement policies (e.g., appeasement, compromise, bilateral and multilateral binding) rather than a containment strategy, which is the preferred policy of hawks and owls, with respect to the dissatisfied state(s). In addition, doves avoid "tight" alliances directed against the revisionist state(s) for fear that this will simply provoke unnecessary conflict and perhaps war. Instead, doves prefer to distance themselves from available allies, particularly when the status-quo coalition is too weak to provide sufficient defense or deterrence.

Lambs are countries that will pay only low costs to defend or extend their values. In a world of predators and prey, these states are prey. Lambs are weak states in that they possess relatively few capabilities and/or suffer from poor state-society relations for a variety of reasons: their elites and institutions lack legitimacy *vis-à-vis* the masses; they are internally divided along, ethnic, political, class, religious, or tribal fault lines; the state's ideology conflicts with and is imposed on the popular culture; or they are what Samuel Huntington calls torn countries—states "that have a fair degree of cultural homogeneity but are divided over whether their society belongs to one civilization or another."[90]

Because lambs are unwilling to sacrifice to extend their values, their foreign policy is not driven by irredentist aims. This distinguishes them from jackals, which may also be weak states. Lambs often bandwagon, as Walt implies, to divert and appease threats. But some, especially torn countries, engage in wave-of-the-future and domino bandwagoning. Others ally with the stronger side for protection from more pressing dangers or out of fear of being despoiled if they wind up on the losing side. As a strategy for long-term security, however, allying with a stronger power will fail miserably when it is an insatiable predator. In such cases, "an alliance between a big and a small power is an alliance between the wolf and the sheep, and it is bound to end with the wolf devouring the sheep."[91] When possible, lambs will choose not to align with either side but instead to distance themselves from more directly threatened states.

Good examples of lambs are Czechoslovakia, Romania, Austria, and Yugoslavia during the 1930s. In every case except Romania,[92] the country's decision to bandwagon with Hitler was facilitated by the successful penetration of Nazi fifth columns into the state and large segments of society.[93]

Foxes are limited-aims revisionist powers of the first rank that use their cunning to make easy gains at the expense of their rivals. Foxes feign indifference to the status quo in order to hold the balance of power between the rising, dissatisfied states and the established powers. Having cleverly maneuvered themselves into a position of decisive power, foxes benefit from—and so foment and incite—other people's conflicts, in which they can assume the role of either the balancer, dividing and conquering the others, or kingmaker, extorting maximum profit from the desperate bidders on both sides.

Foxes do not always "out-fox" their rivals, however. Sometimes their greedy designs prove to be too clever by half. The Soviet Union, for example, held the balance of power in 1939, as Stalin had planned all along. Unfortunately for the Russians, however, Stalin misperceived the actual distribution of capabilities in the system. Specifically, he was misled by the inflated prestige (reputation for power)[94] of France and Britain and so overestimated their military power relative to that of Germany. In consequence, by directing the Nazi threat westward, Stalin thought he was playing the role of balancer but was instead playing the role of kingmaker. This misguided strategy backfired when Germany—with Russia as an unwitting accomplice—swiftly defeated France, Stalin's last potential ally on the Continent.

Jackals are limited-aims revisionist states. Like wolves, jackals are dissatisfied powers; but, unlike wolves, they are either too weak to have unlimited revisionist goals and/or they are not entirely dissatisfied with their place in the existing order. For these reasons, they tend to be risk-averse, opportunistic expanders. To use a biblical metaphor: the jackal trails the lion to scavenge the scraps it leaves behind. In our scheme, jackals are often found trailing wolves (revisionist leaders), but they will also trail lions (the status-quo leaders) when they are on the verge of victory—what I call piling-on bandwagoning. Both forms of bandwagoning are examples of predatory buckpassing: attempts to ride free on the offensive efforts of others.

Wolves are predatory states with unlimited aims. They are very hungry, revolutionary powers that consider the international order oppressive and intolerable. As states that value what they covet far more than what they possess, they are willing to take great risks—even if losing the gamble means extinction—to improve their condition. Like terminally ill patients, wolves are uninhibited by the fear of loss and so are free to pursue reckless expansion. Thus, Hitler told his commanders in chief on the eve of war: "It is easy for us to make decisions. We have nothing to lose; we have everything to gain. . . . We have no other choice, we must act. Our opponents will be risking a great deal and can gain only a little."[95]

Though usually offensive, the motivation of the wolf may be defensive as well; it may be sincere in its claim of feeling threatened. What distinguishes it from other states that feel threatened, however, is that only absolute security—its complete domination of everyone else—can reassure it.[96]

The historical record is replete with examples of states that sought to maximize or significantly increase their power; that put their own survival at risk to improve, not maintain, their positions in the system. Alexander the Great, Rome, the Arabs in the seventh and eighth centuries, Charles V, Philip II, Frederick the Great, Louis XIV, Napoleon I, and Hitler all lusted for universal empire and waged "all-or-nothing," apocalyptic wars to attain it. Seeking to conquer the world or a large portion of it, wolves do not balance or bandwagon; they are the bandwagon.

b. Balance of Interests at the Systemic Level

At the systemic level, balance of interest theory suggests that the distribution of capabilities, by itself, does not determine the stability of the system. More important are the goals and means to which those capabilities or influence are put to use: whether power and influence is used to manage the system or destroy it; whether the means employed to further such goals threaten other states or make them feel more secure. In other words, the stability of the system is a function of the balance of revisionist and conservative forces. When status-quo states are far more powerful than revisionist states, the system will be stable. When a revisionist state or coalition is more powerful than the defenders of the status quo, the system will eventually undergo change—only the questions of when, how, and to whose advantage remain undecided. As figure 3.2 shows, revisionist forces far outmuscled those in support of the

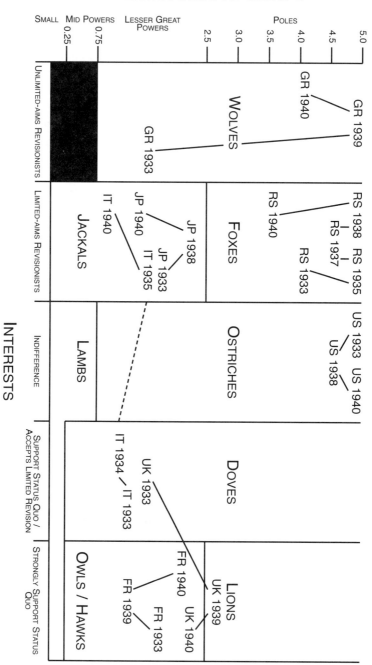

FIGURE 3.2

established order; and this is the deadly imbalance to which the title of the book refers.

In history, revisionist powers have been the agents of change in international politics; status-quo states are the "reactors." Wolfers writes: "Because self-extension almost invariably calls for additional power, countries that seek self-extension tend to be the initiators of power competition and the resort to violence. Herein lies the significant kernel of truth in the idealist theory of aggression."[97] Aggressor states must exert initial pressure (that is, present a significant external threat) before satisfied Powers will respond, often slowly and reluctantly, with counterpressure. The vernacular of modern realism refers to this reaction as "balancing behavior," which the theory generalizes to apply to all states. But what, then, is the initial pressure exerted by the revisionist states called? In this light, it can be seen that the opposite of balancing is not bandwagoning, as today's realists claim, but rather aggression. In the absence of a reasonable external threat, states need not, and typically do not, engage in balancing.

It is not surprising, therefore, that the Concert of Europe replaced the balance of power system in 1815, when all the war-weary Great Powers accepted and warmly embraced the status quo.[98] The balance of power system was restored with the outbreak of the Crimean War, when a revitalized France no longer accepted the status quo and instead sought to reestablish its prior hegemony over the Continent. This suggests that the presence of Great Powers that are all known to accept the status quo and are unlikely to pursue unilaterally expansionist goals is a necessary and sufficient explanation for a Concert system; balance of power systems simply cannot survive under such conditions.[99] Balance of interest theory, by focusing on variations in actors' preferences, can account for this change; structural balance of power theory and balance of threat theory cannot.

Chapter 4

Hitler's Tripolar Strategy

This chapter offers a structural interpretation of Hitler's grand strategy based on the discussion of equilateral tripolarity with two revisionist poles presented in chapter 2. Aware of the tripolar structure of the international system, Hitler constructed a grand strategy to destroy the other two poles, Russia and the United States, and thereby establish German global mastery.

Hitler's program consisted of four stages. First, Germany would rearm and secure alliances with two key LGPs—Britain and Italy. Next, Germany would unleash several lightning wars against its neighbors in order to bolster its military and economic resources and to pacify its Western flank in preparation for the Eastern campaign. Under the shelter of British neutrality or, better still, with British help, the Reich would then strike quickly to eliminate the nearest pole, the Soviet Union, before the more distant pole, the United States, could intervene. The defeat of Soviet Russia would transform the tripolar system into a bipolar one, pitting the stronger German-led European continent against the weaker North American continent (Hitler believed that the U.S. would annex Canada). Germany would now be "entirely self-reliant and capable of withstanding any economic blockade which might have been staged by the major maritime powers."[1]

With Europe as the nucleus of the German empire, Hitler would then set in motion the next step of his Program: the defeat of America and the creation of a global German empire. In preparation for this final war, the Reich would expand overseas from its continental base and retool its armed forces—with the Luftwaffe and navy receiving priority over the army. After establishing power bases in Europe, Africa, and the Atlantic, Germany would attack and crush the United States, converting the international system from bipolarity to unipolarity.

The War of Stages

The roots of Hitler's Program, the *Stufenplan* as set down in *Mein Kampf* in 1925, are easily traced to the Bismarckian and Wilhelmine eras. By the late nineteenth century, German geopoliticians had proposed a two-stage plan for Germany to achieve the status of a world power: first, the creation of a continental base, followed by overseas, colonial expansion. To these two stages, Hitler added a third: a final hegemonic war between the European and American continents that would end in German world dominion.[2]

In his discussions of the balance of power, Hitler, unlike his nineteenth-century predecessors, spoke of the international system in tripolar, rather than multipolar (5 or more poles), terms. France and Britain, he believed, were decaying powers that had long ago fallen to second-class status.[3] Of the remaining great powers, only Stalinist Russia and the United States were capable of thwarting Germany's drive for hegemony. Luckily for Germany, however, during the 1930s, Russia and the United States were both preoccupied with internal problems, and so showed little interest in the fate of Europe. Likewise, Europe seemed scarcely to notice the affairs of the two great powers on its flanks. This state of affairs—the unactualized potential power of Germany's most dangerous rivals and the mutual disinterest among Russia, the U.S., and Europe—offered Germany a window of opportunity to defeat Russia and grab the Continent.

The Two Rival Poles

The tripolar image of a united Europe withering under the shadows cast by American and Russian power surfaces throughout Hitler's writings. Similarly, Karl Haushofer, Hitler's leading geopolitician, warned of the force inherent in vast spaces, which made Russia and America the twin threats posing the great-est danger to European civilization.[4] Only a united Europe under German leadership could prevent the tyranny of North America and Bolshevik Asia. Accordingly, Hitler argued that German needed to expand not merely for its own sake but also to ensure the independence of Europe. Hitler's propaganda of defending European civilization against alien barbarism attracted adher-ents from all parts of Europe to the Nazi cause. The crusade to create a united Europe "appealed to . . . young men from Holland, Belgium, and Scandinavia, who joined the Waffen SS to save Europe from Asiatic barbarism, by which they meant the Soviet Union."[5] Of the American threat, Hitler remarked, "Since today Germany's economic fate vis-à-vis America is in fact also the fate of other nations in Europe, there is again a movement . . . to oppose a European union to the American Union in order thereby to prevent a threat-ening world hegemony of the North American continent."[6]

Hitler did not believe that he would live to see the German-American war for world supremacy. The fight against the United States was a goal reserved for future generations of racially superior Germans after the Führer's death. Instead, Hitler's primary task was to defeat the Soviet Union, the nearest polar power and so Germany's primary target, and establish hegemony over the Continent. The key for Germany was to avoid a two-front war. This could be accomplished, the Führer believed, by defeating France quickly and then, with Germany's rear secure and Britain's blessings, attacking and crushing the Soviet Union. Several decades later, Britain and Germany would be in position to conquer the North American continent. Of the latter task, Hitler said: "I rejoice on behalf of the German people at the idea that one day we will see England and Germany marching together against America."[7]

The American Threat

In his speeches of 1919–20, Hitler displayed grudging respect for American economic and political power and an awareness of the scope of its potential strength. Explaining the Senate's rejection of Wilson's League of Nations and Versailles Settlement, Hitler said, "she is mighty enough and does not need the help of others . . . and she feels restricted in her freedom of action."[8] Several years later, in *Mein Kampf*, Hitler made several references to the awe-some power of the United States. At one point, he touts American power in order to point out the superiority of continental growth as opposed to colo-nial expansion as a method to acquire power:

Many European States today are comparable to pyramids standing on their points. Their European territory is ridiculously small as compared with their burden of colonies, foreign trade, etc. One may say, the point is in Europe, the base in the whole world; in comparison with the American Union, which still has its bases in its own continent and touches the remaining part of the world only with its points. From this results, however, the unheard-of strength of this State and the weakness of most of the European colonial powers.[9]

In his second book (1928), Hitler argued that Europe's privileged place in the world order was endangered by the North American Continent. "With the American Union, a new power of such dimensions has come into being as threatens to upset the whole former power and orders of rank of the states."[10] Continuing on this theme, Hitler wrote:

That this danger threatens all of Europe has, after all, already been perceived by some today. Only few of them wish to understand what it means for Germany. Our people, if it lives with the same thoughtlessness in the future as in the past, will have to renounce its claim to world importance. . . . As a state in the future order of world states, [Germany] will at best be like that which Switzerland and Holland have been in Europe up to now.[11]

As early as 1937, Hitler and Göring, the head of Germany's air force, had authorized the development of bombers to strike at New York and other East Coast cities; and, as Gerhard Weinberg puts it, "if nothing much eventually came of these projects, it was not for lack of trying."[12] Returning from a visit to the United States in 1938, Karl Haushofer declared, "Potentially, the United States is the world's foremost political and economic power, predestined to dominate the world once it puts its heart into power politics."[13] By January 1939, Hitler's statements indicate an obsession with America's shadow on the European scene. "From that time on," John Lukacs asserts, "he began to consider Roosevelt as his principal enemy—a conviction that Hitler held to the end."[14] Of the American danger to Germany, Hitler commented, "Confronted with America, the best we can do is to hold out against her to the end."[15]

It is clear from the way Hitler orchestrated Germany's relations with the United States up until December 1941, that he feared most the war potential of the United States. According to the *Stufenplan*, Germany would not be ready to take on the U.S. until the Reich had consolidated its imperial hold over Europe and obtained a vast colonial empire overseas.

The success of the *Stufenplan* depended on keeping the United States on the sidelines until Germany held the Continent. In Hitler's view, Germany had already lost one war by carelessly provoking the U.S. into active belligerence—a mistake he was determined not to repeat. Thus, despite constant pressure from his naval chiefs during the period 1939 to 1941, Hitler forbade any attacks on American ships and all passenger steamers, though this seriously diminished the effectiveness of German submarine warfare against France and Britain. Similarly, when Roosevelt, in his famous "shoot at sight" speech on September 11, 1941, ordered American warships escorting British freighters to destroy any German submarines or raiders, Hitler responded by instructing his submarines not to instigate any attacks on American shipping.

In line with the plan, Hitler tried to minimize the appearance of German meddling in American politics. To this end, he directed the German press to refrain from printing articles denouncing Roosevelt or supporting his isolationist enemies. The Reich Chancellor feared that outright German support for American isolationists would be the surest way to provoke an American backlash, namely, public support for a more active U.S. foreign policy.[16]

Perhaps more than any other German official, Hans Dieckhoff, the German Ambassador to the United States, warned that American isolation could not be assumed indefinitely. From 1938 on, and particularly after Roosevelt's quarantine address of October 5, 1937, Dieckhoff worried that events were "leading to a war in which Germany would have to face the combined power of Great Britain and the United States."[17] In a memorandum to the German Foreign Ministry on the subject of American foreign policy, Dieckhoff concluded that Germany

must not count on American isolationism as an axiom. According to all indications the United States will continue to follow an essentially passive foreign policy as long as Britain is not prepared to become active herself, or as long as the United States is not subjected to intolerable provocation, or values which vitally concern the United States are not at stake. Should any of these occur, the United States, despite all resistance within the country, will abandon its present passivity. In a conflict in which the existence of Great Britain is at stake America will put her full weight into the scales on the side of the British.[18]

In separate letters to Baron Hans Georg von Mackensen (German Ambassador in Rome and acting head of the German Foreign Office) on November 24, 1937 and to Ernst von Weizsäcker (State Secretary in the Foreign Ministry) on December 20, 1937, Dieckhoff criticized the "increasing activity of Racial Germans abroad, especially by the German-American Bund in the United States" for creating widespread "suspicion [in America] that this activity is promoted by Germany" and "that both Germany and Italy have given up their previous postulate that National Socialism and Fascism were not for export."[19] In a long memorandum on the subject of the German-American Bund, Dieckhoff implored the Foreign Ministry to sever all official ties with German-Americans:

> In my opinion, any political connection between any authorities in Germany and the German-American element, if any such exists, must be broken off. As I have explained above, no good can come of it, only injury to Germanism in America and to our relations with the United States. . . . Just as, in deference to the Russian Government, Bismarck abstained from any contact with the Germans in the Baltic provinces . . . and just as today we consider it necessary to sacrifice the German element both of Alsace and in the South Tyrol for the sake of our relations with France and Italy, respectively, we must absolutely avoid political contact with the German-Americans if we do not wish to disturb or seriously prejudice our important relations with the United States. Here no compromise is conceivable; we must make a clean sweep of it.[20]

The German Foreign Ministry responded quickly to Dieckhoff's concerns. In a reply to Dieckhoff's letter of November 24, 1937, Mackensen related the actions he and Konstantin von Neurath (German Foreign Minister) had taken to curb "German interference in the American domestic situation":

> Until a few months ago there had been no correspondence between German governmental or Party offices and the German-American Bund. It was found 4 weeks ago, however, that several persons in the *Volksdeutsche Mittelstelle* [author's note: the central agency for problems concerning ethnic Germans of non-German citizenship] had established relations with this organization. We took immediate steps against that, stopped all correspondence, and instructed the Consulate

General in New York to demand of Mr. Kuhn, the leader of the German-American Bund, the surrender or destruction of this correspondence. This was all the more necessary, since the American Embassy here had shown great interest in the matter and brought up at the Foreign Ministry the subject of alleged connections between American citizens and German governmental authorities.[21]

Just as the press had been restrained from printing anti-Roosevelt stories and the Foreign Office had severed official ties to German-Americans, Hitler tried to impress upon his allies that, unlike in 1914, American neutrality was not a firmly fixed policy. Accordingly, it was in their interest to calculate how their actions might affect American public opinion. More often than not, however, Hitler's attempts to curb his allies proved unsuccessful. Such was the case in October 1940, when Hitler berated Mussolini for attacking Greece before the American presidential election.[22]

The Soviet Threat

In contrast to the threat posed by America's enormous war potential, the Soviet Union, according to Hitler, endangered "the freedom of the world" through "an inundation by disease bacilli [international Jewry] which at the moment have their breeding ground in Russia."[23] Hitler argued that the Jews had controlled Russia since the Bolshevik Revolution, and that a global Jewish conspiracy, radiating outward from its Russian base, threatened the continued survival of the Aryan race and its German core. The solution for Germany was to wage a racist war of annihilation. The Program itself had been built on anti-Semitism, anti-Bolshevism, and *Lebensraum*, all of which served to integrate German society in support of Hitler and the National Socialist party. Thus, while the ideas of Hitler's grand strategy were partially grounded in rational power politics, the aims of the Program were inextricably linked with, and intensified by, his irrational racist plan to exterminate the Jews.[24]

Hitler's obsession with defeating Russia appeared to be greatly simplified by Stalin's purges. Of the Soviet Union, Hitler said, "this State ha[s] recently butchered four thousand high-ranking officers. Such a country could not wage war."[25] Russia's weakened position afforded Germany a window of opportunity, which Hitler was determined to jump through.

By 1941, however, Hitler had reassessed Soviet military strength. Justifying the timing of the German attack on the Soviet Union, he asserted:

> A few days before our entry into Russia, I told Goering that we were
> facing the severest test in our existence. . . . What confirmed me in my
> decision to attack without delay was the information . . . that a sin-
> gle Russian factory was producing by itself more tanks than all our
> factories . . . if someone had told me that the Russians had ten thou-
> sand tanks, I'd have answered: "You're completely mad!"[26]

As the German-Soviet war dragged on, Hitler grew more convinced that he
had made the right decision to attack Russia when he had:

> The more we see of conditions in Russia, the more thankful we must
> be that we struck in time. In another ten years there would have
> sprung up in Russia a mass of industrial centres, inaccessible to attack,
> which would have produced armaments on an inexhaustible scale,
> while the rest of Europe would have degenerated into a defenceless
> plaything of Soviet policy.[27]

Hitler's Tripolar Strategy

The first stage in Hitler's *Stufenplan* envisaged the establishment of a Greater
Germany through the *Anschluss* with Austria and the absorption of Czechoslovakia and adjacent areas in Poland occupied by German-speaking people.
These lightning wars would cement German economic and political hegemony over central Europe and secure the additional strategic resources and
personnel (i.e., the 35 Czech divisions) needed for the next military campaign,
the swing westward. The *Wehrmacht* would then smash Belgium, Holland,
and France, neutralizing the Western flank and gaining direct control over the
raw materials, food supplies, and labor reserves of Western Europe—all of
which would serve to keep the German war economy afloat.[28]

Having brought Hungary, Yugoslavia, and Romania firmly into the
German economic sphere of influence and having secured through conquest
free access to the resources of Poland, Denmark, Norway, the Low Countries,
and France, Nazi Germany would finally be ready to engage in the titanic
struggle against the Soviet Union, the success of which would determine the
fate of Hitler's goal of *Lebensraum*: living space in the East, particularly the
Soviet Ukraine. Under Hitler's grand design, "What India was for England,
the territories of Russia will be for us."[29]

A final war against the United States had occupied Hitler's thoughts since 1928. In its drive for world supremacy, Germany required hegemony over the Eurasian landmass. After absorbing the resources of the nearest pole, Germany could then unleash the inevitable conflict against the more remote rival pole, the United States. In this battle, Germany could confidently expect victory. Gerhard Weinberg explains:

> [T]he Americans were the real threat to German predominance in the world. Hitler's deduction from this analysis was simple: only a Eurasian empire under German domination could successfully cope with this menace. A third war was now added to the original two. After the first two wars had enabled it to construct a continental empire from the Atlantic to the Urals, Germany would take on the United States. One of the major tasks to be performed by the National Socialist movement, therefore, must be the preparation of Germany for this conflict.[30]

Emphasizing demographics, Hitler viewed German Continental hegemony as a prerequisite for the ultimate war with the U.S.: "It is ridiculous to think of a world policy as long as one does not control the Continent. . . . A hundred and thirty million people in the Reich, ninety in the Ukraine. Add to these the other States of the New Europe, and we'll be four hundred millions, compared with the hundred and thirty million Americans."[31]

In summary, Hitler's grand strategy consisted of a series of isolated wars of escalating magnitude. First, Germany would win easily obtainable objectives in short and decisive campaigns in the east. Next, Germany would defeat France and coerce the British into an alliance against Russia and America. Finally, Germany would be ready to unleash successive polar wars against the Soviet Union and the United States.

For Hitler, the success of this sequence of events, from the *Anschluss* to the final war against America, rested on four elements: the *blitzkrieg*, two strategy innovations, and the advantage of offensive over defensive alliances.

1. Blitzkrieg

The consistency of Hitler's statements and actions from *Mein Kampf* to his death suggest that he was faithful to the *Stufenplan*, which was to culminate in Germany's unrivalled world supremacy (*Weltherrschaft*).[32] Within his lifetime, Hitler expected to see the completion of the first stage—eastward expansion (*Drang nach Osten*) followed by the initiation of a major-power war to gain complete control over Europe. These expansive goals required total war against France and the Soviet Union. Accordingly, economic and military preparations for total war were initiated in 1936 with the second Four Year Plan, and they were expected to be completed between 1943 and 1945.

The precondition for Germany's waging total war, however, was achievement of *Mitteleuropa*, the creation of a central European area dominated economically and politically by Germany. For this initial phase of German imperialism, Hitler devised the strategy of *blitzkrieg*: localized, lightning wars fought with the minimum of economic effort and social discomfort.[33] *Blitzkrieg* was a military strategy oriented toward disruption and routing the enemy's armies, conceived and conducted along classic Clausewitzian lines. Recalling Bismarck's famous "nightmare of coalitions," Hitler hoped that the speed of these wars would prevent escalation to major war against the other Great Powers. Short wars and piecemeal expansion were the keys to avoiding, for as long as possible, an overpowering counter-coalition of the kind that had defeated Germany in 1918.

2. "The Friend of My Enemy Is My Friend"

Another, less discussed strategic innovation by Hitler was his reversal of the Arab proverb that "the enemy of my enemy is my friend." Esmonde Robertson's explanation of this genuinely original stroke merits quoting at length:

Hitherto . . . the law of odd and even numbers, was taken as axiomatic: any given power would make common cause with its opponents' opponent. But Hitler with a singleness of purpose aimed his offers, not at France's potential enemies, which his immediate predecessors had done, but at her allies. He succeeded because he alone knew where the inherent weakness of the French security system lay. Whereas it was a fixed principle of French policy to resist every increase of German strength, others only feared it in certain directions and in limited quantities. Poland was averse to German expansion in the North-East, but might be kept quiet if Germany confined her claims to Czechoslovakia and Austria. For a short time Italy was prepared to challenge Germany, but only when a specified area was threatened. Britain, too, feared Germany in the air, but within certain limits might be prepared to accept expansion of German strength on land and sea. France had a host of allies, but none was entirely dependable: by implication they had each made some provision which would enable them to withhold support. Wherever France restrained them he could give them a free hand. France could thus be forced to transfer her favours continually until the system which she had been at such pains to establish was rent asunder.[34]

Spearheading the movement for revision in Europe, Hitler realized that Germany had an advantage over his status-quo opponents: they, unlike the Reich, could not attract other revisionist powers with promises of territorial rewards at the expense of the Old Order. States with irredenta, such as Hungary, Bulgaria, Italy, and the Soviet Union, adopted jackal policies, climbing aboard the Nazi bandwagon to satisfy their appetite for expansion as well as to increase their security. Encouraging jackal-type bandwagoning behavior, Hitler lured states into the German orbit by skillfully playing on their territorial aspirations and desire for protection from other revisionist powers.[35]

3. Hitler's Strategy of Individual Losses, Overall Gains

Neorealism's core tenet is that states under anarchy fear for their survival as sovereign actors, and so they must guard against relative losses in power. States are security-maximizers or, in Grieco's phrase, "defensive positionalists," and not power-maximizers. This is what distinguishes Waltzian structural realism from traditional realism.[36]

The "avoid relative losses" assumption of state interest posited by contemporary realists would be universally applicable if the primary goal of *all* states were security. This is not the case, however. The chief objective of an unlimited revisionist state, like Nazi Germany, is to dramatically improve its relative power position in the international system, even at the temporary expense of its security. Toward that end, it makes sense for such a state to enter into cooperative arrangements by which it gains relatively less than its partners. Let me explain.

Suppose revisionist state *A* makes separate bilateral deals with states *B, C, D,* and *E,* whereby *A* gains 5 utiles, and its partners each gain 7 utiles. In each individual cooperative arrangement, *A* gains 2 utiles less than its partner. But overall, *A* increases its absolute wealth by 20 utiles. If *A* can prevent the other players from concluding deals with each other and from which *A* is excluded, it gains a relative advantage of 13 utiles with respect to each partner and 20 utiles vis-à-vis all other states (*F, G, H,* and so on) outside the cooperative arrangements. This is a classic divide-and-conquer strategy. It is also consistent with Anatol Rapoport's TIT FOR TAT strategy, which lost every individual contest but nevertheless was the winning entry in Robert Axelrod's Computer Prisoner's Dilemma Tournament.[37]

By trading gains in individual plays for volume of deals, A enhances both its power and security, except against a hypothetical future coalition of $BCDE$.[38] As long as A's resources exceed the combined strength of a $BCDE$ coalition by 8 utiles or more, however, even defensive positionalists should not disapprove of A's making these uneven deals.

This offensive TIT FOR TAT strategy is precisely the one that Hitler followed so successfully in his dealings with Britain in 1935, Russia in 1939, Italy in 1940, and Japan in 1941. It was also the strategy used in Germany's economic relations with its East Central European neighbors. Specifically, Germany deliberately fostered a condition of asymmetric interdependence with its neighbors through what Albert Hirschman calls "the influence effect" of trade: country A (Germany), seeking to increase its influence in country B, alters the terms of trade in B's favor, e.g., by paying above world prices for B's exports; by changing the structure of B's economy to make it highly and artificially complementary to A's economy.[39] Here, country A accepts losses in national income in exchange for gains in national power. In summary, one can argue that Germany, in each case, gave more than it received. Overall, however, Germany got the best of its partners and, in the process, retained the greatest freedom of action.

4. The Superiority of Offensive Alliances

Hitler's misguided notion that Britain would support Germany's quest for continental supremacy is partially explained by his firm belief in the advantages of revisionist over status-quo alliances. This idea surfaces in a discussion in *Mein Kampf* on Germany's foreign policy failures prior to the First World War. There, Hitler concluded that, for a host of reasons, the alliance with Austria destroyed Germany. For one thing, Austria was strictly interested in a status-quo alliance "for the conservation of eternal peace" to preserve "this mummy of a State."[40] The defensive orientation of the alliance proved to be its undoing:

> The value of the Triple Alliance was psychologically modest, as the stability of an alliance increases in the measure in which the individual

contracting parties hope to attain certain seizable, expansive goals through it. On the other hand, an alliance will be the weaker the more it restricts itself to the preservation of an existing condition as such. Here also, as everywhere, the strength lies not in defense but in attack.[41]

With Austria, he claimed, "one could really not set out on 'martial' conquest, let us say, even in Europe. In this fact lay the inner weakness of this alliance from the first day."[42]

Hitler went on to argue that Austria's weakness was a double-whammy for Germany. It not only prevented an offensive alliance with Germany but also provided the glue that held the opposition together:

> Never would the world coalition have come together that began to form itself with King Edward's initiating activity, had not Austria, as Germany's ally, represented a too tempting legacy. Only thus did it become possible to bring States, which otherwise had such heterogeneous wishes and aims, into one single front. With a general advance against Germany, every one of them could hope to receive enrichment at the expense of Austria. The danger was increased exceedingly by the fact that now Turkey also seemed to be a silent partner of this unfortunate alliance.[43]

In a brilliantly absurd twist, Hitler saw the Triple Entente, not the Triple Alliance, as the revisionist coalition. Consequently, Germany and its pusillanimous allies did not stand a chance against the opposing force. Convinced that Britain had joined the revisionist, not the status-quo, alliance in 1914, Hitler thought that London would be inclined to do so again, providing that Germany sweetened the pot.

German Rearmament and the Wooing of Britain, 1933–35

Hitler's principal task upon assuming power in 1933, was to rebuild Germany's military forces. Rearmament would serve several purposes: it was a precondition for territorial expansion; a proven method to overcome Germany's lasting economic depression; and a means to consolidate Nazi power on the domestic front. As an internal matter, Hitler's plan for massive rearmament appealed to a wide range of societal interest groups in

Germany, from the conservative army to the moderate Foreign Office to the extremism of Hugenberg's Pan-German movement. Added to these domestic groups, Germany's economic community, particularly its mining and steel and iron industries, were strongly in favor of rearming, since they stood to make a sizable profit from the proposed armament boom.

For all its benefits, however, this initial stage in the *Stufenplan* would be extremely dangerous for the Reich. It would soon become clear whether France, as guardian of the status quo, possessed statesmen willing to hazard the risk of a preventive war against Germany.[44] Prior to rearming, the Reich had no intention of provoking a showdown with France. To this end, Hitler made a series of "peace speeches," which, he hoped, would create a peaceful international climate as diplomatic cover for the acceleration of Germany's military buildup.[45]

For most of 1933, Hitler and his Cabinet were preoccupied with settling the economic crisis and dealing with the Geneva disarmament conference that had opened on February 3, 1932, prior to Hitler's appointment. Germany's position at the conference was one of rough equality of armaments among the Great Powers. Essentially, Germany demanded that the other major powers reduce their armaments while the *Wehrmacht* rearmed until some specified level had been attained by all parties.

Having devised a divide-and-conquer strategy in Europe based on a bilateral relationship with Britain, Hitler sought to disengage the Reich from all multilateral arrangements. Thus, Germany withdrew from the Disarmament Conference and the League of Nations in October 1933, shortly after Britain and France had adopted hardline stances against arms equality with the Reich. Then, in an attempt to preempt the hostility of the world community, Hitler initiated a series of bilateral negotiations with various powers, focusing his energies on winning over Britain, the keystone in his Program.

To appreciate the importance of the British alliance as a prerequisite for the Reich's expansionist aims, we must digress for a moment to examine Hitler's *Lebensraumpolitik*. Rooted in traditional German geopolitics, the concept of *Lebensraum* centered on the notion that Germany had to acquire economic self-sufficiency in order to achieve true security and control over its destiny. In a Darwinian world, dependence on other nations for war materials meant certain defeat, as was demonstrated by Germany's collapse in 1918.

In *Mein Kampf*, Hitler described the international system as an intense Great-Power competition, in which "the right of self-preservation comes into effect; and what has been denied to kindness will have to be taken with the fist."[46] Years later, in a meeting with his top advisors, Hitler reiterated the theme:

> A balance of power had been established without Germany's partici-pation. This balance is being disturbed by Germany claiming her vital rights and her reappearance in the circle of the Great Powers. . . . This is not possible without "breaking in" to other countries or attacking other people's possessions. Living space proportionate to the greatness of the State is fundamental to every Power. One can do without it for a time but sooner or later the problems will have to be solved by hook or by crook. The alternatives are rise or decline.[47]

Echoing the ideas of many geopoliticians, Hitler argued that Germany's self-preservation demanded an aggressive foreign policy of continental expansion; only thus could the Reich secure autarky and fulfill its destiny. Favoring a policy of contiguous land expansion, Hitler rejected a policy of German *Weltpolitik*. As a land power, Hitler reasoned, Germany could not achieve the goal of self-sufficiency by means of colonial exploitation. Even the most determined of policies to make Germany a formidable maritime power would take generations to complete and would require, as a pre-condition for its success, German control over Europe. In Hitler's words, because Germany's "foreign trade was carried on over sea routes domi-nated by Britain, it was a question . . . of security of transport . . . which revealed in time of war the full weakness of our food situation." Hence, in *Mein Kampf*, he argued: "For Germany . . . the only possibility of carrying out a sound territorial policy was to be found in the acquisition of new soil in Europe proper."[48] He reiterated this view in 1938:

> [T]he space needed to insure [German self-sufficiency in raw mate-rials] can only be sought in Europe, not, as in the liberal-capitalist view, in the exploitation of colonies. It is not a matter of acquiring population but of gaining space for agricultural use. Moreover, areas producing raw materials can be more usefully sought in Europe, in immediate proximity to the Reich, than overseas; . . . The question for Germany ran: where could she achieve the greatest gain at the lowest cost.[49]

Alliances with Britain, Italy, and Japan

In the winter of 1922–23, Hitler began making statements that committed him for the first time to a foreign policy strategy of alliances with Britain and Italy. Prior to that time, Hitler consistently favored a Russo-German over an Anglo-German alliance. In his 1921 analysis of prewar German policy, Hitler declared that war between Russia and Germany could have been avoided because Russia had adopted an exclusively "Asiatic policy of conquest" that did not conflict with German interests. Hitler described the decision to support Austria-Hungary at the expense of Russian friendship as the "first huge error" made by Wilhelmine diplomats. This foolish pro-Austrian policy, Hitler believed, had resulted in the Franco-Russian alliance of 1893, which ultimately led to the outbreak of war in 1914.[50]

From 1923 on, however, Hitler pinned the success of *Lebensraumpolitik* on securing a partnership with Britain. "For such a policy," Hitler wrote, "there is only one single ally in Europe: England. With England alone, one's back being covered, could one begin the new Germanic invasion."[51] Hitler now believed that Germany's irresponsible colonial strategy and naval race with Britain had led to its defeat in the Great War: "To gain England's favor, no sacrifice should have been too great. Then one would have had to renounce colonies and sea power, but to spare British industry our competition."[52] In contrast to "a healthy European land policy," Imperial Germany had adopted *Weltpolitik*, "a colonial and trade policy" that had promised few gains at high costs, namely, conflict with the Anglo-Saxon sea powers.[53]

Britain's opposition to France on the question of Upper Silesia[54] and the Ruhr crisis of 1923 were turning points in Hitler's thinking about a Anglo-German alliance. Here was proof, he thought, that Britain was reasserting its traditional balancer role vis-à-vis Europe. Along these lines, Hitler pointed out that "England has an interest in seeing that we do not go under because otherwise France would become the greatest continental power in Europe, whilst England would have to be content with the position of a third-rate power."[55] Moreover, "England does not want a France whose military might, unchecked by the rest of Europe, can undertake to push a policy which, one way or another, must some day cross English interests."[56]

In addition to its concerns over French power, England would seek German friendship, he believed, to counter America's growing economic and naval strength. The British government's treasonous behavior at the Washington Naval Conference, Hitler claimed, had alerted the British people to the "Jewish conspiracy," the goal of which was to undermine British imperialism in India and Ireland. Regarding the Naval Conference, Hitler agreed with his ideological mentor, Alfred Rosenberg, that "for centuries, England had fought ruthlessly for her naval supremacy . . . and always realized the need to drive the strongest from the field. In Washington, this England gave up her position with a grand gesture and without a struggle and renounced the alliance with Japan and transferred the leadership of world politics to the United States."[57] Up until his death, Hitler continued to believe that Britain would align with Germany to protect its overseas possessions: "[Roosevelt] wants to run the world and rob us all of a place in the sun. He says he wants to save England but he means he wants to be ruler and heir of the British Empire."[58] Given his misguided notion of an underlying Anglo-American rivalry, Hitler confidently expected Britain to join a German-led European coalition against the North American Continent.[59]

While arguing in the 1920s that friendship with Britain was vital to German expansion, Hitler recognized that this goal could not be achieved in the foreseeable future. An alliance with Italy, however, was within Germany's grasp, provided that Mussolini came to power. In a 1922 conversation with Kurt Lüdecke, a fellow member of the NSDAP, Hitler articulated his views on alliances with Italy and Britain:

The natural future alliance of our new Germany, we agreed, should be England and eventually the northern European states, therefore, our logical effort—when we had the power—would be to alienate England from France. As a corollary of our growth, a German-English alliance was imperative. Forces currently dominant in England were, and would indefinitely remain, opposed to Nazi Germany, that we envisioned. With France holding a military trump card, and Germany isolated politically and economically, we were in no position to bargain with England. If we had any hope of understanding amongst the major powers, we should find it in Italy—if Mussolini came to power.[60]

He was confident that Italy would ally with Germany because they were birds of a feather, destined to flock together: both countries shared a fundamental interest in overturning the Versailles settlement, which meant opposing French hegemony in Europe. For Italy, "every added continental reinforcement of France means . . . a future restriction on Italy."[61] The main impediment to a future alliance with Italy—one that would have to await a Nazi takeover of Germany—was the planned *Anschluss* with Austria. To surmount this problem, Germany would have to renounce all claims on South Tyrol:

> Germany must collaborate with Italy, which is experiencing her national rebirth and has a great future. For that, a clear and binding renunciation by Germany of the Germans in South Tyrol is necessary. The idle talk over South Tyrol, the empty protests against the Fascists, only harm us since they alienate Italy from us. In politics there is no sentiment, only coldbloodedness.[62]

On the German side of the ledger, Hitler saw many benefits accruing from a union with Italy and Britain:

> The most important is first *the fact that an approach to England and Italy would in itself in no way evoke danger of war. . . . The alliance . . . would give Germany a chance to make quite calmly those preparations which, one way or another, must be undertaken within the bounds of such a coalition for a reckoning with France. . . . A further consequence would be that Germany would be freed from its adverse strategic situation at one blow.* The most powerful protection of the flank on one side, the complete guaranty of our supply of the necessities of life and raw materials on the other side, would be the blessed effect of the new order of States.
>
> *But almost more important would be the fact that the new union of States comprises a capacity for technical performance which, in many respects, is almost mutually complementary.* For the first time Germany would have allies who do not suck like leeches on our own economy, but which both could and would contribute their share to the richest completion of our technical armament.[63]

"In Europe," he declared, "there can be for Germany in the predictable future only two allies: **England and Italy.**"[64] Outside Europe, however, Hitler predicted an alliance with Japan. The rivalry between Japan and the Soviet Union over "spheres of influence" in China indicated to Hitler that 'international Jewry' was bent on undermining the healthy structure of the Japanese state. In *Mein Kampf*, Hitler argued:

> Today [the Jew] can ape Germans and English, Americans and French, but he has no bridges to the yellow Asiatics. Therefore, he strives to

break the Japanese national State by the power of existing similar structures, to finish off the dangerous opponent before the last State power
is transformed in his hands into a despotism over defenseless beings.

He dreads a Japanese national State in his millennial Jew empire,
and therefore wishes its destruction in advance of the founding of his
own dictatorship.

Therefore, he is now inciting the nations against Japan, as against
Germany . . .[65]

In Germany during the 1920s, Karl Haushofer, of whom Hitler was a close
student, was also expounding on the theoretical advantages of an German-
Japanese-Italian alliance. Japan had space for expansion in the Pacific and so
there was no reason to fear a collision with German *Lebensraum*.[66]

For many reasons, Germany and Japan were "natural" allies. Both countries shared a long tradition of authoritarian rule characterized by similar
political institutions; and they opposed democratic ideals and violently
denounced Communism and the spread of "Bolshevist influence." In terms
of culture and ideology, the seeds of German thinking had been planted in
Japan at the time of the Meiji Restoration. Indeed, in 1883, Ito, a passionate
admirer of Moltke and Bismarck, adopted the Prussian Constitution for
Japan.[67] Many years later, Matsuoka, the Foreign Minister responsible for the
Tripartite Pact, declared that Germany had had the greatest influence of all
Western civilizations in the building of post-Restoration Japan.[68]

The Germans, for their part, similarly admired the Japanese character and
spirit. When Hitler assumed power, German propaganda referred to the
Japanese as the "Prussians of the East" and the Bureau of Race investigation
excluded the Japanese from the prohibition of marriage between Germans
and non-Aryans, since "the blood of Dai Nippon contains within itself virtues
closely akin to the pure Nordic strain."[69]

Germany and Japan also claimed a common denominator in their economic interests. Both Japan and Germany viewed themselves as "have not"
countries, to whom markets and resources were denied. Both countries had
been disinherited at Versailles by the established Western democracies, who
had all along been cheating them out of their fair share of raw materials
and colonies.

Hitler's desire to secure alliances with Britain, Japan, and Italy is consistent
with the hypothesis that revisionist powers seek minimum winning coalitions. A combination of these four powers would afford Germany the greatest
gains at the least cost. With British consent, Germany would be in a position

to gain control over the European continent and become the strongest land power in the world. Moreover, Germany could accomplish this task solely by means of its own military efforts; all that was required of Britain, Italy, and Japan was that they did not fight on the other side.

Hitler confidently expected Italy and Japan, as revisionist states, to side with Germany and its vision of a New Order. Joined by a common destiny, all three states would find their own *Lebensraum*, provided that each member limited its territorial reach to its preassigned sphere of interest. The idea of a global partition meant that Germany would not have to share the spoils of its victories with superfluous allies. To profit by the alliance, Italy and Japan would have to win their own victories. As for Britain, Hitler would gladly offer to guarantee its overseas empire in exchange for a free hand on the Continent.

The Failed Attempt to Gain British Friendship

In November 1933, Joachim von Ribbentrop visited London with a proposal for a naval agreement that would serve as a basis for an Anglo-German nonaggression pact. This meeting was followed up on December 5, when Hitler himself met with the British Ambassador, Sir Eric Phipps, to discuss the armaments question. Complaining of the "intolerable situation for Germany" created by its frontier being "completely undefended" to the point where "the French could walk into the country whenever they liked," Hitler pointed out that an increase in German strength would also benefit England by counterbalancing French and Italian power: "[Germany] must . . . be in a position to throw her weight into the scales at some future time, and, in this connexion, might not Great Britain herself be glad of other alternatives to her present friendships?"[70]

Aiming to drive a wedge between Britain and France, Hitler proposed an agreement that would limit France, Poland, and Czechoslovakia to their present level of armaments but would not apply to Germany and Britain. Phipps records Hitler saying:

As far as Britain was concerned, not only should she not be included in any such standstill agreement, but he would even welcome considerable additions to the British fleet and air force. . . . He then repeated what General von Blomberg had told me . . . that Germany would never dream of competing against England at sea . . .[71]

Figure 4.1 illustrates Hitler's plan in 1934. As the figure shows, assuming that America retained its isolationist policy, the alliance Hitler sought to create with Japan, Italy, and Britain was a minimum winning coalition (power ratio = 6.7) against an opposing Franco-Soviet alliance (power ratio = 5.66), the two powers expected to oppose German expansion. Hitler's alliance scheme is consistent with the hypothesis that revisionist states form minimum winning coalitions.

The Führer went to great lengths to convince the British that he desired only freedom of action on the Continent and would not threaten Britain's naval supremacy or colonial possessions. In directives to his negotiators, Hitler exclaimed: "An understanding must be reached between the two great Germanic peoples through the permanent elimination of naval rivalry. One will control the sea, the other will be the strongest power on land. A defensive and offensive alliance between the two will inaugurate a new era."[72]

F. H. Hinsley writes:

> According to [Admiral] Raeder, Hitler, immediately after assuming power in 1933, laid down, as "the basis for future German naval policy, his strong determination to live in peace with Italy, Japan, and England. In particular, he had no intention of contesting England's claim to a naval position corresponding with her world interests, which view he

FIGURE 4.1
Hitler's alliance scheme shown with 1934 power ratios

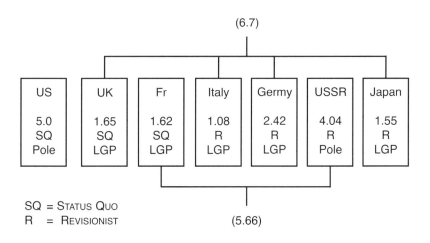

intended to establish in a special treaty concerning the comparative strength of the German and English Fleets. . . . His plan was to win England permanently over to a policy of peace through a proportional naval strength of 35:100." . . . Germany took the initiative in the negotiations; she did so in the spirit of making a gesture in Great Britain's interest; the German proposals themselves were clearly aimed at reassuring this country on the question of German naval rivalry.[73]

While the British were relieved to hear that Hitler would not reintroduce Wilhelmine naval and colonial policies, they were not persuaded to disown the French or to give Germany a free hand in the East. Hitler's courtship of Britain was doomed from the start, for it was based on the prospective gains Britain and Germany could make relative to the other great powers. As a satisfied, status-quo power, Britain could scarcely consider a deal that called for the total unraveling of the established order in exchange for a slight increase in its relative power—one that would have afforded Britain, at best, a precarious position as Germany's junior partner.[74] Instead, London desired better relations with Germany solely for the purpose of bringing the Reich back into the European fold, with the ultimate objective being Germany's loyal participation in various European multilateral security arrangements.

In light of the generous terms the Reich had offered for British friendship, Hitler could not understand how the deal had misfired. How could they fail to see that only Germany would fully support Britain's world ambitions? Only Germany could save them from the threats posed by the United States, France, and the Bolshevik menace. And who could deny that the Franco-Soviet alliance negotiations (started in November 1933) threatened Germany's security, or that Russia was "now the greatest power factor in the whole of Europe"?[75] Surely, this made an Anglo-German combination the most natural of alliances.[76]

German Rearmament and Isolation

Anxious over Germany's departure from the League of Nations and the Disarmament Conference in November 1933, Poland sought a guarantee of Germany's peaceful intentions. On January 26, 1934, Germany concluded a ten-year nonaggression pact with Poland. Hitler was, of course, delighted to remove another peg from France's crumbling alliance system. But he was not surprised, as Taylor points out:

He recognised that Poland, like Italy, was a "revisionist" Power, even though she owed her independence to the Allied victory of 1918; hence he believed that Poland, like Italy and Hungary, would be won to his side. For such a gain, Danzig and the corridor were a price worth paying. . . . As his later policy showed, he had no objection to preserving other countries so long as they acted as Germany's jackals.[77]

In June 1934, Hitler visited Venice to calm the Duce's uneasiness over German intentions in Austria and thereby pave the way for the alliance with Italy. Mussolini was unmoved. Their meeting, the first between the two fascist leaders, only reinforced the Duce's initial assessment of the new German leader as a buffoon. The German foreign minister, Konstantin von Neurath, recalled that "their minds didn't meet; they didn't understand each other."[78]

Shortly after returning to Berlin, the Führer's policy of courting Italian friendship suffered yet another severe setback when Austrian Nazis launched a coup d'état against the Dollfuss Government in Vienna. The coup failed but Dollfuss, a close friend of the Duce, had been assassinated. In retaliation, Mussolini ordered troops to the Austrian border at the Brenner Pass, and relations between Rome and Berlin grew more tense.

Further complicating matters for Hitler, German rearmament had, by early 1935, progressed to the point where it could no longer be disguised. In response to Germany's military production, the British defense White Paper of March 4, 1935, proposed an accelerated arms program. Seven days later, Hitler confirmed the existence of a German air force. Four days later, the French government introduced legislation to extend the period of military service to two years. The following day, Germany announced that it would return to compulsory, universal conscription and amass a peacetime army of thirty-six divisions.

Europe's great powers not only condemned Hitler's renunciation of the military restrictions of Versailles, but also began to harmonize their efforts to counter the growing German threat. On January 7, 1935, Mussolini and then French Foreign Minister Pierre-Etienne Laval signed a complicated series of agreements, referred to as the "Rome agreements." Then, in early April, the heads of state of Italy, Britain, and France, respectively Mussolini, James Ramsay MacDonald, and Laval, met at Stresa and issued a joint declaration to protect Austria's independence against German aggression. According to Prime Minister Pierre-Etienne Flandin, France and Italy exchanged definite promises of military assistance: Italy promised to defend the Rhineland demilitarized zone as the price paid for France's pledge to defend Austria's integrity.[79] In this spirit of cooperation, France and Russia concluded a formal alliance pledging mutual assistance against unprovoked aggression. The same revolutionary state that had consistently denounced the "slave treaty" of Versailles now joined the League of Nations and even preached respect for international law.

The alliance situation in 1935 (shown in figure 4.2) represents the highwater mark of major-power cooperation in Europe to isolate Germany. The size of the alliance supports the hypothesis that status-quo states form overlarge coalitions to deter or defeat revisionist powers.

Britain: Entrapment Fears of a Dove

Britain, according to the scheme laid out in chapter 3, was a dove, that is, a lesser great power that supports the status quo but accepts limited revision to satisfy the legitimate claims of dissatisfied states. Doves seek to be honest brokers, and so their foreign policy must maintain the appearance of equi-

FIGURE 4.2

The alliance situation and power ratios in 1935

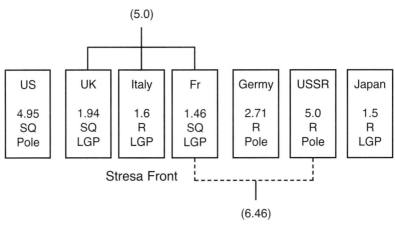

SQ = STATUS QUO
R   = REVISIONIST

Franco-Soviet Mutual Assistance Pact (5/35)
[Dotted line indicates that, for France,
the pact was a paper commitment]

distance between all contending parties. Above all, doves resist tight defensive alliances, which, they fear, will embolden their would-be allies and provoke and unite their potential enemies.

In game-theoretical terms, the dove's policy is one of cooperation with regard to its adversary (a "C" strategy, e.g., an engagement policy), and defection with regard to its allies (a "D" strategy, e.g., the avoidance of tight defensive alliances.) The dynamics of this type of policy, as Glenn Snyder explains, are as follows:

> A "C" strategy of conciliating the adversary will have the desirable effect of restraining the ally, thus reducing the risk of entrapment. The ally, observing one's improving relations with the opponent, will have less confidence that one will stand four-square behind him in a crisis; consequently, he will be more cautious in his own dealings with the opponent. . . . The most undesirable side effect of conciliating the adversary is that it entails the risk of abandonment by the ally.[80]

Throughout the interwar period, Britain's troubled relationship with France was infused by entrapment/abandonment fears. France was the more dependent partner on the alliance because its need for assistance in a war with its potential adversary (Germany) and its degree of conflict and tension with that adversary were both greater than that of Britain. In consequence, France perceived the costs and risks of British abandonment as outweighing the costs and risks of British entrapment. Britain, as an insular power with greater war potential than France and with no irreconcilable differences with Germany, was less dependent on the alliance with France; and so, for it, the costs and risks of French entrapment outweighed those associated with French abandonment.[81]

After the Paris Peace Conference, the primary problem facing British foreign policy was to resolve or, at a minimum, manage the Franco-German cold war. Lloyd George, the British prime minister, disdainful of the Foreign Office's "old diplomacy" of balance of power, brought foreign policy under Downing Street's control and proceeded to subordinate Britain's narrow interests to the League and collective security. With the fall of Lloyd George from power in 1922, however, the Foreign Office recaptured control of British diplomacy and held it until 1937, when Neville Chamberlain became prime minister. During those years, the Foreign Office steered British policy along its traditional strategic lines: the maintenance of the global balance of power.[82] With regard to Europe, the most vital theater for British security, this meant attempting to play its traditional role as balancer and become, in Austen Chamberlain's words, "the honest broker" in continental affairs.[83]

The first task of British diplomacy was therefore "to arrange a postwar European balance between the French, now the strongest power on the continent, and Germany, whose defeat had whetted its neighbours' appetite for territory and revenge."[84] The Franco-German problem came to a head in 1923, when France invaded the Ruhr. Determined to end the continuing crisis, Austen Chamberlain, the British foreign secretary, and Sir Eyre Crowe, the Foreign Office permanent undersecretary, commenced policy planning that would culminate in the Locarno Pact of 1925.

While the French desperately sought to include Britain in its security system against Germany, British foreign policy toward its former ally remained ambiguous, alternating between two conflicting impulses. On the one hand, France remained Britain's most reliable continental ally and its security was seen by many in the Foreign Office as essential to Britain's own. On the other hand, many British policy elites were suspicious of France's true motivations for keeping Germany in a weakened position. Far stronger than Germany in the 1920s, France, in its attitude toward its defeated neighbor, appeared as a bully seeking not security but the reestablishment of its hegemony over Europe—a policy at odds with Britain's desire for a restored balance of power on the continent.

To many British observers, it appeared that France exaggerated the danger of German revanchism. But the reality of French fear could not be denied. As Sir William Tyrrell, assistant undersecretary at the Foreign Office, lamented in 1925: "We have failed to remove the feeling of fear from our chief ally, France, who came out of the war a victor mainly in a technical sense. Her victory did not enable her to provide for her own security."[85] In this view, the solution to the Franco-German cold war was a British security pact with France to eliminate the fear of abandonment in Paris, which had been the driving force behind France's repeated attempts to throw Europe out of balance, e.g., by instigating separatist movements in the Rhineland, occupying the Ruhr, and refusing to evacuate Cologne. Added to this, Austen Chamberlain worried that, if Britain did not offer France reassurance in the form of a firm Anglo-French axis within Locarno, "we shall lose all influence over French policy. . . . We shall be dragged along, unwilling, impotent, protesting, in the war of France towards the new Armageddon. For we cannot afford to see France crushed."[86]

Those who perceived France as a bully counseled against an Anglo-French security pact, which, they claimed, would only embolden Paris with respect to Germany and entrap Britain in a new war initiated by its would-be ally. In addition, a more confident, less frightened France would be essentially immune to British influence. Thus, Nicolson observed: "The French dread of Germany is hereditary and inevitable, nor would we wish to see it entirely removed. Within limits, it serves as a corrective to the enterprising vanity of the French character which, if unchecked, would undoubtedly bring our two countries into conflict."[87] Similarly concerned about the prospect of British entrapment by an emboldened France, Sterndale Bennett, a member of the Central Department, warned as the first steps of the Locarno settlement were being taken: "The French are putting the onus upon us, i.e. they are refusing to make any concessions to Germany unless we pay the price by guaranteeing French security."[88] Churchill, then the chancellor of the exchequer, agreed: "It is by standing aloof," he told Chamberlain, "and not by offering ourselves that we shall ascertain the degree of importance which France really attaches to our troth."[89]

In the end, Stanley Baldwin, the British prime minister at the time, sided with the Foreign Office and Austen Chamberlain—who threatened to resign if Britain chose to remain isolated from continental politics—and agreed to proceed with the Locarno Pact. But Britain's commitment to the continent and France's security remained tenuous at best.

After the Hoare-Laval debacle and with the advent of Anthony Eden as foreign secretary, criticism of the Foreign Office and its pro-French, balance-of-power policy increased. The Anglo-French plan (December 9, 1935) had been designed to settle the Italo-Ethiopian war. It aimed to maintain friendship with Italy at the expense of Ethopia and the principles of the League of Nations. The pro-League British public repudiated the plan. Once Neville Chamberlain became prime minister in 1937, the fear of British entrapment by France, which by now appeared considerably weaker than its revitalized neighbor, assumed far greater importance than France's fear of abandonment by Britain. As Brian McKercher observes: "Anxious to avoid war—and believing that international conferences solved nothing, Chamberlain and his supporters believed that bilateral settlements with British adversaries could better preserve international peace."[90] Driven by entrapment fears, Britain embarked on an appeasement policy toward its enemies and a distancing policy toward its allies that lasted until March 1939.

Throughout the interwar period, the British desired to reestablish themselves as the balancer/honest broker in Europe. This strategy failed because Britain was no longer a Great Power of the first rank, and so it was too weak to assume its traditional role, much less play it effectively. Of the great powers, Britain alone worried about Germany's complete isolation. This was the case in 1935, after the Stresa Conference. Fearing that Hitler might lash out in "mad-dog" fashion, London continued its bilateral negotiations with Berlin in the hope that it could moderate Hitler's conduct and still keep on fair terms with France. Though these talks resulted in nothing more than a meaningless Anglo-German naval agreement, they effectively destroyed the Stresa Front. By sabotaging Western solidarity and condoning a flagrant violation of treaties, the naval agreement has rightly been called an "epochal event whose symptomatic importance was greater than its actual content."[91] Britain's mistake was in not discussing the matter with either Italy or France prior to signing the Naval Treaty on June 18, 1935. Across the Atlantic, the American reaction was also one of horror. In a letter to President Roosevelt, the American Ambassador to Germany, William E. Dodd, observed that it was the first time "in modern history that England has sided with a threatening imperialist European power, rather than guide a combination of weaker powers against a threatening one."[92]

For his part, Hitler was "convinced that the British regarded the agreement with [Germany] in this sphere as only a preliminary to much wider cooperation"; it fed his hope for a grand alliance to partition the world. "An Anglo-German combination," he insisted, "would be stronger than all the other powers."[93] Events were to prove him wrong on both counts.

Chapter 5

The Path To War, 1935–1939

French foreign policy after the Great War fixated on the inevitability of a future attack by a revitalized Germany seeking revenge for its defeat. Attempting to forestall the feared power shift that would reestablish Germany as the dominant power on the Continent, French elites at Versailles cited Germany's economic and military *potentiel de guerre* as justification for French claims for relatively greater armaments and for military control of German territory. The French military, for their part, resolutely argued that permanent allied occupation of the Rhineland constituted the only natural barrier to another German invasion against France or its eastern allies. "If we hold the Rhine solidly, France can set its mind at ease," Marshal Foch declared. "If [France] doesn't hold the Rhine. . . . anything offered or given in exchange is mere illusion, appearance, and vanity."[1] But Clemenceau traded the military's demands for a Rhineland zone permanently under allied control for a stillborn Anglo-American guarantee of French security. The allied military occupation of the zone was to end no later than 1935, and it was understood that it would probably be bartered away long before that time.

Dismayed that the allied occupation would be only temporary, the French general staff argued that French security would require (1) fortifications to compensate for France's demographic weakness and (2) *espaces de manoeuvre* in Poland, Czechoslovakia, and Belgium, so that French forces would not be pinioned behind the Maginot line.[2] The central imperatives that guided French military planning were that any future war should be fought on foreign soil and that France could not expect to defeat Germany without allied support. Thus, throughout the interwar period, French diplomacy centered on the construction of a massive defensive alliance system as a makeweight against Germany. As the theory predicts, a status-quo LGP confronting a revisionist pole will seek a large alliance (not a minimum winning coalition) to deter or defeat the threatening state.

Yet, France found itself deserted by its former allies at Versailles. The U.S. turned its back on the Old World, refusing to ratify the treaty or to join the League; the Soviet Union, treated as an outcast by the West, drew closer to Germany; Italy and Japan left the conference as dissatisfied powers; and although a superficial semblance of allied solidarity with Britain remained throughout the interwar period, Anglo-French disagreement centered on the crux of the matter for France: the need to enforce the peace settlement upon Germany. As Sir Maurice Hankey, Secretary to the Cabinet, observed in 1920: "The fact is that they [the French] wanted a stiffer treaty and we wanted an easier one. Moreover, from the first we always intended to ease up the execution of the treaty if the Germans played the game."[3]

France's traditional strategy against Germany required an eastern counterweight in a two front war. Prior to the First World War, France relied on Czarist Russia (then a status-quo power) as its main ally in the eastern coalition. After the war, France's inferior demographic and industrial potential relative to Germany coupled with the loss of Russia to Bolshevism dictated a strictly defensive military posture and the creation of a ragbag set of treaties with Belgium (1920), Poland (1921, 1925), Czechoslovakia (1924, 1925), Romania (1926), and Yugoslavia (1927).[4] Because the population of France was a third less than that of the Third Reich, Germany could not only field far more fighting units than France but was also assured a great advantage in its industrial workforce, on which its army depended for provisions. By necessity, therefore, French strategy was based on the assumption of defensive advantage and the idea of a long war, which would be fought in two stages. In the first stage, France prepared to fight a defensive war, which was predicted to last up to two years. During this period, France would try to secure a draw with Germany while launching its own national mobilization effort to assemble the means for the second stage: the strategic offensive. As Robert Young explains, the success of the first stage would enable France "to await the tie-breaking contributions of her allies before undertaking the great strategic offensive upon which all hopes of victory were pinned. . . . Yet this belief in the victorious potential of a long war was constantly imperilled by the logical if disturbing conclusion that had to be drawn about the dangers of a short war, one likely as not begun by a sudden German *attaque brusquée*."[5]

To avoid the twin dangers of either a quick German victory or a repetition of the Franco-German bloodletting of 1914–1918, France's traditional two-front war strategy would have to be recast in a radical new light. In contrast to the pre-1914 military assumption that France would bear the brunt of the German attack, leaving Russia free to open a second front in the east, General Maurice Gamelin, French Commander in Chief, and the French general staff reconstructed the eastern-counterweight strategy on the assumption that the next conflict would begin in the east. France would act as a secondary force against Germany, while its eastern allies did the bulk of the fighting. The historian Nicole Jordan describes Gamelin's strategy as France's search for a "cut price war on the peripheries."[6] In the parlance of international relations theory, Gamelin planned a buckpassing strategy for France.

France's interwar military and political strategy suffered from three intractable problems, however. First, France's increasingly defensive war plans contradicted its desire for a coalition effort in the east to contain Germany. Second, all the Great Powers on the Continent were revisionist states that could not be counted on to support the current political order in Europe. Third, as France grew weaker relative to Germany and more dependent on other powers, it began losing faith in its satellite system of small states. Paul-Boncour asked rhetorically in late 1932: "Facing the great powers, can we lean on our small allies?"[7] The problem for France was that it could not forge an alliance with a Great Power on the Continent without simultaneously weakening its satellite system and support for the League. To contain Germany, therefore, France had to decide between, on the one hand, an alliance with one or both of the revisionist Great Powers (Soviet Russia and Italy) or, on the other hand, revitalizing its status quo alliance system by strengthening its commitments to Poland and the Little Entente.

The first clash between France's satellite system and its desire for a Great-Power entente came in 1933, when Germany left the disarmament conference and withdrew from the League, dooming the Four Power Pact. The moment seemed appropriate for France to decide either to repair the damages done to its eastern alliance system by the Four Power Pact (its breach of the League principle of equality of nations) or "revise [its] policy based on ineffective alliances with weak countries, and base [France's] security on the entente of the great powers capable of containing Germany."[8] Remarkably, France did neither because, as Paul-Boncour put it, "no French statesman would ever think of reversing the by now traditional direction of our foreign policy."[9] Unwilling to renounce its ties to the small powers of East Central Europe, France tried instead to keep but not strengthen its existing obligations to Poland and the Little Entente while working for a Great-Power solution to the German threat. In the end, the two policies proved irreconcilable, leaving France with the worst of both worlds.

For Gamelin and the General Staff, the key to France's military and political problems was Italy.[10] Mussolini's show of force against Hitler in July 1934 in response to the assassination of the Austrian Chancellor Dollfuss by Austrian Nazis changed Gamelin's prior assumption of Italian hostility. At that point, the French General Staff formulated a buckpassing strategy, in which Italy would shoulder the burden of defending Czechoslovakia and Austria.

Prior to the Ethiopian crisis, Mussolini seemed more than willing to play into Gamelin's hands. Shortly after Laval's visit to Rome in January 1935, Mussolini, anxious to secure Italy's rear for the invasion of Ethiopia, tantalized France by offering Italo-French staff talks for the joint defense of Austrian independence. In terms too good to be true, the Italian general staff pledged to commit Italian forces to fight in Austria or send nine divisions to France in exchange for the dispatch of two French divisions to the central European front, which Gamelin had designated as the main area of fighting in the next war.

Talks of June 1935 between Gamelin and his staff and Marshal Pietro Badoglio and his staff sealed the deal, creating in Laval's words, "a veritable military alliance" between Italy and France.[11] The French agreed to send an expeditionary force to northeast Italy as a liaison between the Italian and Yugoslav armies in a joint drive upon Vienna. In exchange, Italy pledged to send an army corps to France's northeastern front in Belfort for operations against Germany. For France, the added bonus of the rapprochement with Italy was the release of ten French divisions from the Alps and seven from North Africa, which were no longer needed to deter Italian aggression. Most of the French alpine units would be transferred to the Belgian theater, with the balance of the units supplying the personnel for the French expeditionary force to Italy. The Italian general staff also agreed to cooperate with France in a large-scale army intelligence program directed against Germany.[12]

Mussolini's offer appeared to be designed to encourage France to ride free on the balancing efforts of Italy and France's eastern allies. As Nicole Jordan puts it, "the exorbitantly generous terms of the Italian military offer promised a cut price war on the peripheries. Others, Italy and the Balkan states with their reservoirs of peasant soldiery, would do most of the fighting on the central European front."[13] But Mussolini's pro-French maneuverings soon proved illusory. The Duce's ultimate goal of turning the Mediterranean into an Italian lake inevitably set Italy on a collision course with Britain and France. Thus, even before the military pact with France, Mussolini was telling the Germans that he planned a basic reorientation of Italian policy away from the Stresa Front and against the status-quo, western democracies.[14] This meant abandoning Italy's prior policy of "equidistance," that is, playing the other powers against each other for Italian advantage. No longer willing to be the honest broker—a role which carried the risk of alienating all the Great Powers, Italy was left to drift into a subordinate relationship with its stronger revisionist partner, Nazi Germany.

When it became clear that Mussolini envisaged military action on a grand scale in Ethiopia, a serious rift developed in the newly created Stresa front. At first it appeared that Italy was on one side and France and Britain were on the other. The most acute divergence appeared to be developing between France and Italy, whose relations had been strained by the German-Italian détente and the Franco-Russian agreement. Recognizing the danger of this situation, France quickly switched over to the Italian side. The French move was facilitated by Britain's adoption of a very critical attitude toward Italy. This conveniently enabled the French to let Britain raise the objections that were of fundamental interest to Paris as well, while France offered itself to Italy as a reliable and understanding friend.[15]

In light of France's dependence on Italian support, one cannot overestimate the dismay of the French military over the Italo-Ethiopian war, which caught France squarely between Britain and Italy. But it was not simply a matter of choosing Britain or Italy; the League and France's eastern alliance system were also involved. As Laval observed in July 1935, "France's entire European policy is based upon the League of Nations. The League of Nations is the basis of the Locarno treaty, which is an essential element of French security, and it is within a League framework that the agreements which bind us to our friends in central Europe are inserted."[16]

For most French elites, an alliance with Italy was unthinkable if it came at the expense of British friendship and if it meant rejection of the League. Even

Gamelin, who supported Laval's policies of weak sanctions and the pursuit of peace negotiations with Italy, "stated that while Italian support was 'desirable' that of the British in the long run was 'essential.'"[17] Luckily for Gamelin and the French general staff, Britain had no intention of going to war with Italy over its expansion in Ethiopia. For the British, naval considerations were decisive. Recognizing that the Royal Navy would carry the weight of Anglo-French actions against Italy, the chiefs of staff urged that the fleet be kept intact for use against Japan, which it regarded as the greater threat.

Then came the disastrous Hoare-Laval Plan of December 1935, which further estranged France and Britain. On the French side, Britain's disavowal of the plan deepened the mistrust created by the Anglo-German Naval Agreement. From Britain's perspective, the chiefs of staff called the naval contacts with France "profoundly unsatisfying," which showed France to be an unreliable partner.[18] As France and Britain bickered over the Italo-Ethiopian war, Hitler took the opportunity to reoccupy the Rhineland. The Nazi dictator's first blow against the territorial status quo threw French diplomacy into total disarray.

In light of the relatively mild sanctions Britain and France had imposed against Italy, "Hitler concluded that both England and France were loathe to take any risks and anxious to avoid any danger. . . . The Western governments had, as he commented at the time, proved themselves weak and indecisive."[19] Seeing his enemies as irresolute, Hitler decided to exploit the conflict among the former members of the Stresa Front by reoccupying the Rhineland on March 7, 1936. This move destroyed with a single stroke France's entire Central European alliance system by denying the French their main area of offensive operations; it also made it more likely that the next Franco-German war would again be fought on French soil, nullifying the major strategic advantage the Allies had won in the First World War. Years later, Hitler described the remilitarization as his most daring move: "We had no army worth mentioning; at that time it would not even have had the fighting strength to maintain itself against the Poles. If the French had taken any action, we would have been easily defeated; our resistance would have been over in a few days."[20]

The timidity of the Anglo-French response to the Rhineland remilitarization exposed the main weakness of France's military and diplomatic strategy. The French assumed, like Kenneth Waltz and Stephan Walt, that states automatically balance against greater power and threats. Hitler thought otherwise. Consistent with the logic of my jackal bandwagoning and distancing hypotheses, Hitler was confident that demonstrations of Nazi Germany's greater strength and dynamism relative to the western democracies would produce two results: (1) revisionist states of all sizes would rapidly jump on the Nazi bandwagon; and (2) less immediately threatened status-quo states would not rush to balance against Germany but instead would try to distance themselves from France and other more proximate targets of German aggression, such as Czechoslovakia. In the words of Nicole Jordan:

> [Gamelin] complacently assumed that the reoccupation, by creating an obvious German menace in the east, would unite the threatened states. But as the Nazis were already demonstrating domestically with resounding success, a blatant threat to a vulnerable segment of a community did not generate solidarity. Gamelin's strategic preference for a war in the east left Hitler with ample leeway to mark out Czechoslovakia and to pit against it other French allies whom the Reich could treat as less menaced so long as it served German purposes.[21]

The Ethiopian war, the Spanish Civil War, and the Rhineland crisis cemented the Rome-Berlin Axis. Because revisionist states are searching not for greater security but rather for increased power and prestige, they will not hesitate to take advantage of an opportunity to disrupt the international political order by joining the stronger revisionist side. Thus, as Alan Cassels observes, Italy's foreign policy was being driven by raw Social Darwinism: "Mussolini's simplistic division of the powers into 'rising' and 'declining' states seemed validated by the events of 1935–6. The feebleness of British and French opposition to his Ethiopian venture was at hand to testify to the 'decadence' of these nations. In contrast stood Nazi Germany's 'virility' in outfacing the First World War victors—over rearmament and in the Rhineland." The "jackal bandwagoning" motivation behind Italian foreign policy was no secret to the British Foreign Office. In 1939, for instance, the British Ambassador in Rome, Sir Percy Loraine warned Halifax that "even if we . . . persevere in our attempts to avoid a breach with Italy and keep held out a hand that she may grasp, we cannot blind ourselves to the more ominous factors, e.g., the Duce's belief that the Italo-German combination alone is able to produce dividends for Italy; the underlining by Gayda of the predatory nature of the next war on the part of the have-nots against the haves; the gradual succumbing of Italy, which seems inevitable, to political vassalage and economic inferiority to Germany."[22]

The Formation of the Axis, 1935–37

The spirit of cooperation between the Western democracies and Italy at the Stresa Conference, which was supposed to inaugurate a complete understanding among the three powers with regard to the European order and Germany, was destined to be short-lived, since their interests diverged significantly and could not be reconciled. France was a hawk demanding strict enforcement of the status quo; Britain was a dove attempting to bind the dissatisfied states, particularly Germany, to a revised European order by engaging their legitimate grievances through peaceful revision; and Italy was a jackal with revisionist aims that threatened the existing postwar order and territorial status quo. As Wolfers suggests, the "decisive obstacle to co-operation between France and Italy lay in the fact that Italy . . . was a dissatisfied country and could not be attracted to France by mere guarantees of the established order. She was out for change, not for the enforcement of the *status quo*, and many of the changes which she desired could be effected only by far-reaching French concessions."[23]

Since his political takeover in 1922, Mussolini had portrayed Italy as a "have-not" state, whose major objective was to break the prison bars imposed by the established powers. "States," he claimed, "are more or less independent according to their maritime position." Italy, in his eyes, was "a prisoner in the Mediterranean, and the more populous and powerful she becomes, the more will she suffer from her imprisonment." "To break the prison bars," Italy would have to "March to the Ocean." For Italy, therefore, the only question was:

> Which Ocean? The Indian Ocean linking across the Sudan and Libya to Abyssinia; or the Atlantic Ocean across French North Africa? In the first, as in the second, hypothesis we find ourselves face to face with Anglo-French opposition. To brave the solution of such a problem without having secured our backs on the Continent would be absurd. The policy of the Rome-Berlin Axis therefore answers the historical necessity of a fundamental order.[24]

Mussolini clearly understood that Italy's revisionist ambitions could be satisfied only at the expense of vital French and British interests, which they would never voluntarily concede. For Italy, bandwagoning with Germany meant satellite status, but it was still preferable to joining France and Britain in support of the status quo. On this point, Denis Mack Smith writes, "As one of his Ambassadors said, better be number two with Germany than a bad third after France and Britain; only with Germany could he challenge the dominant powers in the Mediterranean and break out of what he called Italy's 'imprisonment' in the inland sea."[25]

As the only uncommitted great power in the West, Italy held the balance and so enjoyed a strong bargaining position as kingmaker, and both sides recognized it as such: Hitler worried about an Anglo-Franco-Italian combination, while the British and French feared an Italo-German combination. Yet, France could only offer Italy military assistance for the defense of the status quo on the Brenner and some small colonial concessions in Africa, while Germany promised its full support for Mussolini's dreams of empire and expansion as compensation for the loss of Austrian independence. An alliance with Germany, the greatest European land power, would secure Italy's continental position and thereby free Mussolini to pursue his ambitions in the Mediterranean and Africa. Hitler had assured Mussolini that he considered North Africa and the Eastern Mediterranean (primarily Greece and Yugoslavia) to be within Italy's sphere of influence.[26] At the time, Germany was "completely isolated" and "possessed no really reliable friends," Hitler worried, and so "he could only welcome it if relations of mutual trust between Italy and Germany were restored."[27]

As the reader will recall, Hitler's *Stufenplan* called for alliances with both Italy and Britain. The Anglo-Italian rift, however, forced Germany to choose between the two. Frustrated by Britain's unwillingness to ally itself with Germany, Hitler embraced Italy, though not without anguishing over the decision: "It is a terribly difficult decision. I would by far prefer to join the English. But how often in history the English have proved perfidious. If I go along with them, then all is over between Italy and us. Afterwards the English will drop me, and we will sit between two stools."[28]

Britain was unwilling to deal Germany a free hand in Europe in exchange for protection for the British Empire: "The process of German-English understanding would at best bring Germany this or that colonial strip, which it would not be able to defend in an emergency, and where based on direct German-English agreement would not be large enough to bring Germany significant economic advantages, but would be large enough to drive Belgium, Portugal and France properly into a united anti-German front."[29]

Closer ties with London, Hitler reckoned, promised only a renewal of the old Franco-Italian alliance against Germany. His logic was that an Italy denuded of German assistance would be forced to capitulate to Britain in the

Mediterranean. Italy would then seek compensation in Southeastern Europe at the expense of German expansion. To prevent this, Hitler withdrew the olive branch he had earlier extended to Britain and strengthened the fragile entente with Italy by signing the so-called Gentleman's Agreement with Austria in July 1936, by which Germany recognized the sovereignty of Austria and agreed not to interfere in its domestic affairs. In exchange, the Austrian Chancellor Kurt von Schuschnigg pledged to pursue a foreign policy based on the principle that "Austria acknowledges herself to be a German State" and to share some political responsibility with the "national opposition."[30] One week later, civil war broke out in Spain, where Italian troops were to be heavily committed in yet another attempt to revive the Roman Empire. In Spain, as in Ethiopia, Germany was the only great power to offer Italy support, which included the dispatch of German troops. In October 1936, the Italian foreign minister, Count Ciano, signed a secret treaty with Germany recognizing the common political and economic interests of the two countries. Mussolini referred to the relationship as the Rome-Berlin Axis.[31]

Hitler's strategic considerations now began to focus on Japan. Uppermost in his mind was the threat presented by the Soviet Union, which, by its treaties with Czechoslovakia and France, had proven itself to be, as Hitler had argued all along, Germany's mortal enemy. An alliance with Japan would divert from Europe the military power of the Soviet Union. With Japan on its side, Germany would have "an ally that ranked as a world power, whereas he was not convinced that Italy was in the same class."[32] The two countries shared fundamental interests—their desire for revision and fear of Soviet military power and the subversive activities of the Comintern—that had been drawing them together since 1933. In 1935, a German-Japanese alliance became the subject of negotiations between Colonel Oshima and Ribbentrop that resulted in the Anti-Comintern pact, signed on November 25, 1936.[33]

Initially, Hitler remained hopeful that Britain, given its traditional Russophobia, might someday join the Anti-Comintern pact. One year later, however, Stalin's purges had caused the German High Command's estimate of Soviet military power to decline dramatically.[34] This coupled with Britain's refusal to come to terms with the Reich compelled Hitler to rethink certain aspects of his Grand Strategy. The thrust of the Anti-Comintern pact, Hitler decided, would be redirected against Britain, which, of course, better served Mussolini's interests as well. Hitler now accepted the reality that Britain might have to be regarded as an enemy. This did not mean that Germany would have

to defeat Britain, for he was confident that London, in view of its recent performance, could be bullied into neutrality.

Curiously, as Japan further antagonized the West by attacking China,
Tokyo found itself in negotiations with Italy for the conclusion of a bilateral Anti-Comintern agreement ostensibly against Russia. But consistent
with Hitler's new anti-British policy, Mussolini's interest in an alliance with
Japan was primarily directed against the West. On September 8, 1937, the
German Ambassador to Japan, Dirksen, noted that "Italy is very anxious to
make far-reaching concessions to the wishes of Japan . . . with the ulterior
aim of obtaining a freer hand in the Mediterranean by committing Japan
against England."[35]

On November 6, 1937, Italy joined the Anti-Comintern Pact, described
by Ribbentrop as "a military alliance between Italy, Germany and Japan in
anticipation of the inevitable conflict with the Western Powers."[36] The
Italian Foreign Minister Ciano noted that he had "seldom seen [Mussolini]
so happy. The situation of 1935 has been transformed. Italy has broken out
of her isolation: she is the center of the most formidable political and military combination which has ever existed."[37] Since the pact threatened the
British Empire on three fronts (the North Sea, the Mediterranean, and the
Far East), it was, in Ciano's words, "anti-Communist in theory but unmis-
takenly anti-British."[38] Creating "the strongest coalition in the world," the
pact would force "England to seek an understanding with the Axis.'"[39]

While clearly developing into something more than an ideological man-
ifesto, the Anti-Comintern Pact was not yet a military alliance and Japan
insisted that its participation was limited to the pact's nominal target, the
Soviet Union. Nevertheless, by 1938, three of the four revisionist great powers, Fascist Italy, Imperial Japan, and Nazi Germany (the USSR being the
exception) had formed an alliance. Added to this, Germany now began to
support Japan with concrete actions, e.g., by refusing to participate in the
Brussels conference held in November 1937, in response to China's plea and
by recognizing the Japanese puppet state of Manchukuo in exchange for
which Germany received a preferential trade position.[40] To Hitler, cooperation among the "have not" states was only natural. As he explained to a Polish
delegation in 1935: "There were in the world nations that were satiated and
other nations whose needs were not properly satisfied. But he would fail to
understand it, if those of the second category should hinder each other in
improving their condition, thus making it easier for the sated nations to keep
the less fortunate nations in their unfavourable situation."[41]

FIGURE 5.1
The alliance situation and power ratios in 1936

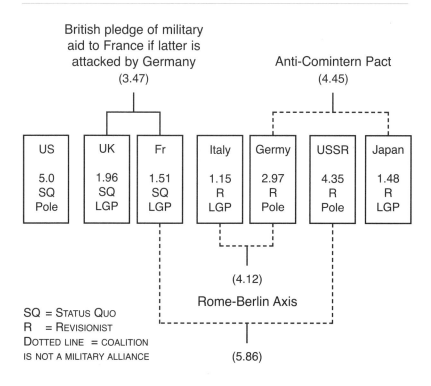

To The Brink of War, 1938–39

Anschluss and the Czech Crisis

In a secret conference with his principal advisors on November 5, 1937, recorded in the infamous "Hossbach Memorandum," Hitler introduced his new thinking on the prospects of an alliance with Britain.[42] The Führer's speech opened with an attempt to persuade his skeptical staff of the dispensability of British friendship. Britain and France, he claimed, had shown themselves to be "two hate-inspired antagonists . . . to whom a German colossus in the center of Europe was a thorn in the flesh."[43] A future war in the West had become inevitable. In the meantime, Germany would have to settle old scores with Czechoslovakia and Austria. The "annexation" of these

FIGURE 5.2
The alliance situation and power ratios in 1938

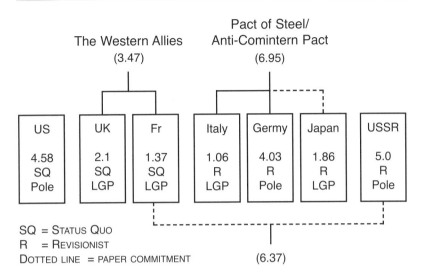

Pact of Steel/
The Western Allies   Anti-Comintern Pact
(3.47)   (6.95)

US	UK	Fr	Italy	Germy	Japan	USSR
4.58	2.1	1.37	1.06	4.03	1.86	5.0
SQ	SQ	SQ	R	R	R	R
Pole	LGP	LGP	LGP	Pole	LGP	Pole

SQ = STATUS QUO
R = REVISIONIST
DOTTED LINE = PAPER COMMITMENT   (6.37)

two states would provide Germany with "foodstuffs for 5–6 million people" and, "from the politico-military point of view, a substantial advantage because it would mean shorter and better frontiers, the freeing of forces for other purposes, and the possibility of creating new units up to a level of about 12 divisions, that is, 1 new division per million inhabitants."[44] Most important in economic and strategic terms, the absorption of Prague into the Nazi orbit would go along way toward solving the chronic problem of shortages in German holdings of foreign exchange and raw-material imports necessary for military production.[45]

Hitler named the years 1943–45 as the last possible date for Germany to complete the series of preventive wars that would culminate in Nazi hegemony over Europe. After that time, Germany would no longer have a relative power advantage over its probable enemies. The Czech operation, he believed, would go without a hitch because Britain and France had already silently written off the Czechs; the USSR was unlikely to intervene given the Japanese threat to the Soviet Far East. Unforeseen complications would be minimized by carrying out the military campaign with lightning speed; it would be over before any Great Power could intervene.

Hitler's first task was to bring the Austrian Republic back into the fold of the German Reich. In January 1938, the Austrian police raided Nazi headquarters in Teinfaltstrasse, Vienna, where they uncovered incriminating documentary evidence that the Austrian Nazi Party expected a German invasion later in the year. In February, Hitler called Schuschnigg, the young Chancellor of Austria, to the Berghof and presented him with an ultimatum essentially demanding that he hand over power to the Nazi Party and merge Austria's economy with the Reich's.[46] In a desperate move to save his country, Schuschnigg decided on March 8, 1938, to call a plebiscite for the 13th of March. Knowing that the vote would favor Austrian independence, Hitler responded by ordering the invasion of Austria by noon on the 12th. On the 11th, Schuschnigg cancelled the plebescite, but to no avail, as German troops were already on the march.

Of the great powers, Italy stood to lose the most by the *Anschluss*. Yet Hesse reported from Rome that the Duce "had accepted the whole thing in a very friendly manner." The Führer "was thrown into transports of joy and said, repeating himself hysterically many times: 'I will never forget him for this.' "[47]

After the Austrian *Anschluss*, Hitler prepared for the next step on the path to Continental hegemony: absorption of Czechoslovakia behind the smokescreen of liberating the Sudeten German minority. For this operation, Hitler preferred a military solution, but Anglo-French appeasement at Munich resulted in Germany's being offered most of the spoils of victory without a fight. In a conversation with the Hungarian Foreign Minister Csaky, Hitler asked: "Do you think that I myself would have thought it possible half a year ago that Czechoslovakia, so to speak, would be served up to me by her friends?"[48] Nevertheless, Hitler was furious that war had been averted and vowed never to repeat this mistake.

Perhaps the most significant development arising out of Munich was the West's total disregard for the Soviet Union, which had been deliberately excluded from the conference, even though the Soviets had continually voiced their willingness to aid the Czechs. "It is indeed astonishing," Churchill later commented, "that this public and unqualified declaration by one of the greatest powers concerned should not have played its part in Mr. Chamberlain's negotiations, or in the French conduct of the crisis." With the advantage of hindsight, Churchill concluded: "The Soviet offer was in effect ignored. . . . They were not brought into the scale against Hitler, and were treated with an indifference—not to say disdain—which left a mark in

Stalin's mind. Events took their course as if Soviet Russia did not exist. For this we afterwards payed dearly."[49]

Haushofer's Vision: Land Powers vs. Sea Powers

From the beginning, Haushofer and Ribbentrop disagreed with Hitler's pro-British, anti-Russian, anti-colonial policies.[50] Influenced by Mackinder's theories of the Eurasian pivot and the natural rivalry between land and sea powers, Haushofer championed Russo-German cooperation against the Anglo-Saxon sea powers. In 1913, he wrote, "A community of interests between Japan, Russia, and the Central European Imperial Power would be absolutely unassailable;" and quoting Mackinder in 1939: "It is vitally necessary that Russia and Germany unite their powers."[51]

For Haushofer, cooperation with Russia was the only way to dethrone the despotic hegemonic rule of the Anglo-Saxon sea powers: "Such an alliance does not aim at 'world domination,' but to be sure, at the abolition of the capitalistic rule of Western Democracy over the 'have nots' and at the establishment of a juster world-order, free from such exploitation."[52] A Russo-German-Japanese transcontinental bloc would counterbalance the Anglo-Saxon powers; free German forces for the conquest of Western Europe; and, once these resources were in hand, create a Greater Germany capable of crushing the USSR. With sole control over the vital core of the Eurasian landmass (Mackinder's "Heartland"), Germany could safely build its naval and air forces to defeat the U.S. and establish its world hegemony.

By the spring of 1939, world events had conspired to make Haushofer's vision of a German alliance with Soviet Russia a reality. After Hitler had made good on his promise to wipe Czechoslovakia off the map of Europe[53] and then four days later (on March 20) to seize the Baltic port of Memel from Lithuania, world attention focused on Romania and Poland—the most likely targets of the next German attack. It is worth pointing out that the seizure of the rest of Czechoslovakia significantly strengthened the Nazi war machine. As Williamson Murray points out, in this case, conquest paid:

> The booty from Czech arms dumps was enormous. In April 1939 an average of twenty-three trains per day, filled with ammunition and weapons, left Czechoslovakia for the Reich. . . . All in all, occupation of Czechoslovakia provided extensive military and economic help to the Reich. It enabled Germany to overcome for the time being serious eco-

nomic difficulties. It provided the Wehrmacht for the first time since the beginning of rearmament with a substantial arms surplus that could either earn foreign exchange or be devoted to equipping reserve units. Lastly, the seizure of Czechoslovakia and domination of the Slovakian puppet state gave the German an important jumping-off position for attacking Poland.[54]

Convinced, finally, that the aims of Hitler's revision were not limited to recovering the German minorities outside the Reich, the British government declared on March 31 that it would protect the existence of Poland by armed intervention if necessary. London strengthened its paper commitment to Poland by introducing conscription (for the first time ever during peace) and opening negotiations with France and the Soviet Union, albeit with great reluctance, to re-create the pre-war, anti-German alliance. Unimpressed by this show of Western resolve, Mussolini ordered Italian troops to invade Albania on April 7, in response to which the British and French extended similar guarantees to Greece and Romania.

While it is true that the guarantees to Poland, Greece, and Romania signaled a greater willingness on the part of the British (and, to a lesser extent, the French) to stand up to the dictators, it did not mean, as is commonly believed, that Britain had abandoned its policy of appeasement and was now ready for war with Nazi Germany. Rather, Chamberlain and other British elites still believed that Hitler could be appeased by economic concessions and some revision of the German-Polish frontier that would leave the Polish state essentially intact.[55]

The end of March and most of April were a time of intense diplomatic shuffling among all the European great powers and Poland. Britain was negotiating with the Soviets, the French, and the Poles for an anti-German front. Germany was engaged in trade negotiations with the British and the Soviets; while, at the same time, Hitler and Ribbentrop were presenting the Poles with an ultimatum: either align with Germany against the Soviets or expect total annihilation at the hands of the *Wehrmacht*. Courted by both the democracies and Germany, the Soviet Union held the balance of power and would use its bargaining strength as kingmaker to extort concessions from both sides.

This bargaining advantage was lost, however, when Chamberlain, realizing that he could not have an alliance with both the USSR and Poland, chose the Poles over the Soviets. Foreign Secretary Halifax told the American ambassador, Joseph Kennedy, that the decision had been based on the latest

information on the Soviets, which showed "their air force to be very weak
and old and of short range, their army very poor and their industrial back-
ing for the army frightful, and the most they could expect from Russia, if
Russia wanted to be of help, would be that they might send some ammunition to Poland in the event of trouble."[56] Britain's decision ensured that
events would not be shaped in London but rather in Berlin and Moscow.

The Nazi-Soviet Pact

It was clear to Stalin that Poland would be the next victim of German aggression. If Britain failed to honor its pledge and left Poland to its fate, the Soviet
Union would probably find itself fighting Germany alone. If, on the other
hand, Britain honored its guarantee by declaring war on Germany, the Soviet
Union could safely stand aside as the capitalist powers exhausted each other
in a war of attrition from which Russia would gain enormously. This was
precisely the scenario that the British Foreign Office feared in arguing for an
Anglo-Soviet agreement:

> It would seem desirable to conclude some agreement whereby the
> Soviet Union would come to our assistance if we were attacked in the
> West, not only in order to ensure that Germany would have to fight a
> war on two fronts, but also perhaps for the reason, admitted by the
> Turkish Minister for Foreign Affairs to General Weygand, that it was
> essential, if there must be a war, to try to involve the Soviet Union in it,
> otherwise at the end of the war the Soviet Union, with her army intact
> and England and Germany in ruins would dominate Europe. (There
> are indications that the real Soviet policy is—and would be—to get us
> involved and then to try to keep out herself.) Even though we may not
> be able to count implicitly on the Soviet Government either honestly
> wishing to fulfil, or being capable of fulfilling, their treaty obligations,
> nevertheless, the alternative of a Soviet Union completely untram-
> meled and exposed continually to the temptation of intriguing with
> both sides and of playing off one side against the other might present
> a no less, perhaps more, dangerous situation than that produced by
> collaborating with a dishonest or an incompetent partner.[57]

In short, without an Anglo-Soviet agreement, the stronger the British commitment to Poland, the more Stalin could extract from Hitler in exchange for

Soviet neutrality. In any case, the Soviet Union stood to profit from an agreement with Germany to destroy what remained of the Old Order in Europe.[58]

If this logic were not enough to convince Stalin to accept a neutrality pact with the Reich, his information that Japanese Premier Kiichiro Hiranuma had just opened negotiations with Germany to transform the Anti-Comintern Pact into a more effective military alliance against the Soviet Union pushed him over the edge. These negotiations came on the heels of renewed military action (May 28, 1939) by the Japanese Kwantung Army against the Soviet satellite state of Outer Mongolia.[59]

Hitler's interest in a neutrality pact with the USSR was heightened by the Anglo-Franco-Soviet negotiations. Many British strategists were critical of Chamberlain's anti-Soviet policy, as Harold Nicolson's diary entry of September 26, 1938 notes: "Winston says (and we all agree) that the fundamental mistake the P.M. has made is his refusal to take Russia into his confidence. Ribbentrop always said to Hitler, 'You need never fear England until you find her mentioning Russia as an ally. Then it means that she is really going to war!' "[60] Now that Britain was "mentioning Russia as an ally," Hitler worried that it might succeed in recreating the Triple Entente. To prevent this, the Soviets had to be lured in to the Axis camp.

Another factor favoring a German rapprochement with Russia was Hitler's failure to secure an unrestricted military alliance with Japan. Such an alliance, Hitler thought, would have a great effect on the Western powers, given their many interests in Asia. Japanese naval authorities, however, felt that Japan was not yet prepared to take on the Anglo-Saxon powers. Thus, as Gerhard Weinberg points out, "by the last half of April 1939, it was becoming apparent that the pact desired by Germany—namely a pact with universal application—would almost certainly not materialize within the time desired by Hitler."[61]

Hitler's interest in a Nazi-Soviet pact was also driven by economic considerations. The cost of rearmament, warned Hjalmar Schacht and every other director of the Reichsbank, was dragging the Reich to the brink of bankruptcy.[62] "German trade with eastern Europe," David Kaiser writes, "had reached its limits by 1939, partly because of limited production and transport capacity in eastern Europe, but above all because the European countries needed many industrial goods and raw materials which the Germans could not or would not supply, and therefore were seeking to divert their exports to hard-currency nations whenever possible."[63] The economic clauses of the Nazi-Soviet pact would solve this problem by ensuring "Germany of long-term supplies of critical raw materials, obtained on extremely generous terms, since the German industrial goods which the Soviets demanded in exchange would be delivered much more slowly."[64]

Unlike Hitler's failed attempt to court an alliance with Britain by tempting it with relative gains, the Soviet Union, a revisionist state, took the bait. As the theory predicts, revisionist powers bandwagon for profit and safety, often from each other. While Britain could only offer the Soviets, in the words of Ambassador Schnurre, "participation in a European war and the hostility of Germany,"[65] Hitler promised them a handsome reward from the partition of Poland. Thus, Ribbentrop "could not see why Russia should want to associate itself with England as England was in no condition to offer 'any *quid pro quo* really worth the trouble.' "[66] Always the opportunist, Stalin agreed.

Yet, Hitler had heartfelt reservations about the Nazi-Soviet pact. Prior to its signing, he decried the West's failure to grasp the true meaning of the Russian menace and to come to terms with Germany. Accurately predicting the flow of the coming war, Hitler raged: "Everything that I undertake is directed against Russia; if the West is too stupid and too blind to understand this, then I will be forced to reach an understanding with the Russians, smash the West, and then turn all my concentrated strength against the Soviet Union."[67] For Hitler, then, the agreement with Russia was clearly intended as a short-term strategy; it did not signal a change in his long-run policy with regard to the Soviet Union. Ultimately, Germany would have to defeat Russia in order to gain control of the Continent. In a diary entry on August 29, 1939, the German Ambassador Ulrich von Hassell accurately described Hitler's true motives for the Soviet pact: "About the Russian pact Hitler said that he was in no wise altering his fundamental anti-bolshevist policies; one had to use Beelzebub to drive away the devil; all means were justified in dealing with the Soviets, even such a pact as this. This is a typical example of his conception of 'Realpolitik.' "[68]

Chapter 6

The Western and Polar Wars, 1939–1945

By 1938, Hitler had already conceived of war with Britain and France in preventive terms: war was inevitable and it was better to fight now than later. Given the increased pace of Anglo-French rearmament after Munich, Germany's window of opportunity would eventually be shut:

> Let us assume that because of our rapid rearmament we hold a four to one advantage in strength at the present time. Since the occupation of Czechoslovakia the other side has been rearming vigorously. They need at least one and a half to two years before their production will reach its maximum yield. Only after 1940 can they begin to catch up with our relatively large headstart. If they produce only as much as we do, however, our proportional superiority will constantly diminish, for in order to maintain it we would have to go on producing four times as much. We are in no position to do so. Even if they reach only half of our production, the proportion will constantly deteriorate. Right now, on the other hand, we have new weapons in all fields, the other side obsolete types.[1]

Germany was at the peak of its relative power (power ratio = 4.95) and the combined strength of the Axis (7.59) far exceeded that of Britain (2.6) and

France (1.18), which had reached its nadir for the interwar period (see table 6.1 below). The only problem, then, was to decide on a strategy for the Western attack. On May 23, 1939, Hitler outlined the plan. He would occupy Holland and Belgium with lightning speed, and then quickly defeat France. Afterward, if London did not sue for peace, he would try to eliminate England by a final decisive blow. In the event that air strikes failed to gain London's capitulation, the Reich Chancellor was confident that Germany could still win a long war against Britain:

> If Holland and Belgium are successfully occupied, and if France is also defeated, the fundamental conditions for a successful war against England will have been secured. England can then be blockaded from Western France at close quarters by the Air Force, while the Navy with its U-boats can extend the range of the blockade. When that is done, England will not be able to fight on the Continent.[2]

On May 25, 1940, Hitler's goal to destroy the Allied armies in the West was on the verge of fulfillment. Of the Channel ports, only Dunkirk and Ostend remained as avenues of escape for the Belgian, British, and French armies. At

FIGURE 6.1
The alliance situation and power ratios in 1939

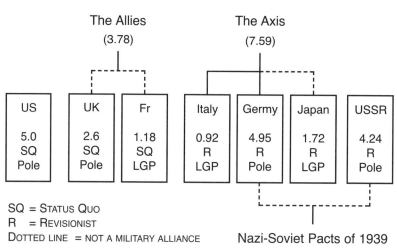

SQ = Status Quo
R = Revisionist
Dotted line = not a military alliance   Nazi-Soviet Pacts of 1939

this point, Hitler made arguably one of his most crucial mistakes of the war. Worried (unjustifiably as it turned out) that France would succeed in forming a new front along the Somme, Hitler chose to disregard Dunkirk and the British and concentrate instead on Paris and the French. This time, Germany would not be stopped on the Somme, as von Moltke had been stopped on the Marne through excessive concern about the British on the flank and through failure to maintain the momentum of the right wing. Any troops that escaped from Dunkirk would be imprisoned on the British Isles.[3]

Thus, Hitler ordered Rundstedt's tanks and troops, which were only 15 miles from Dunkirk, to stop and actually withdraw slightly in order to hold a blocking position along the line Gravelines-St. Omer-Béthune. There they were to wait for the arrival of von Bock's forces, which were 35 miles away, but to whom Hitler had given the task of crushing the allies. Rundstedt protested that he already held the position and strength to close the trap; but if he waited for Von Bock's forces, the British would escape. Hitler responded that the main objective was to defeat the French Army.

Bitterly opposed to Hitler's orders, Halder's diary entry of May 24, 1940, records: "The left wing [Rundstedt's forces], consisting of armor and motorised forces, which has no enemy before it, will so be stopped dead in its tracks upon direct orders from the Fuehrer! Finishing off the encircled enemy army is to be left to air force!!"[4] In their effort to join up with Rundstedt's forces, von Bock's troops advanced slowly (taking 48 hours) and suffered heavy losses. On May 27, Hitler finally ordered the panzer divisions to push forward. It was too late. The British, having used the three-day respite to shore up their southern flank, thwarted the German attack. On May 30, Halder noted: " . . . bad weather has grounded our air force and now we must stand by and watch how countless thousands of the enemy are getting away to England right under our noses."[5]

Of the 400,000 troops pinned at Dunkirk some 360,000 were saved, though not without the near-total sacrifice of their equipment—only 25 of 704 tanks came back from France. In Churchill's words, "the nucleus and structure upon which alone Britain could build her armies of the future" had been preserved.[6] More important, the initial shock of the disaster in Flanders had been quickly dissipated by the miracle at Dunkirk. Rather than feeling resigned to defeat, the British people drew encouragement from the escape of 225,000 British troops from what had appeared to be certain destruction. To many, the British Expeditionary Force (BEF) had been saved by divine intervention. With God on its side, Britain would surely win the war. Hitler's generals grumbled: "With a more powerful Navy, at the outbreak of that war, or a wheeling movement by the Army towards the Channel Ports, the end would have been different."[7]

Nevertheless, after the defeat of France, Hitler again had high hopes of negotiating an end to the war with Britain. Convinced that Britain would "come to its senses" after the French armistice, Hitler rebuffed Franco's promise to intervene on the Axis side if Spain received considerable rewards for doing so. This was the second and most critical mistake that Hitler made—one that probably cost him the war. Germany needed Spain's cooperation in order to occupy Gibraltar and North Africa and thereby deny the Mediterranean theater to the British and later the Americans. Acting like a revisionist leader seeking to limit the coalition to a minimum winning one, however, Hitler turned down Franco's request for the expansion of Spanish holdings in Morocco. As Paul Kecskemeti exclaims: "He wanted to take certain territories for himself, and the problem of getting enough for Germany—while also satisfying Italy without thoroughly alienating France—seemed arduous enough without the further complication of Spanish demands. It is probable, therefore, that Hitler said no to Franco primarily because he did not think Spanish help was really necessary."[8] Seeing no need to incur the costs of a North African campaign in order to bring Britain to terms, Hitler desperately sought to preserve a cheap victory in the West, which he believed (as did most observers at the time) Germany had already "objectively" accomplished.

But Churchill stubbornly refused to capitulate to Germany, no matter how generous the terms. Encouraged by Dunkirk and backed by U.S. material assistance, the British people chose to fight rather than surrender. London's decision for war was eased by progress in its civil and air defense systems that greatly moderated the public's fear of a German "knockout blow." Hitler and Admiral Raeder felt that an "invasion should be undertaken only as a last resort to force Britain to sue for peace."[9] In the absence of any other means to coerce Britain to give up the struggle, on July 16, 1940, Hitler, after six weeks of deliberation, reluctantly issued "War Directive No. 16"—the invasion of Britain, code-named "SEALION." Still clinging to his dream of a world divided between Germany and England, Hitler did not want this war. In a speech given three days after the directive, he claimed that Germany had made

> determined and honest efforts to achieve friendship with the British Empire—an empire which it was never my intention to destroy or

even to harm. I do realise, however, that this struggle, if it continues, can only end with the complete annihilation of one or the other of the two adversaries. Mr. Churchill may believe that this will be Germany; I know it will be Britain. . . . I can see no reason why this war must go on. I am grieved to think of the sacrifices which it will claim.[10]

The German fleet, having suffered heavy losses during the Norwegian campaign four months earlier,[11] was woefully unprepared for war.[12] Estimating that the minimum demands of the army for SEALION required 1,722 barges, 471 tugs, 1,161 motorboats, and 155 transports, the German Naval Staff concluded: "The task allotted to the Navy is out of all proportion to its strength."[13] Hitler was not optimistic, but he agreed with Raeder that the key to victory was air supremacy. No invasion fleet could be put to sea until the Royal Air Force (RAF) had been destroyed, giving the Luftwaffe complete air mastery. In the Battle of Britain, Hitler once again blundered. In late August, Hitler shifted the Luftwaffe attack from the RAF Fighter Command bases to London.[14] Had the Luftwaffe persisted in bombing the airfields, the already exhausted Royal Air Force might have collapsed under the strain. Seemingly unaware of this, Hitler missed an opportunity to gain the required air supremacy for the amphibious assault against Britain.

British Policy Toward France: Buckpassing or Distancing?

Historians and political scientists have wondered why Britain did so little to help France against Germany and allowed Hitler to pursue piecemeal aggression. Recent interpretations of the case argue that Britain perceived defensive advantage in military technology and thus attempted to ride free on the balancing efforts of France. In short, Britain passed the balancing buck to France.[15]

I maintain instead that unlike 1914, when the relative power ratios favored the status-quo alliance (Britain, France, and Russia), 1938 saw German power (4.03) alone exceed the combined strength of the European status-quo states, Britain (2.1) and France (1.37). (If Italy and Japan are added, the equation becomes more lopsided in favor of the revisionist coalition.) In this situation (where $A > B + C$), the theory predicts no coalition, since B and C cannot combine to defeat A and A does not require a coalition to defeat either B or C. I will attempt to show that, on both theoretical and empirical grounds, this interpretation is superior to the more widely accepted view.

The buckpassing argument is part of a larger theory that predicts the effect of perceived offensive/defensive advantage on multipolar alliance patterns.[16] When offense is perceived to have the advantage, the theory posits, states balance aggressively and unconditionally: Once one state goes to war, its allies must follow immediately, as if on a chain gang. Conversely, when defense is perceived to have the advantage, states attempt to ride free on the balancing efforts of others: allies pass the buck. The perception of offensive advantage in 1914 and defensive advantage in 1939 is said to explain the difference between the alliance dynamics prior to the two World Wars. The logic is consistent and compelling, but does the theory successfully explain the British case? For several reasons, I think not.

First, how does the theory account for the reversal of British policy after Munich? According to Christensen and Snyder:

> One of the reasons that Chamberlain appeased Hitler at Munich was his exaggerated estimate of German strategic bombing capabilities and his fear that Britain's own retaliatory capability would not deter attacks on British cities. After the Munich crisis, Chamberlain pushed for a reorientation of British air power expenditures from bombers to fighters. Believing these efforts to be successful, he concluded by mid-1939 that a German attack on Britain would probably fail. This allowed him to guarantee Poland with less fear of the immediate casualties that this might produce.[17]

In Christensen and Snyder's own words, Britain's behavior directly contradicts their hypothesis. Perceived offensive advantage (a German knockout blow) causes Britain to buckpass, not chain-gang, while defensive advantage (faith in their air defenses) causes it to balance more aggressively, i.e., guarantee Poland and pledge to station troops on French soil.

My distancing hypothesis, by contrast, predicts Britain's partial policy reversal. After Munich, Anglo-French rearmament began closing the gap in Germany's military advantage and Britain saw itself and not France as the more immediate target of German aggression.[18] As a result, Britain drew closer to France and actually pledged troops to a continental defense. The Chiefs of Staff (COS) paper "The Strategic Position of France in a European War" (February 1, 1939) supports this view. While indicating that "British defenses were in the process of being strengthened," the COS stressed that "improvements would be shown during the next two years."[19] Taking pains to contrast the "expected brighter future with the present," the COS concluded: "We shall be in a position to defend ourselves at home and at the same time to afford considerably more assistance at sea, in the air and on the land, than we could today."[20] When war came, however, the strength of Britain and France did not yet equal that of Germany. Thus Britain, having accepted a limited commitment to the Continent, did not entirely reverse its distancing policy regarding France, though it might have had war not come until 1941.

Second, a central theme of the buckpassing argument is that British elites feared that higher military spending, particularly for a larger and better-equipped army, would tempt the French to reduce their own military expenditures. By passing the costs on to France, Britain could confidently believe that Germany would be balanced at minimal cost to itself.

The actual military expenditures of the Great Powers tell a different story, however. In the crucial period 1934–38, Germany increased military expenditures by 470 percent, Japan by 455 percent, the Russians by 370 percent, and Italy by 56 percent. By contrast, the British increased spending by 250 percent, and the French by a pitiful 41 percent.[21] Hence, while one can argue that Britain should have spent more on the military to keep up with its potential enemies, it is implausible that Britain refused to do so because it worried that France would spend less. As Timothy McKeown points out, "increases in [French] military spending from 1934 to 1938 were so anemic that it is difficult to imagine them doing less, even had a stronger British effort offered them a greater opportunity to free ride."[22]

Third, the buckpassing argument relies on the assumption that the defense of Britain and France constituted a collective good. None of the authors, however, explicitly makes this case, which is particularly troubling in light of the obvious differences between British and French security requirements. Britain was threatened by an air and sea assault; France by a land invasion. Thus, if one of the allies was able to secure its borders against a German attack, it does not follow that the other's frontiers were thereby defended.

In fact, both British and French leaders believed that Germany could launch a successful air and amphibious assault against Britain's home territory independent of a German occupation of France. Douglas Johnson observes that beginning in 1939, "the idea began to be put about that Germany was contemplating a move against Great Britain, perhaps preceded by a move against Holland and Belgium, rather than a move against France. If that was the case then France might well be able to stand by and allow that to happen. She could then do a deal with Hitler, or Mussolini, or both."[23]

As early as November 1938, Chamberlain advanced the "British-first" hypothesis at an Anglo-French meeting of ministers. In response to Daladier's request "for greater support from Great Britain," particularly more motorized divisions, Chamberlain denied that Germany would strike first against France on land and actually claimed that Britain would be Germany's first target from the air:

> The present attitude of Germany had brought before His Majesty's Government the possibility of a quarrel between Great Britain and Germany rather than between France and Germany, and the first blow might well, therefore, be struck against Great Britain rather than France. . . . The development of aviation had seriously altered the position in Europe, to the disadvantage of Great Britain. So long as Great Britain could only be attacked by sea, her defence was easy. But London was now the most vulnerable capital in the world. Within 24 hours of warfare London might be in ruins, and most of the important industrial centres in Great Britain as well. The principal armament centres were within range of enemy aircraft. His Majesty's Government was bound to take account of the fact that the nerve centres of Great Britain might be paralysed at the outset of war. This was a vital point, and it was their first duty to make Great Britain as safe as possible. . . . The result of their considerations of the problem had been that they had decided to give priority to anti-aircraft defences over the demands of the land forces, whenever they competed.[24]

This view is supported by Harold Nicolson's diary entry on October 31, 1939, of a discussion he and other British politicians had with French political leaders, including Edouard Daladier and Paul Reynaud: "[The French] think that we shall suffer very much from the air and that this time *it will be we and not they who are invaded.*"[25] Finally, on May 9, 1940, one day before the German attack on the Low Countries and France, the Chamberlain cabinet discussed a review of the strategic situation prepared by the Chiefs of Staff. The report predicted that Germany's "most likely course . . . would be to launch a major offensive against Britain, and the main threat to the United Kingdom was an intensive air offensive which, if successful, might culminate in an attempt at actual invasion. An enemy occupation of the Low Countries would seriously aggravate this menace."[26]

The very fact that Britain survived after France's defeat suggests that Anglo-French security lacked the property of jointness required of a collective good. Of course, this is not to imply that there was no relationship between British and French security or that British leaders expected that the fall of France would not affect the risk of a successful German invasion of the British Isles. It is simply to say that Britain's frontiers would have been even less secure had Britain done more to bolster France's defenses and so less to strengthen its own.

The nonrivalry property of a collective good is also suspect in this case. Anglo-French forces assigned to defend one of the allies' frontiers could not simultaneously be used for the defense of the other's. As Wallace Thies observes:

> Because defensive forces generally could not be transferred quickly and easily from one ally to another, alliance members did not view the forces of their allies as substitutes for their own. The French might take comfort in the knowledge that the British would almost certainly take their side in the event of war with Germany, but this did not relieve them of the requirement to build an army as large or nearly as large as Germany's; the British navy might rule the seas but it would be of little help in shielding France against a German attack.[27]

And until the British had secured their own borders, they had no intention of shielding France against a German attack. To do so would be to make Britain a more inviting target than France. Thus, the British Chiefs of Staff, convinced precisely of this, predicted in their last prewar strategic appreciation (February 20, 1939) that a German attack would be concentrated against Britain rather than France because "the vulnerability of the islands to combined air and sea attack would make [Britain] a tempting target."[28] The COS gave four reasons for expecting the initial German assault to be directed against Britain:

> France could not resist alone after the defeat of Great Britain; a full-scale attack on France would involve heavy losses which might have a serious effect on German morale; British support to France under attack was likely to prove more effective than French support to Great

Britain; and lastly, by use of her air force alone against this country Germany would exploit her relatively strongest weapon with the least expenditure of life and economic resources.[29]

Believing that it would be attacked first, Britain made every effort during the final weeks of the twilight war to hasten the production of anti-aircraft equipment, especially Bofors guns, bomber and fighter aircraft, and fully trained crews.[30] The outcome of the Battle of Britain confirms the Chiefs of Staff's belief that, for Britain, the "crux of the matter is air superiority."[31]

Even if the British had understood how quickly France would fall, it is far from clear that they would have, could have, or should have acted otherwise. According to J. L. Richardson, "even if more adequate resources had been available, the Army would probably not have adopted the kind of strategy and equipment likely to have made a crucial difference to the campaign in France in 1940."[32] Indeed, many British elites expressed relief over France's defeat. Chamberlain thought the French "terrible allies" and that Britain would be "better off without them." Britain though "alone" by the end of June, was "at any rate free of . . . the French who ha[d] been nothing but a liability" and "it would have been far better if they had been neutral from the beginning."[33] Like Chamberlain, Churchill and Halifax thought that Britain would be better off without the French. In Sheila Lawlor's words, both Churchill and Chamberlain did not see "French survival as necessary to British survival."[34] Sir Alexander Cadogan, too, "had been unsympathetic to the French 'howling for assistance (and even a 'token' would, in his view, be 'so much down the drain'). It would not 'do any good' and he would 'sooner cut loose and concentrate on defence of these islands . . . We should really be better off.' . . . He hoped the British were 'not uncovering [themselves] to help a helpless France' and would 'like to see the French put up a much better show' before he would 'risk all help to them.' They must concentrate on their 'own defence and the defeat of Germany, instead of dribbling away to France all that we have that is good—and losing it.'"[35] Eleanor Gates points out that many British policymakers "openly viewed France as a heavy burden, which it was necessary to slough off, and gave full vent to their feelings after the French defeat." In addition to those figures already mentioned, Lord Hankey "felt that France had been 'a debit rather than an asset in the present war' and found it 'almost a relief to be thrown back on the resources of the Empire and America.' . . . Air Marshal Dowding, who had jealously guarded his fighter squadrons throughout the Battle of France, went farthest of all. At the end of this agony, he actually said to Halifax: 'I don't mind telling you that when I heard of the French collapse I went down on my knees and thanked God.' "[36]

To many British elites, the rise of air power had made France and the Continent less important for British security—just as, years later, ICBMs and mutual assured destruction made the balance of power in Europe largely irrelevant for U.S. security. Changes in the Air Ministry's programs that obviated offensive and defensive deployment of the RAF in the Low Countries bolstered this belief in the expendability of the Continent, as Michael Howard observes:

"The Royal Air Force was [in autumn 1937] developing weapons-systems which were beginning to make a foothold on the continent of Europe, from their point of view, expendable. Consciously or unconsciously this may have affected the attitude of the Air Staff to the continental commitment."[37] Resources devoted to the RAF were "believed to increase British capability both autonomously to deter a German attack on Britain and to deal with that attack should deterrence fail."[38] Even Churchill called Britain's fighter squadrons: "in effect our Maginot Line"[39]—a statement in considerable contrast to Baldwin's claim in 1934 that Britain's frontiers lay on the Rhine.

Finally, according to the buckpassing interpretation, Britain attempted to ride free on the *strength* of France's balancing efforts. By contrast, the "distancing" hypothesis posits that alliances will not form among status-quo states when their combined strength is *less* than the opposing revisionist state(s). According to this view, the main reason Hitler was able to pursue piecemeal aggression unopposed was the power asymmetry in his favor, not the perception of defensive advantage.

The empirical record supports the distancing hypothesis. Contrary to the buckpassing view, Chamberlain never considered relying on the efforts of other states to provide for Britain's security. Sidney Aster comments:

[Chamberlain] held France and its statesmen in near contempt. "She [sic] never can keep a secret for more than half an hour, nor a government for more than nine months," he observed in January 1938. Of particular concern were French economic and industrial troubles which hindered its rearmament programmes. His attitude to the United States was equally reserved. He never neglected to pay the usual homage to the "special relationship," but his opinion of Anglo-American relations was that "it is always best and safest to count on *nothing* from the Americans except words." With regard to the Soviet Union . . . his private letters indicate that he had no faith in Soviet military capabilities and considered the Russians untrustworthy as a potential ally. . . . Consequently, *Britain could only look to its own resources for protection, having no reliable allies.*[40]

Among British elites, Chamberlain was not alone in detesting France for its military weakness and political instability:

French weakness and despair between the wars owed much to cold and sometimes callous treatment from London, and Baldwin was not exceptional when he counted as a major comfort of retirement "that he should not have to meet French statesmen any more." Repugnance was increased when a left-wing government like Blum's—"hazardous associates," Garvin called them—were [sic] involved. Those like Lord Lothian and Geoffrey Dawson, editor of *The Times*, who admired Hitler's strength often made no secret of their detestation for a weak and untrustworthy France, and they were even less restrained once France had allied with the Soviet Union.[41]

Upon succeeding Baldwin as Prime Minister on May 28, 1937, Chamberlain formulated a double policy of deterrence and appeasement, which was designed to provide for Britain's security without relying on allies:

His over-riding principle, articulated as early as 1934 while he was Chancellor of the Exchequer, was that Britain's best defence policy "would be the existence of a deterrent force so powerful as to render success in attack too doubtful to be worthwhile." As he wrote on 9 February 1936, in practical terms this meant "our resources will be more profitably employed in the air, and on the sea, than in building up great armies." Nothing, including the outbreak of war with Germany in 1939, ever changed his view on this subject. Given this strategy, his priorities were to maintain fiscal stability, providing for home and imperial defence, and absolute opposition to Britain ever again committing itself to raising a 1914-style continental army.[42]

Seeing only weak and unreliable allies, Chamberlain reacted to the Czech crisis by "dismiss[ing] as impractical the Churchillian alternative of a 'grand alliance' against the dictators." Support for Czechoslovakia, Chamberlain declared, "would simply be a pretext for going to war with Germany. . . . [and] that we could not think of unless we had a reasonable prospect of being able to beat her to her knees in a reasonable time, and of that I see no sign."[43] In other words, Britain could not join or put together a winning coalition, and so, as the theory predicts, no coalition formed. Rejecting the military option, Chamberlain instead redoubled his efforts to mediate possible areas of conflict with Germany—at least until the British rearmament effort had begun to pay off.

This "distancing" interpretation of British foreign policy also accords with Ribbentrop's assessment of the possibility of Germany reaching a settlement with Britain in 1938:

> . . . the conclusion must be drawn that a war between Germany and England on account of France can only be prevented if France *knows from the very beginning* that England's forces would not suffice to guarantee the common victory. Such a situation could force England and thereby France to accept many things which a *strong* Anglo-French combination would never tolerate. . . . If England with her alliances is stronger than Germany and her friends, she will in my opinion fight sooner or later. Should Germany, however, be so successful in her alliance policy that a German coalition would be stronger than its British counterpart, or perhaps as strong, it is quite possible that England would prefer to try for a settlement after all.[44]

Arguing that Britain was behind in its rearmament program and was therefore playing for time, Ribbentrop concluded that Germany should pursue "[q]uiet but determined establishment of alliances against England, i.e., in practice, strengthening our friendship with Italy and Japan and in addition winning over all countries whose interests conform directly or indirectly with ours."[45]

Ribbentrop's analysis proved essentially correct. Painfully aware of the imbalance of power between the British and German coalitions, Chamberlain continued to try to conciliate Hitler even after German troops occupied Prague on March 15, 1939. On March 19, he wrote "I never accept the view that war is inevitable."[46] A week later he expanded on his view: "I see nothing for us to do unless we are prepared ourselves to hand Germany an ultimatum. We are not strong enough ourselves and we cannot command sufficient strength elsewhere to present Germany with an overwhelming force. Our ultimatum would therefore mean war and I would never be responsible for presenting it."[47]

As discussed, the German move did provoke a limited British commitment to the European continent. However, in light of the woeful state of the Territorial Army, Britain's pledge could only be a symbolic gesture designed to encourage France to fight and not to remain neutral or, worse, side with the enemy if Germany attacked Britain directly.[48] Barely equipped for survival, Britain was in no position to help France.

In sum, during the 1930s the combined strength of Britain and France was less than that of Germany, and so no coalition formed. Instead, Britain distanced itself from France and adopted a dual policy of deterrence and appeasement. As the rearmament programs of Britain and France began closing the gap in Germany's military lead, Britain drew closer to France and began to stand up to Hitler. That the gap was never entirely closed explains Britain's not doing more to aid France.

The World Triangle Against Britain

After the *Luftwaffe* failed to deliver the knockout blow against Britain, Hitler realized that, as in 1914, what had been envisioned as a short campaign in the West had become a grinding war of attrition. To prevail, Germany would have to spend several years reconfiguring its forces for sea-based operations. Meanwhile, Hitler's primary goal, victory over the USSR, would be delayed for the duration, perhaps for a decade or more. In addition, a slugfest with Britain greatly increased the risk that the United States would actively enter the war.

Seeing little to gain and much to lose, Hitler cancelled Operation SEA-LION. He never intended to destroy Britain, only "to make Britain compliant to the aims of his Programme by striking military blows against her."[49] Having abandoned plans to invade England, Hitler realized that the war would continue well into 1941. Germany now required a more-lasting security in the East. This could be accomplished in one of two ways: either by drawing the Soviet Union into an anti-British coalition (and then smashing the USSR in 1942) or by attacking the USSR immediately. The latter option called for a two-front war.

For its part, The High Command of the Armed Forces had been urging Hitler to adopt Ribbentrop's concept of a massive continental coalition composed of Germany, Russia, Japan, Italy, Spain, and France, whose purpose would be the destruction and partition of the British Empire. The formation of this anti-British bloc stretching from Madrid to Tokyo called for a diplomatic effort of herculean proportions on Hitler's part. All of the revisionist states would have to agree, first of all, on participating in the onslaught of the British Empire, and secondly, on the division of the spoils, that is, who would get what piece of the former British Empire. To achieve this task, Ribbentrop had planned to designate each country its own mutually exclusive sphere of influence. All of the allies would be permitted southward expansion: Italy into North Africa, Japan into the Pacific, Germany into Central Africa, and the Soviet Union toward India. Though he remained extremely skeptical, Hitler went along with the project, which lasted from September to November of 1940.

The peripheral strategy against Britain commenced with the signing of the Tripartite Pact on September 27, 1940. For years, Ribbentrop had been urging the creation of a "world triangle" against the British Empire, consisting of Japan, Italy, and Germany. This had been the aim of Germany and especially of Italy in concluding the Anti-Comintern agreement of November 1937. But at that time, Japan, fearing that it might be drawn into a war with the United States, insisted that its only target be the Soviet Union.

For Japan, Hitler's military successes in the summer of 1940 changed everything. Europe's lost colonies in the Far East were there for the taking, if only Japan came to terms with Hitler, who, as conqueror of the Netherlands, France, and possibly Britain, could no longer be ignored. Thus, as soon as the Konoye-Matsuoka Cabinet was formed in July 1940, Japan let it be known that it was now anxious for a spheres-of-interest agreement with Germany based on a military pact with the Axis powers. An alliance with Italy and Germany, Matsuoka believed, would also provide Japan with insurance against a Soviet attack. Hitler and Mussolini so desperately wanted a military alliance with Japan that, "in return for recognition of Japan's far-reaching aspirations and the good offices of Germany in effecting better relations with Soviet Russia, Japan was asked only to sign up with Germany and Italy and to take a 'strong and determined attitude' toward the United States."[50]

The signatories to the Tripartite Pact pledged to "cooperate with one another in regard to their efforts in Greater East Asia and the regions of Europe respectively" and "to establish and maintain a new order of things."[51] The crux of the agreement resided in Article 3, whereby the three Axis powers agreed "to assist one another with all political, economic and military means when one of the three contracting parties is attacked by a power at present not involved in the European war or in the Sino-Japanese conflict."[52]

FIGURE 6.2
The alliance situation and power ratios in 1940

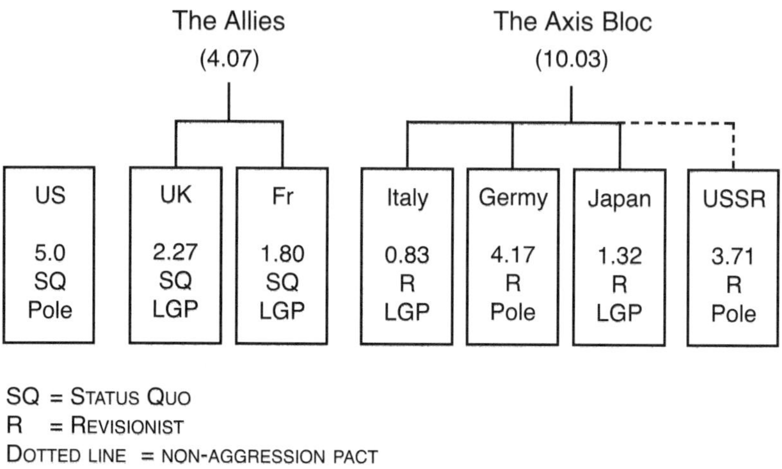

The Allies (4.07)			The Axis Bloc (10.03)			
US	UK	Fr	Italy	Germy	Japan	USSR
5.0	2.27	1.80	0.83	4.17	1.32	3.71
SQ	SQ	SQ	R	R	R	R
Pole	LGP	LGP	LGP	Pole	LGP	Pole

SQ = STATUS QUO
R   = REVISIONIST
DOTTED LINE = NON-AGGRESSION PACT

Hitler could not have been more pleased. The Germans had already persuaded the Italians to accept an offensive and defensive alliance in May of
1939; but Tokyo, despite intense efforts by Germany, had balked at a similar
proposal. Finally, the *Wehrmacht's* success on the battlefield had convinced
the Japanese to climb aboard the Axis bandwagon. With regard to the military requirements of Hitler's grand strategy, the navies of Japan and Italy
would help to make up for Germany's deficiency in naval armaments, which
it had not yet remedied and needed for war with Britain and the United
States.[53] The alliance, Hitler argued, would not only win Britain over to his
policy by the threat of force but also prevent the United States from intervening in the European conflict by threatening it with a two-ocean war.[54] In
his diary entry of September 27, 1940, General Halder described the pact as
"an undoubted political success and a warning to America."[55]

Molotov Visits Berlin, November 1940

In the month following the Tripartite Pact, Ribbentrop's "continental bloc"
strategy misfired badly. Hitler was unable to devise a formula for the division

of spoils that would satisfy Mussolini, Pétain, and Franco. Nevertheless, Hitler grudgingly agreed to give the peripheral strategy one last try. The occasion would be the visit by the Soviet Foreign Minister, Vyacheslav Molotov, to Berlin from November 11 through November 13, 1940.[56] If the talks failed, Hitler would be confirmed in his belief that war with Russia, not Britain, was the solution to Germany's problems. If the meeting proved successful, however, Germany stood to gain two advantages in its relations with the Soviet Union, as Martin Van Creveld points out: "By offering the Russians the prospect of expansion at the expense of Britain in the direction of the Persian Gulf and India, Hitler and Ribbentrop hoped not only to hurt the British but to 'divert' the Russians from their traditional European aims and relieve Germany of their pressure."[57] Indeed, the crucial aspect of the continental bloc strategy from Germany's perspective was to divert Russian expansion southward, away from Eastern Europe.

From Moscow's perspective, Molotov was sent to Berlin to sound out Hitler's intentions with regard to Russia and to begin negotiations for a new Nazi-Soviet pact on Soviet terms. Specifically, Molotov and Stalin wanted the withdrawal of German troops from Finland; placement of Bulgaria in the Soviet sphere of influence; and Soviet control of the Straits.

The first issue Hitler raised with Molotov was Finland. The Führer pointed out that "Germany did not desire any war in the Baltic Sea and that she urgently needed Finland as a supplier of nickel and lumber." Consequently, "the decisive question for Germany was whether Russia had the intention of going to war against Finland." According to the record, Molotov "answered this question somewhat evasively." Hitler responded by repeatedly warning "that there must be no war with Finland, because such a conflict might have far-reaching repercussions." Specifically, Hitler worried that Germany's vital raw material shipments from the Baltic would be cut off and that "Allied bases might be established in Scandinavia."[58] When Molotov replied that he could not understand the sudden danger to Germany of a second Baltic War, especially now—after Germany's victories in the West, Hitler revealed a surprising concern:

... the Führer ... considered it entirely possible that the United States would get a foothold in those regions in case of participation by Sweden in a possible war. He (the Führer) wanted to end the European war, and he could only repeat that in view of the uncertain attitude of Sweden a new war in the Baltic would mean a strain on German-

Russian relations with unforeseeable consequences. Would Russia declare war on the United States, in case the latter should intervene in connection with the Finnish conflict?

When Molotov replied that this question was not of present interest, the Führer replied that it would be too late for a decision when it became so. When Molotov then declared that he did not see any indication of the outbreak of war in the Baltic, the Führer replied that in that case everything would be in order anyway and the whole discussion was really of a purely theoretical nature.[59]

Putting this issue aside, Hitler then outlined the projected anti-British bloc, saying that:

> he wanted to create a world coalition of interested powers which would consist of Spain, France, Italy, Germany, Soviet Russia, and Japan and would to a certain degree represent a coalition—extending from North Africa to Eastern Asia—of all those who wanted to be satisfied out of the British bankrupt estate. To this end all internal controversies between the members of this coalition must be removed or at least neutralized. For this purpose the settlement of a whole series of questions was necessary. . . . It was a matter of determining in bold outlines the boundaries for the future activity of peoples and of assigning to nations large areas where they could find an ample field of activity for fifty to a hundred years.[60]

As Ribbentrop put it to Molotov, "the decisive question was whether the Soviet Union was prepared . . . to cooperate . . . in the great liquidation of the British Empire."[61]

While agreeing in principle to the idea of a continental bloc, Molotov made it clear that Hitler would not succeed in his attempt to delimit the Soviet sphere of influence to Asia. To the contrary, Molotov repeatedly raised precisely those European questions that had been responsible for German-Soviet tensions in recent months: Poland, Finland, Romania, and particularly Bulgaria. With regard to the Balkans, Molotov issued several complaints and proposals for rectifying the situation:

As a Black Sea power, the Soviet Union was tied up with a number of countries. In this connection there was still an unsettled question that was just now being discussed by the Danube Commission. Moreover, the Soviet

Union had expressed to Romania its dissatisfaction that the latter had accepted the guarantee of Germany and Italy without consultation with Russia. The Soviet Government had already explained its position twice, and it was of the opinion that the guarantee was aimed against the interests of Soviet Russia. Therefore, the question of revoking this guarantee came up. To this the Führer had declared that for a certain time it was necessary and its removal therefore impossible.

Molotov then came to speak of the Straits which, referring to the Crimean war and events of the years 1918–19, he called England's historic gateway for attack on the Soviet Union. The situation was all the more menacing to Russia, as the British had now gained a foothold in Greece. For reasons of security the relations between Soviet Russia and other Black Sea powers were of great importance. In this connection Molotov asked the Führer what Germany would say if Russia gave Bulgaria, the independent country located closest to the Straits, a guarantee under exactly the same conditions as Germany and Italy had given one to Romania.[62]

Hitler replied that the German-Italian guarantee to Romania "had been the only possibility of inducing Romania to cede Bessarabia to Russia without a fight. Besides, because of her oil wells, Romania represented an absolute German-Italian interest, and lastly, the Romanian Government itself had asked that Germany assume the air and ground protection of the oil region, since it did not feel entirely secure from attacks by the English." Emphasizing this last point—that Romania had requested the guarantee— Hitler concluded that, if the Russian guarantee to Bulgaria "was to be given under the same conditions as the German-Italian guarantee to Romania, the question would first arise whether Bulgaria had asked for a guarantee. He [the Führer] did not know of any request by Bulgaria."[63] In any event, Hitler would have to discuss the matter with Mussolini before anything concrete could be laid down.

On the final day of meetings, Molotov made it painfully clear to Hitler and Ribbentrop that Soviet interests could not be diverted to Asia but would continue to extend throughout Eastern Europe, the Balkans, the Baltic, and the Mediterranean.[64]

Two days after Molotov's departure from Berlin, Hitler told his closest advisors that "the talks have shown the direction in which the Russian plans are moving. Molotov has let the cat out of the sack. They did not even try to hide their plans. To allow the Russians into Europe, would mean the end of central Europe. The Balkans and Finland are endangered flanks."[65]

In considering the prudence of Hitler's decision to attack the Soviet Union, it is worth noting that Germany's strength relative to the other great powers was at its high water mark during the period 1940–41. DePorte correctly points out:

> By 1940 Germany had become so powerful that it would dominate Europe unless prevented by a coalition of Great Britain, the Soviet Union, and the United States. It took the power of all three to defeat the Third Reich. Britain alone, even with American support short of intervention, could at best have maintained control of its home island and the lanes of communication to its overseas dependencies and friends. The Soviet Union, even with Britain still in the war and with help from the United States, could at best have maintained a core of the Russian state, Brest-Litovsk style, at the farthest eastern end of Europe. Britain and Russia together could not have defeated Germany or disrupted its European empire. As in 1918 only American entry into the war could tip the balance from German victory in Europe to German defeat.[66]

Confronted by the prospect of a war of attrition with Britain that risked bringing the United States into the conflict prematurely, Hitler decided to turn Germany's attention to the defeat of the Soviet Union. With Russia out of the war, Britain would lose its last potential Continental ally and would, according to Hitler, sue for peace. More important, in control of the European Continent, Germany could then wage the final hegemonic war against North America.

Japan Proves a Reluctant Partner

Despite Hitler's efforts not to disrupt American neutrality until Russia had been defeated, by January 1941, the U.S. appeared more likely to enter the war. To ensure that the United States, if it chose active belligerence, stayed out of the war in Europe and the Atlantic, Hitler turned to Japan and the Far East theater. In Hitler's view, any steps taken by Japan against British possessions in the Far East might force Britain to come to terms with Germany, and thereby keep America on the sidelines. Hitler also sought to instigate U.S.-Japanese conflict to divert American energies from the Atlantic theater to the Pacific.

With preparations for the campaign against the USSR already set in motion, Hitler conceived of Japan's role as holding Britain in check and keeping the United States neutral. This, he believed, would prevent an Anglo-American front from opening in Europe and allow Germany to attack the Soviet Union without complicating distractions arising in the West. Within the framework of Japan as a German "dagger" against America, Hitler urged Tokyo to attack Singapore, regardless of the consequences. The German leadership mistakenly believed, as did the military analysts in the U.S. and Britain, that a Japanese attack on Singapore would finish Britain off and allow the transfer of German troops to the eastern front for the planned attack on the Soviet Union, "Operation Barbarossa," scheduled for mid-May 1941. An attack on Singapore would also serve as a litmus test of Japanese loyalty to Germany, which was in question because of Tokyo's ambiguous commitment to the Tripartite Pact. Fearing abandonment, Hitler worried that the Japanese intended to reach an accommodation with Roosevelt, leaving Germany alone to face the United States.

On March 5, 1941, Hitler issued a directive outlining his aims for Japanese-German cooperation in the Far East:

(a) the quick defeat of England is to be designated as the common aim in the conduct of the war, thereby keeping the U.S.A. out of the war. . . .
(b) **The seizure of Singapore**, England's key position in the Far East, would signify a decisive success for the combined warfare of the three Powers.[67]

The directive also stated that "No hint of the *Barbarossa Operation* must be given to the Japanese,"[68] who would certainly not attack southward if they knew that the Soviet Union would soon be in the opposing camp. Instead, Ribbentrop told the worried Japanese Foreign Minister, Matsuoka, that "if Russia should ever attack Japan, Germany would strike immediately. He could give this firm assurance . . . so that Japan could push southward toward Singapore without fear of complications with Russia. . . . [If] Germany should become involved in a conflict with Russia, the Soviet Union would be finished in a few months."[69]

For his part, Admiral Raeder, Commander-in-Chief of the German Naval Staff, argued: "Japan wants to avoid war with the U.S.A. if possible, and she could do this if she would take Singapore by a decisive attack as soon as possible."[70] In October 1940, General von Boetticher reported from the German

Embassy in Washington that certain circles within the U.S. military considered "the fate of the [British] Empire to be sealed;" therefore "American advantage lay with an Axis victory," for "you can't go to bed with a corpse."[71] On April 1, 1941, Hitler met the Japanese Foreign Minister, Matsuoka, in Berlin in a final effort to persuade Japan to attack Singapore immediately. The Führer described the overall situation of the war:

> [In] scarcely a year and a half 60 Polish divisions had been eliminated with the occupation of Poland, 6 Norwegian divisions with the occupation of Norway, 18 Dutch divisions with the occupation of Holland, and 22 Belgian divisions with the occupation of Belgium, and of the 138 French divisions there remained only 8 weak brigades. All of the English units had been routed and driven out. These were losses which could not be recouped and the position of England was no longer recoverable. Thus the war had been decided, and the Axis Powers had become the dominant combination.[72]

Continuing, Hitler asserted that Britain had only two hopes, America and Russia. According to the Reich's calculations, American aid "could appear in tangible form only in the year 1942 at the earliest, but even then the extent of such help would bear no relation to the increased productive capacity of Germany."[73] Furthermore, Hitler argued, "If [the U.S.] helped England, she could not arm herself. If she abandoned England, the latter would be destroyed and America would then find herself confronting the Powers of the Tripartite Pact alone."[74] The key was to prevent a U.S.-Soviet rapprochement. Hitler alluded to this possibility:

> Both the British Empire and the United States hoped that in spite of everything they would be able to bring Russia in on the side of England. They believed that they could attain this goal, if not this year, perhaps next, and thus produce a new balance of power in Europe.
>
> In this connection it should be noted that Germany had concluded well-known treaties with Russia, but much weightier than this was the fact that Germany had at her disposal in case of necessity some 160 to 180 divisions for defense against Russia. She therefore did not fear such a possibility in the slightest and would not hesitate a second to take the necessary steps in case of danger.[75]

With Germany keeping Russia busy on its western front and the United States in the initial stages of rearmament, Hitler concluded that, "Japan was the strongest power in East Asia." Surely they recognized that such a propitious "moment would never return" for Japan to realize her own *Lebensraum*.[76]

The Japanese were unconvinced by Hitler's arguments.fearing entrapment, they refused to risk war with Britain—a war that would certainly provoke the U.S. against Japan as well. For now, Tokyo regarded Hitler's scheme as nothing more than a transparent attempt to maneuver Japan into taking the full force of the American blow. And so, just as Ribbentrop's periphery strategy against Britain proved a complete failure, the Three Power Pact had thus far failed to make Japan compliant to Hitler's wishes.

War Among the Poles, 1941–1945

Having shelved the "periphery" strategy against Britain, Hitler concluded that his cherished Eastern campaign could no longer be delayed. The defeat of the USSR, Hitler thought, would not only prevent the danger of a American-Soviet coalition but would also compel Britain to give up the fight: "Britain's aim for some time to come will be to set Russia's strength in motion against us. If the U.S.A. and Russia should enter the war against Germany the situation would become very complicated. Hence any possibility for such a threat to develop must be eliminated at the very outset."[77]

As for Britain's hope of active U.S. support, Hitler argued: "America will have less inclination to enter the War, due to the threat from Japan which will then have increased. A victorious campaign on the Eastern Front will have a tremendous effect on the whole situation [and] also on the attitude of the U.S.A."[78]

As Hinsley notes: "He would not attack Russia simply in order to undermine Great Britain by removing Germany's last enemy on the continent," but also "in the hope that precisely by this action the United States would be deterred from entering the War."[79]

Fortunately for the Anglo-Saxon powers, the Eastern Campaign was not a repeat performance of the Battle of France. Germany's *blitzkrieg* strategy was foiled by the vast expanse of the Soviet Union, which enabled the Red Army to trade space for time. Germany might still have been able to defeat the USSR in 1941, however, if only Mussolini had not entrapped Germany by attacking Greece. To clean up the Duce's mess, in March and April of 1941, Hitler withdraw some of his troops from the regions bordering the Soviet Union in order to crush Yugoslavia and Greece. The rescue of Italy cost Germany precious time and resources needed for the Eastern campaign.[80]

The failure of the *Wehrmacht*'s offensive in 1941 gave the United States a breathing spell to begin mobilizing its enormous war machine and join the Soviet Union in an overwhelmingly powerful "two-against-one" winning coalition. But there was still time for Germany to win the war against the Soviets, turn around and defeat Britain (if it did not sue for peace), and thereby keep the United States off the Continent and out of the war. The question is: How did the Soviets wind up fighting Germany alone? How and why did Stalin allow this most terrible of situations, one that he had feared for years, to occur?

Stalin's Failed Tertius-gaudens Strategy

According to my scheme, the Russian bear was actually a fox: a limited-aims revisionist pole that tries to hold the balance and extort profit from its rivals. Like Hitler, Stalin conceived of the pre-World War II international system in tripolar terms. But unlike Hitler, who saw the European system as bipolar with the U.S. out of the picture, Stalin's tripolar vision was based on his belief that Britain and France together constituted a third European pole—one that could effectively balance Germany. In his speech at the plenary session of the Central Committee in January 1925, Stalin revealed the *tertius-gaudens* strategy that would guide Soviet foreign policy in the next world war:

> The preconditions for war are getting ripe. War may become inevitable, of course not tomorrow or the next day, but in a few years. . . . But, if war begins, we shall hardly have to sit with folded arms. We shall have to come out, but we ought to be the last to come out. And we should come out in order to throw the decisive weight on the scales, the weight that should tilt the scales.[81]

For the Soviet Union to become the enjoying third, Stalin had first to ensure that war would break out in the west, and that it would be a protracted one. And for that both sides must be formidably strong. Consistent with his desire to instigate a "second imperialist" war from which the Soviet Union could safely abstain, Stalin supported the victory of fascism in Germany but not the further spread of fascism throughout Europe. A triumph of fascism in Western Europe would not have produced the division of Europe into opposing armed camps of revisionist and status-quo states upon which Stalin was counting. Furthermore, a total fascist victory would ultimately endanger the Soviet Union.

Given Soviet Russia's *tertius-gaudens* strategy, Stalin pursued a dual diplomacy regarding the fascist and democratic states. If Stalin's grand design was to succeed, he would have to make certain that two potential hostile coalitions—an Anglo-Franco-German combination and a German-Japanese alliance—did not form. Since Germany was the only common member of the two feared coalitions, the solution to the Soviet security problem was, in the long term, a rapprochement with Berlin. And because Stalin did not believe that Britain and France would come to Russia's aid in the event of a German attack in the east, an alliance with the dreaded Nazis in effect offered Moscow its only and therefore minimum winning coalition.

Obviously, Stalin's strategy also required that France be militarily strong enough to keep from being overrun and speedily conquered by German forces. In the short term, therefore, Stalin supported the strengthening of a collective-security coalition led by France and directed against Germany. He also encouraged the democracies to rearm and instructed the French Communists to call off their campaign against the government's plan to extend the period of French military service from one to two years. Robert Tucker comments:

> By his collective-security diplomacy, in combination with his popular-front tactics in the Comintern, Stalin was assisting events to take their course toward a European war. An accord with Germany remained a basic aim because it would offer an opportunity to effect a westward advance of Soviet rule while turning Germany against the democracies in what Stalin envisaged as a replay of World War I, a protracted inconclusive struggle that would weaken both sides while neutral Russia increased her power and awaited an advantageous time for decisive intervention. But to make sure that the European war *would* be protracted, he wanted Britain and France to be militarily strong enough to withstand the onslaught that Germany under Hitler was becoming strong enough to launch against them. That explains his moves to encourage ruling elements in both these major states to rearm with dispatch, and his order to the French Communists to support the French military buildup.[82]

The power side of the model predicts a Nazi-Soviet alliance, but only one in which the Soviets actively participate in the fighting and are assured of receiving along with Germany an equal share of the spoils. (See discussion of equilateral tripolar system with two revisionist poles). By joining Germany to divide Poland, Stalin behaved according to the "Partitioned Third" version of tripolarity. True, Poland was not a pole; but the power configuration of Poland, Germany, and the Soviet Union was $A < B = C$, and so the logic of what I call a "Type 3" tripolar system still applies. In carving up Eastern Europe, the territory that lay between the two revisionist poles was divided equally between them, such that neither side made relative gains *vis-à-vis* the other.

Conversely, by encouraging Germany to attack westward by itself, Stalin acted contrary to the logic of the power side of the model. Stalin's behavior is nevertheless understandable given his misjudgment of the strength of Britain and France. Believing that the Allies were stronger than Germany, the Soviet dictator aided Hitler (that is, he balanced against the Allies) in the hope that the two sides would be evenly matched, and the conflict would evolve into a war of attrition. In the end, Russia paid the price for Stalin's mistake in overestimating the Allies' strength.

The interests side of the model also predicts a Nazi-Soviet alliance; specifically, the pact supports the hypothesis that revisionist states flock together. For Russia, a rapprochement with Germany offered more than security: Soviet expansion was possible only in collusion with Hitler. In the end, the two countries' shared interest in revisionism bridged their ideological divide. As Louis Fischer comments, ideology "proved no barrier when Hitler wanted war and Stalin coveted territory."[83]

Stalin's own explanation for the Nazi-Soviet pact (given in 1940 to the British Ambassador Sir Stafford Cripps) testifies to the strength of shared interests, whether revisionist or status quo, in deciding who aligns with whom: "[The] U.S.S.R. had wanted to change the old equilibrium . . . England and France had wanted to preserve it. Germany had also wanted to make a change in the equilibrium, and this common desire to get rid of the old equilibrium had created the basis for the rapprochement with Germany."[84] Similarly, Sir Nevile Henderson viewed the Nazi-Soviet pact as the inevitable outcome of any concession-making competition between status-quo and revisionist suitors of an unsatiated power: "[By August 11, 1939, Moscow] was asking for a free hand in the Baltic States. Russia's real objective was thus becoming apparent; and, with Germany secretly in the market, the scales were being heavily weighted against the Western Powers. They could not barter away the honor and freedom of small but independent countries, but Germany could."[85]

Stalin's "major blunder," as Isaac Deutscher correctly points out, was that "he expected Britain and France to hold their ground against Germany for a long time; . . . he overrated France's military strength; and he underrated Germany's striking power."[86] Consistent with these observations, in 1939 Stalin stated that "democratic states . . . are without doubt stronger than the fascist ones both militarily and economically."[87] Given Stalin's expressed belief that a bloc of aggressor states consisting of Germany, Italy, and Japan was arrayed against the interests of Britain, France, and the United States, and that the democracies were, in combination, "unquestionably stronger" than the fascist coalition, both militarily and economically, Stalin "could and evidently did calculate also that the oncoming war between them would be a protracted one that would result in their mutual weakening or exhaustion while Soviet Russia was at peace and rebuilding its own strength."[88] After the Second World War, Voroshilov said: "We in spite of it all thought that if Germany attacked Britain and France, it would bog down there for a long time. Who could have known that France would collapse in two weeks?"[89]

Viewing the European system as tripolar, it is easy to see why Stalin made a deal with Hitler. A nonaggression pact with Germany would destroy the status quo, afford easy spoils in Eastern Europe and Finland, and instigate a war of attrition among the capitalist powers. Better still, the Soviet Union enjoyed the role of kingmaker, as both Germany and the democratic powers needed it to form a winning coalition. Thus, Germany would be made to pay heavily for Soviet assistance in a war from which Russia could safely abstain. Stalin used his bargaining power to prolong the Anglo-Franco-Soviet negotiations just long enough to extract additional concessions from Hitler, in exchange for which the Soviet leader put his signature to the pact with Germany that he desperately wanted anyway. It appeared that Stalin had succeeded in the role of abettor: Germany was deflected to the west, while the Soviets comfortably looked on from the sidelines, gaining at the others' expense.[90]

Speaking of the pact, Stalin commented: "Of course it's all a game to see who can fool whom. I know what Hitler's up to. He thinks he's outsmarted me, but actually it's I who have tricked him."[91] Events would soon prove otherwise, however. Hitler had duped Stalin. With the September 1 deadline for the Polish attack only a week away, Hitler was willing to give the Soviet dictator whatever he wanted to secure Soviet neutrality and thereby deter Britain from honoring its pledge to Poland. Indeed, the Führer seemed to be in an especially giving mood, confident that he would attack and crush Russia in the near future, taking back all he had given and more.[92]

In retrospect, we know that it would have been far better for the Soviets to have balanced against, rather than bandwagoned with, Germany. In that case, Stalin would have presented Hitler with the prospect of a two-front war, seriously undermining the Führer's strategy and perhaps causing its abandonment. But because he mistakenly perceived Europe as a tripolar, not a bipolar, system with France and Britain as the third pole, Stalin expected a war of attrition in the West. The fall of France abruptly ended Stalin's dream of easy conquests in a postwar period when the rest of Europe would be exhausted.

This begs the question: When the long war failed to occur, why did not the Soviet Union immediately join Britain in its fight against Germany? The historian James McSherry offers a plausible hypothesis, which, if true, suggests an important limitation of my model. He argues that Bolshevik ideology prevailed over balance-of-power logic:

> With three or more approximately equal states, a balance of power operates almost automatically. Should state *A* appear to be growing too powerful and dangerous, states *B* and *C* combine against it. If state *B* becomes too powerful, *A* and *C* form an alliance. Tsars and foreign ministers in St. Petersburg reacted in this classical pattern almost instinctively. . . . But the Bolsheviks saw themselves winning everything or nothing. They perceived only two powers: the Soviet Union and an implacably hostile capitalist world. As long as the capitalists didn't unite in a crusade against the U.S.S.R., what matter if one capitalist state became more powerful than the others or even brought some of the others under its sway? Once Hitler had conquered France, the Soviet Union was in mortal peril. But Stalin realized the full extent of the danger only on June 22, 1941.[93]

To the extent that ideology overrides the logic of structure and interests, my hypotheses will fail to accurately explain and predict national policy.

But in this particular case, accepting the ideological interpretation may be conceding too much. My distancing hypothesis, which predicts that a state will not join the weaker side when it expects that its added strength will not change the outcome, offers a viable alternative explanation for Soviet behavior. According to this hypothesis, Stalin decided not to join Britain in balancing against Germany because, after the swift defeat of France, he judged that Britain was doomed. This hypothesis is consistent with the view of the British Ambassador to Moscow, Sir Stafford Cripps. In August 1940, Cripps observed that after France collapsed "there is no doubt that the views of the Soviet Government underwent a change, and, instead of proceeding with a rapid *rapprochement*, I was unable to obtain access of M. Molotov." Hence, Cripps concluded:

> It is beyond question that there is not the slightest chance at the present time of producing any kind of rupture in German-Soviet relations, nor do I think that it is possible to reduce in any way the assistance which is being given to Germany by the Soviet Union so long as it appears to the Soviet Government that the German attack on Great Britain may lead to a speedy end of the war in favour of Germany.[94]

In summary, before the war, Stalin overestimated the strength of France and Britain relative to that of Germany, misperceiving the Allies as the stronger side. Thus, the Soviet Union supported Germany, guarding its rear and supplying it raw materials, in the hope that the two sides would be as closely matched as possible, and the conflict would end in mutual exhaustion. By escaping participation in the fighting, the Soviet Union would emerge far stronger in relative terms in the aftermath of war than it had been prior to war's outbreak.

After the collapse of France, when the tide turned strongly in Germany's favor, similar balance-of-power considerations prescribed that Russia should switch sides, supporting the Allies, again in the hope of sustaining the visibly weaker side. By that time, however, Stalin had decided that Germany would soon win the war outright, whatever the Soviet Union did. Reconciled to a German victory, Stalin distanced the Soviet Union from Britain.

Japan's Role in Germany's Eastern War

Throughout the Eastern campaign, Hitler had insisted that Germany would defeat Russia without help from his allies. Even after "Operation Barbarossa" failed to produce a quick German victory, Hitler "rejected the idea of Japan taking part in 'his' Russian war by setting up another front in the East."[95] Instead, he wanted Japan to hold Britain in check and keep America neutral to prevent the opening of a second front in Europe. Ribbentrop and the Foreign Office disagreed with Hitler's "Germany alone" strategy against

Russia. Ever since 1938, Ribbentrop had regarded Britain, not the Soviet Union, as Germany's principal enemy. Fixated on the idea of challenging Britain with a "continental bloc," the German Foreign Minister proposed enlisting the full support of Japan to end the war with Russia as soon as possible. A Japanese attack on Vladivostok would, in Ribbentrop's view, "eliminate quickly the Russian opponent" and "release the German forces sooner for renewed action against England."[96]

In the summer of 1941, the Wilhemstrasse once again began pressuring Japan's decisionmakers to attack British possessions in the Far East. On August 25, 1941, Ribbentrop sent a telegram to the German Ambassador in Tokyo, General Eugen Ott, expressing his frustration with those who were "misjudging the situation with regard to power and the military aspect" and seemed to be "unaware of Japan's own strength and the weakness of the United States and England."

> The fact that the United States has reacted to Japan's occupation of Indochina only with economic sanction ... the fact that the Roosevelt-Churchill meeting produced only words, and the fact that the United States has made the hopeless and almost desperate attempt to keep Japan out by means or insincere negotiations are clear signs of weakness on the part of the United States, proving that it will not risk any serious military action against Japan. This is no news to the military expert, for he has long known that the army and the air force of the United States are not yet ready and that its navy is still inferior to the Japanese navy. Moreover, a large majority of the American people are opposed to war. . . . Japan is still in a position to impose whatever decision she chooses. But the longer she waits, the more the balance of forces will change to her disadvantage . . .[97]

As with the previous German request to attack Singapore, Japan did not take the bait. At the time, Tokyo was engaged in negotiations with Washington to improve Japanese-American relations. The Japanese Deputy Foreign Minister, Amau, reminded Ott that the "aim of the Tripartite Pact is to prevent war with America." Amau further pointed out that bullying tactics made the U.S. more, not less, belligerent, as Berlin already knew:

> Japan first strove to [prevent war with the U.S.] by taking a threatening tone with Roosevelt, but to no avail—on the contrary it merely

made Roosevelt take a firmer stand. . . . Germany, on the other hand, has not reacted to Roosevelt's acts of provocation and . . . has even in the case of the closing down of the consulates, refrained from giving him any pretext for entering the war. Japan therefore considers it tactically correct . . . to use the same methods as those used by Germany.[98]

Determined to prevent an agreement between Tokyo and Washington, Hitler had informed Tokyo in the autumn of 1941, that in the event of a Japanese attack on the U.S., Germany would wage war too. The Führer honored this commitment on December 11, 1941, when Germany declared war on America in accordance with the Three Power Pact. By supporting his Far Eastern partner, Hitler hoped that Japan would tie down the U.S. in the Pacific, keeping American forces well clear of the European theater.[99]

Geography played a major role in Hitler's judgment of the impact of America's entry into the war. He did not deny the tremendous potential power of the U.S., but he questioned its ability to project that power.[100] In a conversation with Matsuoka on April 4, 1941, Hitler remarked:

America's performance depended on her transport capabilities, which in turn would be limited by the tonnage available. Germany's warfare against shipping tonnage represented an appreciable weakening not only of England but of America also. Germany had made her preparation so that no American could land in Europe. She would wage a vigorous war against America with her U-boats and her Luftwaffe . . .[101]

In addition, German intelligence data indicated that the U.S. would not be ready to intervene in the European theater for years to come. By that time, around 1943, the Reich would have established an empire over the Eurasian continent from which it could easily defend against an American attack.[102]

The U.S. in the Eyewitness Role

In the 1930s, the aloofness of U.S. foreign policy during Italy's seizure of Abyssinia; Japan's invasion of China; and Germany's takeover of the Rhineland, Austria, and the Sudetenland in Czechoslovakia, fully accords with the role of the ostrich: a polar power that acts like a weak state, choosing to be an eyewitness rather than a participant in world affairs. Indeed, the historical record offers little room for controversy: Roosevelt pursued an isolationist policy, refusing to commit the United States to the defense of the existing international order. Within the Roosevelt administration, there were competitive "idealist" and "realist" schools. Some officials, such as Secretary of State Cordell Hull, monotonously preached Wilsonian gospel, while others, like Assistant Secretary of State Adolf Berle, championed a brand of realism based on the concept of a separate, viable Western Hemisphere removed from the turmoil of Europe. There was no debate, however, on the essential thrust of U.S. foreign policy: both factions favored isolationism.

To his credit, the President viewed world politics as a relatively tightly coupled system, and for this reason his ideas did not fit neatly into either school. He warned that the U.S. could not expect to remain safe in its Western Hemisphere while the rest of the world was at war. In the age of air power, Roosevelt insisted, the 3,000-mile oceanic barrier, which had traditionally served to insulate the United States from foreign wars, would no longer prove an insuperable obstacle to aggressor states seeking territorial profits in the Western Hemisphere.[103] Moreover, for Roosevelt, the awesome destructive power of the new air technology meant that offense clearly had the advantage over defense. As early as May 16, 1933, in a message delivered to the heads of fifty-four states represented in Geneva, FDR declared that the "overwhelming majority of peoples retained excessive armaments because they feared aggression in an age when *modern offensive weapons were vastly stronger than defensive ones.*"[104] Employing Jervis-type systems thinking, FDR understood the pernicious effect of offensive advantage on the security dilemma.

Roosevelt's systemic ideas about the interconnectedness of world politics, however, did not compel him to seek an activist foreign policy. With little or no chance of selling a forward foreign policy to an isolationist Congress and public, the President responded to aggression abroad in the classic tradition of U.S. isolationism, attempting to play "a passive role as the beacon of liberty to mankind, providing a model for the world to follow, but avoiding any active participation in a foreign conflict."[105] In a speech in mid-1936, for instance, Roosevelt revealed that, while he sympathized with the troubles plaguing the European nations, "they have understood well in these years that [American] help is going to be confined to moral help, and that we are not going to get tangled up with their troubles in the days to come."[106]

Roosevelt's oblique strategy risked several dangers. As an eyewitness to world affairs, the U.S. encouraged the four expansionist Great Powers—Germany, Japan, Russia, and Italy—to disregard the considerable latent power of the United States. Up until March 1941, the U.S. government—for all its high-sounding and idealistic rhetoric about the struggle against Nazism, Bolshevism, and Fascism—proved unwilling to aid frontline status-quo states. The passage of two major pieces of legislation, the Johnson Debt-Default Act and the Neutrality Act of 1939, effectively prevented the U.S. government and private citizens from arranging credit for any belligerent.[107] Uncertainty about when and if the U.S. would adopt a more interventionist policy tempted the Axis powers to try to overturn the status-quo order sooner rather than later.

Moreover, America's military and political weakness compelled the other status-quo Great Powers to try to appease the stronger dictator states. To be sure, had America rearmed and pledged support for the European status quo, France and Britain would not have sat on their hands while the Axis powers leveled successive blows against the established international order.

Roosevelt's passive foreign policy also risked the danger of a direct assault against the American Continent—a scenario that had caused the President himself a considerable amount of anxiety. Though it seemed remote at the time, the possibility remained that the Soviet Union and Germany might put aside their mutual hostility, if only temporarily, for the purpose of ganging up against the U.S. and its allies. Indeed, this is precisely the strategy that Mackinder had warned the sea powers to guard against and that Haushofer had urged upon Hitler.

Finally, the security of the Americas would have been severely compromised had Germany or Russia managed to grab the Continent quickly, before the U.S. could deploy its military forces. That the Soviets could hold out against the Nazi attack long enough to enable the U.S. to mobilize and employ its awesome resources was by no means assured. And the longer the U.S. took to effectively enter the war, the greater the risk that Stalin would make a second deal with Hitler.

Structural-systemic theory cannot explain why the United States did not play a more active mediator or balancer role in Europe; the answer resides at a lower level of analysis, either domestic politics or decisionmaking or some combination thereof. The immovable strength of American isolationist sentiment caused Roosevelt to shy away from any significant U.S. involvement in the affairs of Europe, even after a grave threat was perceived. Domestic politics also explains why, on those rare occasions when the Roosevelt administration did attempt to mediate a settlement, it did so halfheartedly—almost hoping that its efforts would fail.

But systemic theory does provide a partial explanation for the persistence of America's isolationist policy. While Germany and the Soviet Union remained on opposite sides, the U.S. could expect a relatively stable balance in Europe. If war broke out between Germany and the Soviet Union and the power balance on the continent was disrupted, Britain, backed by substantial U.S. material aid, could be expected to assume its traditional role as balancer, throwing its weight on to the scale of the weaker side. For this scenario to have occurred, however, the U.S. would have had to mediate a stable settlement in Western Europe. The expansionary energies of Germany and the Soviet Union, the only two virile giants on the international stage capable of endangering the American continent, would then have been directed at one another.

Hitler Declares War Against the Distant Pole

Aware of the tripolar distribution of power, Hitler nevertheless simultaneously declared war on both of his polar enemies, the U.S. and the Soviet Union. In so doing, he forced into existence the only coalition that could defeat Germany. Indeed, as Hauner notes, "when on 11 December 1941 Hitler had declared war on the USA in a self-destructive fit of absent-mindedness he had to admit to the Japanese Ambassador Oshima three weeks later that he did not know how to defeat America."[108] After all, Hitler had scheduled the decisive duel between the "Teutonic Empire of the German Nation and the American World Empire" to occur after his death.

The entry of the United States into the war threatened a large-scale Allied intervention in the Western Mediterranean and on the Atlantic coast of French West Africa, and with it a greater likelihood of Vichy defection and Spanish reluctance to side with the Axis. Forced to shift his attention from the Eastern Front to the Mediterranean theater, Hitler now advised his Italian and Japanese allies that the key aim of Axis policy in the spring and summer of 1942 should be a meeting in the Indian Ocean. If successful, this rendezvous operation would disrupt the entire Anglo-American supply system, gain Axis control of the Middle East oil resources, cut the southern supply route to the Soviets, and permit the flow of critical materials between Germany and Japan. It was a high-stakes roll of the dice that, one way or the other, promised to tilt irrevocably the balance of the entire war. The Italians, of course, did not need to be convinced of the supreme importance of the Mediterranean theater and the need to defeat Britain. Back in December of 1941, the Duce had already reached the conclusion that the key to victory was "the Suez Canal; the attack must come not only from one side, but 'also from the East.' "[109]

Toward that end, General Rommel's German Expeditionary Corps in Africa were sent to bolster the Italian positions in Libya and Tripolitania with the hope that Egypt could be taken before the expected Anglo-American landing in the Western Mediterranean. The Japanese, for their part, had achieved victory off the coast of Ceylon in April, and, in light of Japan's continued success in Burma and its Axis partners' desire to link up in the Indian Ocean, it appeared that this latest victory would be followed by a further westward push into the area of rapid advance. In early May, German air activity increased over the Central Mediterranean and the Axis built up their supplies in North Africa for Rommel to move eastward from his bases in Libya. On June 21, Tobruk fell to Rommel's forces as they sped toward the Suez Canal. Buoyed by the success of his latest offensive, Rommel convinced Hitler to scrap "Operation Hercules"—the planned attack on Malta that had been conceived by the Italian Supreme Command and strongly supported by Mussolini[110]—and gamble instead on his German expeditionary force continuing its dash to Egypt, from whence it would press on to the Persian Gulf. Simultaneously, the German offensive on the Eastern Front held the promise of a march across the Caucasus into the Middle East with the added prospect of a German thrust through Turkey. It appeared that the Axis rendezvous at Suez would be in sight by summer's end, and with it a tide of Axis victories and Allied defeats.[111]

The southern advance to the Caucasus was going according to plan and, by mid-August, had gained the Axis control of the Maikop oil field. But already the armies' lines of communications and supplies were being pressed to their limits. In early November, the southern advance ground to a halt before the mountainous terrain of the Southern Caucasus, with the Grozny oil fields beyond that, and Baku, the ultimate objective, still further to the south.

To the north, forty German divisions began their attack on September 3 against Stalingrad, the possession of which would divide Central Russia from the Caucasus. As the German forces reached the outskirts of the city, the Russians withdrew behind the Don and created a Stalingrad front. During the early weeks of the fighting, the German air forces were flying up to 2,500 sorties a day but the Soviets were able to amass significant forces east of the Volga to launch an encircling offensive of their own. On November 19, the Russians attacked the Axis forces north of the city and on the following day assaulted the German positions to the south. Within a week, twenty-two German divisions were encircled, fourteen were destroyed. As December approached, the German Sixth Army had been completely encircled.

In an attempt to liberate the Stalingrad pocket, Hitler ordered General von Mannstein, whose forces had stalled in the Caucasus, to redirect his divisions north for the purpose of a combined attack with German forces directed to move eastward from their positions on the Don. On December 16, Mannstein's armies, which had commenced their drive from the south four days earlier, were met and driven back by Russian forces moving southward from their positions east of Stalingrad. By the end of the month, the Red Army had destroyed another twenty-two German satellite divisions. Any hope of an Axis victory on the Eastern Front by year's end had been dashed.

The crisis for the Axis in the East coincided with an equally catastrophic turn of events on the North African Front. On October 23, the British Eighth Army assaulted Rommel's forces at El Alamein and achieved a decisive breakthrough just ten days later. Rommel, recognizing that the battle for Egypt was lost, ordered a general and swift retreat. The Allies now threatened a landing at Rommel's rear in French North Africa. The fate of the Mediterranean campaign and Italy's very survival required that unoccupied France and Corsica not fall into enemy hands. Both the Duce and Hitler feared that Vichy France would bandwagon with the Anglo-Americans.

Uncertain of French loyalty, Hitler summoned Laval to Munich for the purpose of offering the Vichy government a stark choice: full cooperation or occupation of the Free Zone, Corsica, and Tunisia. Laval rejected the formal offer of an alliance with Italy and Germany and then prevaricated on the Axis demand for the use by combined Italian-German forces of the bases of Bizerta and Tunis. Vichy's hostility meant not only that German and Italian divisions—so desperately needed in Russia and North Africa—would be tied down in southern France, but also that the French fleet at Toulon had to be scuttled. On November 11, Axis air forces were in control of the Tunisian airfields and Italian and German armored units landed at Tunis and Bizerta. The establishment of an Axis bridgehead in Tunisia, however, could not change the course of the war. "In the long run," Rommel pointed out, "neither Libya nor Tunisia could be held, for the African war was being decided by the battle of the Atlantic."[112]

To make matters worse, Japan had, for all intents and purposes, abandoned its European partners and their plan for a meeting across the Indian Ocean. Instead of pursuing the offensive in the Indian Ocean initiated so successfully in April, the Japanese foolishly disregarded Hitler's advice and turned in the opposite direction to meet the American forces that had landed on Tulagi and Guadalcanal on August 7. In five months of bitter fighting in the Solomons, Japan suffered heavy losses in warships, ground combat assault troops, and naval air units that precluded the anticipated return to the offensive in the Indian Ocean. With Japan diverting its resources to the South Pacific, the British took Madagascar and the Americans opened a supply route across Iran that sustained the Red Army in its battle against the new German offensive.[113]

The Japanese, by refusing to coordinate their military strategy with the European Axis, had gravely underestimated the obvious importance of the European theater to their own success; indeed, their empire in Southeast Asia had been handed to them by German victories in Europe. As a result of this oversight, the Axis frittered away their best chance to wrest the Middle East from Allied hands and to achieve victory on the Eastern Front in 1942.[114]

For some time, the Japanese had been urging Hitler to reach a new agreement with the Soviet Union in order to focus their energies on fighting the British and Americans. The Axis defeats in the winter of 1942–43 further convinced Tokyo that its advice had been correct all along.[115] On December 15, the Italians joined their Axis partner in raising the issue of a possible settlement with the Soviets, which the Duce believed would be the cardinal issue of 1943. The next day, an Italian delegation led by Ciano and Marshal Ugo Cavellero left Rome by train to confer with Hitler in Berlin. In his subsequent memorandum to Mussolini, Ciano recorded:

> When I spoke of the possibility of a separate peace with Russia, Hitler expressed his own negative point of view in the following words. Germany had already in the past posed the problem of coming to an understanding with Russia, and precisely in the winter of 1940–41 every attempt was made to push the Russians into Central Asia. This was particularly discussed at the time of Molotov's visit to Berlin. But the Russians did not follow this course. Instead they brought up their historic claims on Finland and the Dardanelles, against Roumania, and in the direction of Bulgaria. If Germany had given way at the time, the Russians would first have attacked Finland, and then after they had taken over the Roumanian oil, the Axis would have been placed in an untenable position.
>
> The Russia of Stalin still follows the path chosen by Peter the Great for the expansion of his people to the North and South-West. Russia has in no way shown herself prepared to follow the course proposed to her towards India and the Persian Gulf because she regards these aims

as secondary. If she were first assured of hegemony over Europe, the rest would follow of its own accord.

The break between Germany and Russia arose out of the increasing danger which this latter threat presented. When Hitler knew for certain that nine hundred airfields, an enormous quantity of war material and numerous troops were concentrated on the frontier, he had to take defensive measures. Can yet another attempt now be made to reach a settlement of the struggle with Russia? The Fuehrer asked himself this question some months ago, when rumour was spreading that Japan had sounded the Fuehrer in this sense. But, as we had assumed, we learnt that these rumours had been artificially spread by the Russians themselves to bring pressure on their allies to give more support in armaments, and to obtain the opening of the Second Front.

What would the position be today if we somehow came to an agreement? It is certain that the Russians would devote six months to a complete overhaul of their equipment and strength in order to fall on our rear again. The Brest-Litovsk line is out of the question. These are regions which represent indispensable reserves of foodstuffs and raw materials for Germany and Russia alike. Thus any line drawn which might satisfy the requirements of one people would sacrifice the needs of the other.

Even if we came to an understanding with Russia, we would not be able to move larger forces to Africa, because the only reason for the crisis which has arisen in Africa is to be found in our transport difficulties and not at all from lack of materials and troops.[116]

Ruling out peace with Russia, Hitler stressed instead the utmost importance of the pacification of the Balkans: "Every measure must be taken to prevent the outbreak of fire in our rear in case an Anglo-Saxon landing takes place." In addition, Hitler insisted that the Duce be asked "personally to telegraph to the Italian troops in Russia not to yield an inch of territory."[117]

Not surprisingly, some high German officials violently opposed Hitler's conduct of the war. In July 1943, former Ambassador Ulrich von Hassell, a conservative nationalist dismissed in 1938, roundly criticized from the sidelines the German attacks against both the Soviet Union and the United States:

There is absolutely no foundation for the assertion that Russia wanted to attack, or would have attacked later. We have here the pernicious example of the preventive war which Bismarck condemned. If Germany "stumbled" into the two-front war in 1914, Hitler wantonly brought it on in 1941. Russia had only one feeling about an intact Germany—fear. Russia would never have attacked Germany, or at least never have attacked successfully, so long as Germany possessed an unbroken army. It suffices to imagine what would have happened if Germany, after the fall of France, had remained in possession of a fully intact, powerful instrument of war, instead of wearing it out in battle against an underestimated Russia. The fight against Russia which Hitler started was just as reckless an undertaking as the war in general. After it had started there was at least one chance—the only "morally" good chance, from the propaganda point of view—to wage it exclusively against bolshevism and to make our watchword the liberation of the Russian people, with whom Germany had no quarrel.

The opposite happened. Hitler united Russia behind Stalin against Germany. Incidentally, one might also point out the folly of aligning ourselves simultaneously against Poland as well as against Russia—a violation of the A B C of any Germany policy in the east.

A further ruinous decision was that of declaring war on the United States. Annoying as it was to see this power supporting the other side, it was stupid of Hitler to seize the initiative and turn the United States from a supporter of the other side into our major foe, who would use the full force of her strength against Germany. It may be that Hitler thought he owed this action to Japan. If so, it was the only instance of treaty loyalty in Hitler's career and a truly strange and disastrous one at that.[118]

Most, if not all, historians and political scientists would agree with Hassell's characterization of Nazi Germany's bid for world domination as an extremely reckless strategy, one that was doomed to fail. Such a conclusion, I believe, is too categoric and somewhat difficult to defend in light of the evidence. Confronted by a global coalition of incredible strength and with scarcely any help from its allies, Nazi Germany more than held its own until 1944 and survived into 1945. The relatively narrow margin of the Allied victory suggests that the outcome of World War II might have been different had any one of several events broken another way. Let us therefore engage in what E. H. Carr called "parlour-games with might-have-beens."[119]

Counterfactual Parlour Games

What if, for instance, Germany had knocked the Soviet Union out of the war in 1941 or 1942, as it had done to Russia in 1917? What if Japan had not attacked at Pearl Harbor but instead had joined Germany against Russia? Would America have entered the war and, if so, would it have mobilized as quickly and with as much determination as it did after the Japanese attack? What if Hitler had not declared war against the United States? Would the U.S. Congress have declared war against Germany?

Engaging in similar speculation, Hugh Trevor-Roper claims that any one of four "hypothetical accidents" in 1940, could have put Hitler "in a position to conquer the world" in 1941: if Britain had not had a statesman able to unite the country to continue what looked like a pointless struggle against Germany; if Britain had not, at that precise historical moment, possessed the vital intelligence—"the Ultra secret"—critical to the air victory over Britain; if Franco had not resisted the temptation to rush to the aid of the apparent victor and had allowed an assault on Gibraltar; and, lastly, if Mussolini had not launched a surprise invasion of Greece. Had any one of these conditions been met, Germany would have defeated Britain and achieved a final victory in the West. Under such circumstances, Trevor Roper asks:

> Would Japan wantonly have attacked Pearl Harbor when defeated Britain and Russia offered an undefended prey? Would America have intervened in Europe, when there was no bridgehead left, in order to save Communist Russia? Is it not more likely that Hitler's dream would have been realised: that a German empire would have been established, dominating Europe and hither Asia: that, in Hitler's own phrase, the German age of the world would have begun?"[120]

At the tactical level, what if Hitler had made use of "Russian commissars and Jews as cheap sources of labor [rather] than exterminating this sorely needed potential labor force"?[121] What if Nazi ideology had not prevented the full mobilization of German women (female employment dropped until 1943)? What if the Nazi regime had not brutally treated its foreign workers, forced laborers, and the inhabitants of the occupied territories, particularly in the Soviet republics?[122] Might the Nazis have been seen by these populations as liberators rather than hostile conquerors? With their help, might Germany have gone on to defeat the USSR? Finally, what if Hitler had upheld his original decision to send only a small force to defend a limited area in North Africa?[123] If it were possible to rewind a tape of history and replay the war, any one of these alternative scenarios might have occurred and produced a different outcome.

Conclusions

Hitler's overall strategy accords with the expected behavior of a polar power trying to gain supremacy in a tripolar system. As one of three equal-sized poles, Germany could not defeat the nearest pole without first augmenting its strength by internal and external means, that is, through rearmament, the conquest of its neighbors, and key alliances with LGPs. Strengthened by these preparations, Germany, if it acted quickly, could then isolate and defeat the nearest pole. After several years of consolidating its European base and expanding overseas, Germany would be ready to challenge and defeat the other pole in the bipolar system.

Given the benefit of hindsight, A. J. P. Taylor concluded that Hitler "gratuitously destroyed the source of [his] success" by attacking "two World Powers who asked only to be left alone."[124] And yet, Hitler came within a hairsbreadth of succeeding in his quest for European hegemony. Confronted by the combined military efforts of the entire world, Germany held out until 1945. Had he defeated the Soviet Union, a U.S.-German, rather than a U.S.-Soviet, bipolar system would have resulted.

In the end, Hitler blamed Germany's destruction on British stupidity. He had offered Britain its only chance of holding on to its Empire and world-power status. How, he asked, could anyone have foreseen that the British would elect men who did not possess the intelligence to correctly assess England's true interests? British elites, Hitler charged in 1945, had clung to an outmoded idea of the balance of power, conceiving of it not in global terms but rather as it related to Europe:

[Churchill] has made the same mistakes as those generals make who wage a war according to the principles of the preceding war. . . . The crucial new factor [since Pitt's day] is the existence of those two giants, the U.S. and Russia. Pitt's England ensured the balance of world power by preventing the hegemony of Europe—by preventing Napoleon, that is, from attaining his goal. Churchill's England, on the other hand, should have allowed the unification of Europe, if it wished to preserve that same balance of power.[125]

This passage suggests that Hitler saw a German-dominated Europe as the third pole in a tripolar system. Unlike many of his contemporaries, Hitler therefore accurately predicted that Germany's defeat would bring about a bipolar system:

> . . . with the defeat of the Reich . . . there will remain in the world only two Great Powers capable of confronting each other—the United States and Soviet Russia. The laws of both history and geography will compel these two Powers to a trial of strength, either military or in the field of economics and ideology. These same laws make it inevitable that both Powers should become enemies of Europe. And it is equally certain that both these Powers will sooner or later find it desirable to seek the support of the sole surviving nation in Europe, the German people. I say with all the emphasis at my command that the Germans must at all costs avoid playing the role of pawn in either camp.[126]

Fortunately, the Second World War did not turn out as the Führer had planned in *Mein Kampf*. Instead, the two poles on Europe's flanks were able to activate and combine their enormous resources in time to defeat the Reich and its Axis partners. By partitioning Germany, the Allies solved the "German Problem" that had given rise to two world wars in the space of twenty-five years. The structural effect of the division of Germany was to transform the volatile tripolar system into a stable, but very competitive, bipolar world.

Chapter 7

Conclusions

Most of what has been written about World War II features highly descriptive and often elaborate investigations of the internal decisionmaking processes of the Great Powers with the individual, state, and/or society as the unit(s) of analysis. Far less has been written about the structure of the interwar system and its impact on the origins and outcome of the war. The obvious reason for this bias is the consensus among historians and political scientists that Hitler alone was responsible for World War II. The less obvious reason is the widespread belief that structural properties change at a glacial pace and are not subject to control by statesmen. Hypotheses derived from third-image theory typically pertain to general systemic properties and state behavior. Structure, it is said, does not determine outcomes but rather works to keep them within narrow ranges.[1] It explains meta-history, the driving forces of global change and continuity, and not particular historical events.

Those of us who believe that systemic properties are often decisive in explaining international behavior recognize the partial truth of these arguments but respond that structural properties have not been measured with sufficient precision and that the links between unit-level and structural causes have not been specified with enough clarity. As presently conceived, structural theories cannot explain specific historical outcomes, and they claim no ability to do so. Consequently, there have been precious few structural analyses that connect a theoretical discussion of polarity (or any other structural variable) to a concrete historical case. Instead, empirical tests of structural theories typically employ data-based, quantitative techniques. In search of statistically significant correlations, these studies dredge highly aggregated data, across centuries, places, and cases in an inductive attempt to establish measures of association among various structural variables (e.g., polarity, polarization, the concentration of capabilities) and systemic war proneness.[2] Leaving aside the problem of unspecified scope conditions, identification of such correlations is, to be sure, a worthwhile endeavor, particularly with respect to improving our ability to make accurate predictions. If the ultimate goal of scientific research is explanation, however, understanding the connections between "cause" and "effect" is of greater theoretical and prescriptive value.

Structure alone, however, can take us only so far in the search for sequences of cause and effect. Structural explanations are, as Waltz asserts, "indeterminate because both unit-level and structural causes are in play."[3] To explain outcomes, then, we must uncover and map out the internal dynamics of various international systems, that is, the interactions between unit-level and structural causes. Singer is right in saying that "unless one can illuminate the decisional links between environmental conditions and the behavior of the nations making up the system, any model of systemic effects on the incidence of war must remain less than complete . . . even if the statistical associations to date between system structure and war were both consistent and robust— which they certainly are not."[4]

The failure of existing structural theories to generate precise and falsifiable propositions that exhibit some degree of predictive accuracy should not, however, lead us to abandon systemic study in favor of unit-level theory. The cure for weak systemic theories is not to ignore the effects of structure on behavior and outcomes but rather to create better systemic theories. Such progress requires greater precision in the measurement of structural conditions and more attention to unit inputs and variations, such that outcomes are indeed codetermined by unit-level and structural causes.[5]

In this spirit, the present study attempts to enhance the predictive and explanatory power of neorealist theory by adding two variables: the inequalities of power among the Great Powers and their level of satisfaction with the status quo. These refinements transform neorealism from a theory of international politics to one of foreign policy. The amended theory, which I call balance-of-interests theory, yields more varied and determinate predictions about system dynamics and state behavior and richer explanations of concrete historical cases than does Waltz's theory. Moreover, its design captures realism's traditional concern with the power and interests of states. These gains come at a price, however: the revised theory is admittedly far less elegant than Waltz's. Nevertheless, a theory built on only two elements is quite parsimonious by any standard.

Structure as Relative Inequalities

In contrast to Waltzian neorealism, in which the structure of the international system is determined by counting the number of Great Powers, this study defines structure not just by the number of poles but also by the differences in their relative sizes. This more refined measure of structure allows for nuanced hypotheses about international politics and state behavior and makes it possible to differentiate systems of the same polarity according to differences in their precise power configuration. In Waltz's own words, "inequality is what much of politics is about. The study of politics, theories about politics, and the practice of politics have always turned upon inequalities, whether among interest groups, among religious and ethnic communities, among classes, or among nations."[6]

Yet most balance-of-power theorists, including Waltz, have overlooked the important effects of power inequalities on system stability and the foreign-policy choices of individual countries. By defining polarity as the number of Great Powers in the system, neorealism ignores the uneven distribution of capabilities among the Great Powers themselves, treating structures of the same polarity as if they were all of a piece. The bottom line is that structural theorists have paid insufficient attention to the definitions and measurement of international structure. The debatable quality of the measurement of the critical variables is important for several reasons.

First, imprecise measurement tends to homogenize structures that would otherwise be recognized as significantly different. Since there can be no explanation without covariation between the putative cause and the phenomenon that is being explained, an unrefined measure of structure necessarily results in static theory and, by extension, indeterminate and often nonfalsifiable hypotheses, which cannot be used to explain changes over a relatively short span of time. Given these limitations, the main line of attack against neorealism is that it does not explain very much. Waltz himself admits that the predictions yielded by his theory are so general as to be nonfalsifiable: "Because only a loosely defined and inconstant condition of balance is predicted, it is difficult to say that any given distribution of power falsifies the theory."[7] By lumping all non-bipolar systems under the rubric of multipolarity, neo-realism defines out of existence much of its potential explanatory power. Specifically, Waltz claims that the polarity of the system has changed only once since the birth of the modern state system in 1648. Thus, his theory cannot explain any variation in behavior and outcomes prior to 1945, when the system was supposedly multipolar, or during the bipolar era that commenced after World War II.

I say "supposedly multipolar" because no study of World War II prior to this one has attempted to measure accurately the distribution of capabilities among the Great Powers. The structural analyses that do exist merely posit that the system was multipolar, without first defining what constitutes a pole, specifying how to measure capabilities, and then crunching the numbers to validate the postulated structure. When these crucial tasks are performed, the late interwar system is revealed to be tripolar and not multipolar (four or more poles) as is commonly assumed.

Second, consistent with the realist image of international politics, balance-of-power theory counsels statesmen to identify and prioritize the national interests according to any changes that occur in the relative distribution of power. Thus, a faithful model of the theory requires precise measurement of the capabilities of the relevant states; in more technical terms, it requires, at a minimum, interval scale measurement. Neorealism's independent variable, polarity, is an ordinal scale measure that simply distinguishes Great Powers from non-Great Powers. This kind of rough measure is perfectly fine for Waltz's purposes. But we should not forget that the relatively new concept of polarity did not appear in pre-Waltzian discussions of the balance of power. Instead, traditional realists focused on the relative distribution (balances and imbalances) of capabilities among particular states and coalitions rather than on the number of Great Powers in the system. As Morgenthau writes: "The historically most important manifestation of the balance of power . . . is to be found . . . in the relations between one nation or alliance and another alliance."[8] Traditional realists viewed capability not as a systemic attribute but rather as a unit property or a relationship between states and/or coalitions, e.g., the potential outcome of military interaction.[9] In short, a rough measure such as polarity misses much of the logic of balance-of-power theory.

Finally, more precise measurement would quickly dispel the myth that structure changes at a glacial pace. As this study has attempted to show, the relative capabilities of the Great Powers underwent major shifts during the interwar period. For the first decade and a half after World War I, the international system was unipolar, with the United States as the lone pole. By 1934, Stalin's industrialization drive had elevated the USSR to a polar status equal to that of the U.S., and the system was thereby transformed to one of bipolarity. By 1936, Hitler's domestic consolidation of Nazi power and revision of Versailles' limitations on German rearmament propelled Germany to polar status. This created an unbalanced tripolar system, with the U.S. and the USSR still significantly stronger than Nazi Germany. By 1938, Hitler's acceleration of Germany's rearmament program once again transformed the system from one of unbalanced tripolarity to equilateral tripolarity. Aside from these transformations of international structure, important changes were taking place at the non-polar level. In 1913, for instance, Japan held a 4.4% share of total Great-Power resources, less than one-third of the capabilities controlled by Britain (14.1%). By 1938, its share of capabilities (9.3%) almost equaled Britain's (10.5%). While Japan more than doubled its percentage share of total Great-Power resources, Britain and France found themselves heading in the opposite direction. From 1890 to 1938, Britain's percentage share of total Great-Power capabilities shrank from 21% to 10.5%, while France's share dropped from 12.7% to a mere 6.9%.

One conceptual aspect of system structure should be particularly noticed, for future reference and because of its significance to the argument at hand: polarity must not be equated with the concept of polarization, which describes "the closeness of attachments with a system's alliances and the degree to which a system's coalitions stand apart from one another."[10] To begin with, alliances are not states and so they cannot be considered poles; as Waltz puts it: "Even with the greatest of external pressure, the unity of alliances is far from complete."[11] Further, polarization is one of the behaviors that we seek to explain by means of structural causes; to treat polarization as if it were the structure of the system is to confuse causes with their effects.

I mention the difference between polarity and polarization because, in the context of the present study, it is especially tempting to break the rules. Recall that, in the relevant model (*viz.*, equilateral tripolarity with two revisionist poles), two revisionist poles would gang up and partition the third (status quo) pole. But this is not what happened: Germany and the Soviet Union did not gang up on the United States. Yet, if we were to ignore the difference between polarity and polarization it is possible to view the Anglo-French combination as the third (status quo) pole. Then, the prediction is indeed correct. The story of World War II becomes one of "shifting tripolarity" as follows: From 1936 until the Fall of France in 1940, the system was tripolar with Nazi Germany, the Soviet Union, and an Anglo-French combination as the three poles of the system; from June 1940 to the end of World War II, the system remained tripolar with the Anglo-American bloc replacing the Anglo-French one as the third pole.

The problem with this story is that it makes precisely the mistake that Stalin made: it treats British and French capabilities as if the whole were the sum of its parts. This view is not only nonsystemic in logic but also disconfirmed by the historical evidence. Britain did not see its fate tied to France's and so distanced itself from its neighbor. Far from constituting a pole, the so-called Anglo-French combination was an alliance in name only. As A. J. P. Taylor points out:

> The practical test of an alliance is the military planning which goes with it. Staff conversations were held between Great Britain and France immediately after the German move into the Rhineland. They lasted five days and lapsed. No more were held until February 1939. France did not get increased security or strength from the alliance with Great Britain. Rather she got an ally who was ceaselessly holding her back for fear that the alliance might have to become effective—not that the French needed much restraining.[12]

Moreover, if we treat Britain and France as a pole, why not do likewise with respect to the Axis partners? This would be absurd, of course, since there was virtually no coordination at all among the Axis powers, which largely explains why they lost the war. In short, we must not confuse structure with behavior; polarity with polarization.

State Interests

The interests, or motivations, of states, whether they are revisionist or status quo, is the other element, along with the relative capabilities of the Great Powers, of balance-of-interests theory. Just as microeconomic theory assumes that firms seek to maximize profits, a theory of international politics must assign some goal(s) to states.[13] In social systems, structure constrains and provides opportunities for purposeful, rational action. The effects of structure cannot be known, however, unless we first posit what it is that states desire.

Recognizing the necessity of goal-driven behavior, neorealist theory allows for the full range of state motivations, "from the ambition to conquer the world to the desire merely to be left alone."[14] Because it does not incorporate this wide variation in state aims as a model-based feature, however, neorealism treats state interests as if they were inconsequential for a theory of balance of power. This book argues otherwise. In determining alliance dynamics and system stability, it matters whether the state is revisionist or status quo; that is, whether it values what it covets more than what it possesses or is satisfied with what it already has and seeks only to maintain its possessions. In essence, the distinction is one of maximizing security or power. I do not mean to suggest that power and security are always mutually exclusive goals; to the contrary, power often enhances security and vice versa. There is, as Reinhold Niebuhr says, "no possibility of drawing a sharp distinction between the will-to-live and the will-to-power."[15] I do mean to suggest that the purpose of power is not always security and that accumulations of power do not always bring greater security. Power can be used to threaten others or to make them more secure; to take resources or to defend them; to prevent others from achieving their goals or to assist them in realizing them.

In the final analysis, states are less concerned with power imbalances than they are about who holds power. Interests, not power, determine how states choose their friends and enemies. Revisionist states will readily side with the dominant state or coalition if they believe that its goal is to overturn the established order to their advantage. Status-quo states will favor the more powerful state or coalition if they believe that its goal is to preserve the peace and stability of the system. Thus, Grey of Fallodon explained why, from 1886 to the end of the century, Britain "did not attempt to create any counterpoise to the strongest group [the Triple Alliance]; on the contrary, the British Government sided with that group":

> . . . there was, I think, a belief that the power of the Triple Alliance made for stability and therefore peace in Europe; that France and Russia, though militarily the weaker, were the restless Powers, while the Triple Alliance was on the whole contented. The conclusion I would draw is that Great Britain has not in theory been adverse to the predominance of a strong group in Europe when it seemed to make for

stability and peace. To support such a combination has generally been her first choice; it is only when the dominant Power becomes aggressive and she feels her own interests to be threatened that she . . . gravitates to anything that can be fairly be described as a Balance of Power.[16]

By varying the system's composition of revisionist and status-quo states, systems of the same structure (distribution of capabilities) are predicted to behave quite differently. Further, the relationship between state interests and structure, on the one hand, and system stability and alliance dynamics, on the other, is not a linear one. Instead, the combined impact of structure and unit interests on system stability and the alliance behavior of states often produces counterintuitive outcomes. For example, a system composed of a majority of revisionist states may be just as stable (or more so) than one with a majority of status-quo states, depending on the precise power configuration and the mix of revisionist and status-quo states. For all these reasons, we must distinguish states according to their level of satisfaction with the status quo. I chose to do this by means of five categories: unlimited-aims and limited-aims revisionists, indifference toward the status quo, and soft and staunch supporters of the status quo.

In evaluating the usefulness of balance-of-interests theory, particularly as an alternative to Waltzian neorealism, the question is: Do the gains in predictive and explanatory power outweigh the losses in terms of additional complexity. Obviously, I believe that they do. Waltz's theory predicts that states balance and nothing else. State behavior differs only in the way balancing is accomplished: under multipolarity, alliances are an essential mechanism for balancing power; under bipolarity, the poles balance each other by relying on their own capabilities rather than the capabilities of allies.[17] Waltz's emphasis on the differences between external and internal balancing provides many useful insights about the stability of multipolar and bipolar systems. But history is replete with examples of states that did not respond to greater power by balancing against it. Moreover, Waltzian neorealism ignores altogether state responses to opportunities in their environment. It is a theory about how states react to threats and under what circumstances these responses are more or less likely to trigger systemwide war.

In contrast, this study identifies eleven distinct state behaviors, which include in addition to balancing: buckpassing, distancing, engagement, binding, holding the balance, and jackal and several other forms of bandwagoning. I then presented a typology based on state interests and capabilities that categorizes states as either wolves, lions, lambs, jackals, owls, hawks, doves, foxes, or ostriches. The combination of state interests and relative capabilities tells us a great deal about what kind of behavior to expect from various types of states; whether they will respond to threats and opportunities in their environment and how they will do so. Rather than reiterating all of these behaviors and how they played themselves out during the interwar period and World War II, I will briefly summarize the more salient hypotheses and findings.

Bandwagoning: Birds of a Feather

States do not always have an incentive to check greater power; sometimes their interests are better served by joining the stronger side. I have argued that bandwagoning rather than balancing is the characteristic behavior among revisionist states because their primary goal is to transform, not maintain, the system. System stability is a virtue only for those states that are content with the status quo; political disorder serves the interests of those states that are dissatisfied with the system they have. By working to throw the system into disequilibrium, bandwagoning states can hope to make gains even if they wind up on the losing side—which would be unexpected from their perspective, since, by definition, bandwagoning means joining what appears to be the winning side. Moreover, to the extent that the goal of revisionist states is to maximize power and not security, it makes sense for them to join the side with greater resources. Both motivations for bandwagoning are embodied in Italy's traditional jackal policy of trailing the lion in the hope of picking up the scraps it leaves behind.

It should be pointed out, however, that jumping on the bandwagon of a stronger revisionist power is a risky strategy. The smaller revisionist state becomes a satellite of its more powerful ally and a target for stronger status-quo adversaries. Regardless of which side wins the war, the smaller revisionist state may lose its autonomy and possibly its very existence. Yet, despite the logic of these arguments to balance greater power, the prospect of making gains by joining the revisionist side often proves irresistible for revisionist states. Seeking to maximize their power, not security, revisionist states tend to be risk-acceptant, rather than risk-averse, actors. Thus, Mussolini, tempted by gains in North Africa and Central Europe, readily jumped on the German bandwagon, though this meant a precarious satellite status for Italy. The

Italian leader reasoned that aligning with Britain and France would offer Italy still less room for maneuver, while at the same time, it would make Italy an inviting target for German aggression.

Distancing

In addition to the formation of alliances through balancing and band-wagoning behavior, this study identifies a third type of response to threats: distancing, or no coalition. This hypothesis posits: When the military strength that the status-quo alliance is able to muster is inadequate to deter or defeat the aggressor(s), less directly threatened status-quo powers will distance themselves from available allies that are more immediate targets of the aggressor(s). I have argued that Britain's policy toward France during the period 1938 to 1940 is an example of distancing. Because the sum total of Anglo-French military strength was at the time less than that of Germany, Britain did not seek an alliance with France and was unwilling to commit more than a token number of troops for Continental defense. Instead, Britain distanced itself from France and adopted the dual policy of engagement and rearmament. Chamberlain believed that the success of his dual policy would prevent war with Germany, while failure would at least buy time for Britain to mobilize its domestic and imperial resources; that is, the policy would improve Britain's capacity to deter German aggression and, if deterrence failed, to defend against an attack. Thus, Britain devoted its scarce resources not to land forces for the defense of France but to the production of fighter squadrons and anti-aircraft equipment for home defense. As the rearmament programs of Britain and France began closing the gap in Germany's military lead, Britain drew closer to France and began to stand up to Hitler. That the gap was never entirely closed explains why Britain did not do more to aid France.

Defensive and Predatory Buckpassing

A state may also choose, in response to a threat, to try to direct the enemy's aggression elsewhere in the hope that it will become embroiled in a war of attrition. When the motives for employing this strategy are purely defensive, then it is what is commonly referred to as "buckpassing," that is, the attempt to ride free on the balancing efforts of one's allies. The U.S. policy of letting Britain and the Soviet Union do its fighting for it in 1940–41 is an example of buckpassing. Even though it had not yet been attacked and was not an immediate target of Nazi aggression, U.S. security ultimately depended on the defeat of Third Reich and the prevention of either German or Soviet hegemony over the European Continent. These goals could not be accomplished without active American participation in the war.

It is important to note that buckpassing implies the existence of a collective good, without which it cannot be said that a nation is riding free on the efforts of others. Thus, because an alliance between the U.S. and Britain, and later with the Soviet Union, would have been strong enough to balance Germany and the other Axis powers, it was a collective good. By contrast, the combined strength of Britain and France in 1940 was not sufficient to balance Germany, and so, I have argued, there was no collective good.

When the motives for directing the adversary's energies elsewhere also include aggrandizement, to make easy territorial gains after both sides have bled each other white, then it is what I call predatory buckpassing. When one of three equally powerful poles plays this type of strategy, it is a fox in the role of the "abettor," instigating conflict between the other two members of the tripolar system for its own expansionist purposes. This was Stalin's strategy in 1939–40. Believing, incorrectly, that the combined strength of France and Britain was equal to that of Germany, and thus that Britain and France formed a third (status quo) pole in Europe, Stalin signed the nonaggression pact with Hitler to steer Nazi aggression westward after Germany crushed Poland. The predatory motivations behind Stalin's move were to destroy the status quo, gain easy spoils in Eastern Europe and Finland, and instigate a war of attrition among the capitalist powers—a war the Soviets would initially sit out and that would eventually bring about world revolution.

Stalin's decision for benevolent neutrality toward Germany was also partly motivated by survival instincts. The Soviet leader may have come to the conclusion, in 1939, that Germany would inevitably overrun Poland, in which case, if the Soviets signed a pact with Britain and France, they would find themselves fighting Germany prematurely and without help. An accurate reading of the power situation, however, dictated a pact with Britain and France in 1939. Had the Soviet dictator understood the relative power situation in the West, he would have known that France would fall, sooner rather than later. Consequently, he would have realized that, with or without a pact with France and Britain, Soviet Russia would inevitably have to fight Germany, in which case, it would have been better for the Red Army to have the hope of French and British assistance than not to have this possibility.

Instead, misreading the power situation and thus buoyed by high hopes for unearned spoils, Stalin proceeded to guard the rear of his mortal enemy, Hitler, when the latter was engaged in disposing of the Soviet Union's last potential Continental allies in Western Europe. Meanwhile, the Soviet dictator was busy seizing worthless territory from Finland and Romania, earning their hostility and the Red Army a reputation for weakness.

The French army's swift collapse dashed Stalin's dream of easy conquests in a postwar period when the rest of Europe would be exhausted. More important, Stalin's blunder in postponing the the day of reckoning with Germany (instead of balancing against it in 1939—40) nearly cost the Soviet Union its very survival. Despite Hitler's indecisive military strategies of 1941, the *Wehrmacht* destroyed almost half of the Red Army as it had been in June 1941. As Trumbull Higgins observes, "a little more professionalism and tank production on the part of the Germans might well have achieved a final decision against the Red Army before winter and the Siberians had arrived."[18]

The Size of Alliances

Alliances concluded among dissatisfied powers are offensive; their purpose is to revise or entirely overthrow the status-quo order. Alliances among satisfied powers are essentially defensive; their purpose is to deter an aggressor or, if deterrence fails, to repel an attack. From these two simple statements, it is possible to deduce a good deal about the size and composition of revisionist and status-quo alliances.

Revisionist Alliances: The Minimum Winning Coalition

Revisionist states seek minimum winning coalitions. This is because the purpose of offensive alliances is to maximize one's share of the spoils of victory. Superfluous members, those beyond what is required for victory, will only diminish each member's share of the winnings. Moreover, because the expansionist goals of revisionist states may overlap or conflict with each other (e.g., one state wants to make gains in a theater that another wants to remain stable), revisionist leaders will try to keep their offensive coalition small to simplify military strategy and prevent needless squabbles over the gains from conquest. Hence, revisionist states desire a coalition just strong enough to defeat the target, and no stronger.

Ideally, revisionist states would like to avoid coalitions altogether. By isolating weaker victims and fighting alone, a revisionist state is able to choose the timing, place, and means of attack and, more important, it need not share any of the spoils of its victory. It is not surprising, therefore, that Hitler desperately wanted an alliance with Britain: "Germany as the strongest military power in the world, Britain as the strongest naval power, would represent the most gigantic force in the world."[19] With Britain as its main ally, Germany could keep all future Continental winnings. The Anglo-German alliance never came to pass, however, because Britain, desiring only to maintain the status quo without having to fight for it, wisely refused to become Hitler's junior partner at any price.

Realizing that an alliance with Britain would not be forthcoming, Hitler needed allies on the Continent. Yet, consistent with the logic of the minimum winning coalition, the Führer wanted only benevolent neutrality from the Soviet Union and Italy during the German campaigns of 1939–40. For both offensive and defensive reasons, Hitler sought to avoid coalition warfare, as occurred in 1914, by waging short wars against isolated targets that the *Wehrmacht* could easily overrun. The fewer the number of states actively participating in the fighting, the more Germany would gain and the less likely that other status-quo states would join the conflict against Germany.

With these goals in mind, Hitler's main concern prior to the German invasion of Poland was to secure a promise from Mussolini that Italy would continue its military posturing to keep the British guessing as to Italy's real intentions to the very last moment. After the attack against Poland, the Duce informed Hitler at their meeting at the Brenner Pass in March 1940 that active Italian intervention would be contingent upon Germany military successes against the west. (True to his word, Mussolini declared Italian belligerency only after the French collapse in June 1940.) Thus, Hitler designed his wars against Poland and Western Europe knowing that his two continental allies, Italy and the Soviet Union, would remain neutral.

Another danger of large alliances for revisionist powers is the greater risk of entrapment by weaker coalition members, who sometimes unilaterally initiate undesired conflicts (from the revisionist leader's perspective) that threaten to squander resources, disrupt the unity of alliance, and unite hitherto neutral countries against the revisionist coalition. For example, after the Fall of France, Mussolini seriously considered attacking Yugoslavia but was discouraged by Ribbentrop, who pointed out: The Axis is engaged in a "life and death struggle with England," and it would be "inadvisable to tackle any new problem at all that did not absolutely have to be tackled in connection with this effort to crush England." Ribbentrop went on to say:

> From the purely political standpoint, such a new seat of conflict in the Balkans would in certain circumstances start a general conflagration. How would it affect Hungary? How would Greece react, etc.? Above all, however, it should be remembered that Yugoslavia has close relations with Russia. Moscow, ever mistrustful, would then in certain circumstances be brought into the picture even though only diplomatically, and in the end Germany would be forced again to shift troops to the east. This she does not consider advisable.[20]

Mussolini's ambitions were only temporarily contained. By September, the Italians learned through the press of the dispatch of German units to Romania. Angry at not being consulted by Hitler over the German occupation of Romania and fearful that his ally was growing too strong, Mussolini unilaterally launched an offensive against Greece, declaring: "Hitler always faces me with a *fait accompli*. This time I am going to pay him back in his own coin. He will find out from the papers that I have occupied Greece. In this way the equilibrium will be reestablished."[21] When the Italian forces stalled, German troops had to be diverted from operation *Barbarossa* to Greece.

The stormy relationship between Hitler and Mussolini typifies intra-alliance politics among revisionist states. Contradictory and often competing revisionist goals severely limit the possibility for coordinated action among such states, which explains why offensive alliances tend to be small or crumble under their own weight. Thus, in late 1940, Hitler's halfhearted attempt to put together a Continental coalition to partition the British Empire failed because he could not reconcile the competing territorial ambitions of France, Spain, Italy, the Soviet Union, and Japan.

Status-Quo Alliances: Large, Inclusive Coalitions

In a balance-of-power system, one would expect status-quo alliances to be larger than the minimum winning coalition. This is because the alliance "gain" (*viz.* maintenance of the status quo) satisfies all the members of the alliance.[22] Moreover, the purpose of status-quo alliances is not to make gains from conquest but to deter or, should that fail, to defeat expansionist states or coalitions. For obvious reasons, large, overpowering alliances best serve the purposes of deterrence and defense against would-be aggressors. The larger the alliance, the less likely the status quo will be challenged and the less cost to each member of balancing against the threat. Recognizing that free-rider problems are said to be inescapable in large coalitions, it makes sense to form a coalition that is far stronger—not equal to or slightly greater than—the revisionist threat. Then, if some members do less than their fair share, as expected, the status-quo alliance will still be strong enough to fulfill its purposes. When the expansionist threat is large, moreover, there is less temptation among members of the status-quo alliance to "free ride" with respect to their alliance commitments. "International coalitions," Jervis observes, "are more readily held together by fear than hope of gain."[23]

Articulating this notion that alliances meant to deter will only succeed if they assemble overwhelming force, Strausz-Hupé and Possony write:

> Why did the British-French guarantee of Poland and Romania of April, 1939, fail to avert the Second World War? The answer is that . . . the military strength which the alliance was able to muster was inadequate to deter the aggressor. Germany could . . . reasonably hope that she could win the war, . . . Alliances which do not assemble *superior* military power, or which do so only on paper because some of the allies have no readily available military strength, cannot be counted upon to avert war. This guarantee is given only by alliances which assemble *overwhelming* force.[24]

Further, the unity of the status-quo alliance is only as strong as the members' shared belief that, in combination, they are far stronger than the opposing revisionist coalition; status-quo alliances tend to fall apart at the first sign of weakness in confronting the enemy (states will adopt distancing policies). Hence, the Little Entente collapsed, for all intents and purposes, and Belgium declared neutrality in 1937, after France's timid response to Hitler's remilitarization of the Rhineland in 1936. In this regard, we must be careful not to confuse size in terms of the numbers of members in the alliance with overall strength in terms of their combined resources.

Knowing that war means certain defeat, aggressors are unlikely to disturb their neighbors. This is why Woodrow Wilson championed a community of power over a balance of power. The general moral of this book, so far as it has

one, is that the formation of a large status-quo coalition could have prevented both World Wars. But this would have required a peacetime American
military presence in Europe or, at the least, the active engagement of the U.S.
in European affairs. That this did not occur, that the U.S. behaved as an
ostrich when it alone among the status-quo powers had the capability to act
as a lion, was the decisive factor; it was the "dog that didn't bark in the night."

Implications for the Post-Cold War World

From 1989 to 1992, the unprecedented rate of peaceful change made the task
of political forecasting as difficult as trying to paint a moving train.[25] Since
then, the pace of change has slowed and the outlines of a new, post-bipolar system have begun to take shape. Some observers, let us call them geoeconomists,
see clear signs that the emerging post-Cold War world is again becoming
tripolar with the United States, Germany, and Japan as economic poles—each
in control of a sizable regional bloc.[26] The growing list of members in this new
geoeconomic school of thought includes President Clinton, who, at the Tokyo
summit in July 1993, spoke of "a tripolar world driven by the Americas, by
Europe, and by Asia."[27]

According to the geoeconomic view, the international system has recently
undergone a great transformation from simple bipolarity to organized complexity that has shattered the system's structure into two separate parts: a
unipolar security structure led by the United States and a tripolar economic
one revolving around Germany, Japan, and America. Thus, Thurow declares: "In 1992 there is one military superpower, the United States, standing
alone, and three economic superpowers, the United States, Japan, and
Europe, centered on Germany, jousting for economic supremacy. Without a
pause, the contest has shifted from being a military contest to being an economic contest."[28] Supporting this notion of a "bifurcated system," Leonard
Silk writes:

> If the collapse of the Soviet Union has made the once bipolar world
> "unipolar" with respect to military power, it has become "tripolar" eco-
> nomically, with the United States, Japan and Germany (or, in regional
> terms, North America, the Pacific Rim and the European Community)
> bound together in a complex relationship, both rivalrous and inter-
> dependent like a tempestuous marriage.

Depending on the way the ménage à trois behaves, the relationship may split apart or strengthen and mature. Threesomes are inherently unstable, however; the immediate danger, the Japanese believe, is that the Americans and Europeans will gang up on them.[29]

Geoeconomic logic rests on the assumption that military power with respect to the industrialized powers is no longer important, and should be devalued as a marker of superpower status in the post-Cold War world. The era when Great Powers tried to amass land empires has passed. The Soviet Union collapsed under the weight of its empire, while Japan and Germany were emerging as economic superpowers of the twenty-first century by deemphasizing their military capabilities and focusing instead on export-led strategies to promote economic growth. This divorce between "the 500-year-old linkage between economic and military capability as the path to predominance in world politics" suggests to John Lewis Gaddis "that a fundamental tectonic shift has taken place in what is required to gain influence in the world: that the old path of using economic capacity to build military strength no longer produces the results it once did; and that it may indeed have reduced, rather than adding to, the influence of those nations that have persisted in following it since the end of World War II."[30]

Simply put, "geoeconomics is turning geopolitics and all warfare into a provincial phenomenon."[31] As evidence, the geoeconomists point out that national security is increasingly being defined in economic rather than military terms; that the primary task of national intelligence involves economic rather than military espionage;[32] and that, today more than ever, scholars, leaders, and citizens alike appreciate the links between security and economic issues and conceive of political power more in terms of its economic than its military dimension. Typifying this new awareness of the interactions between economic and security concerns, Leslie Gelb points out that "in the absence of the Soviet military threat, the Americans, West Europeans and Japanese have lost incentives to set aside economic differences. As a result, economic conflicts have become the most pronounced source of tension between nations, and disputes are becoming more difficult to resolve."[33]

As this passage suggests, geoeconomists do not forecast the end of Great-Power rivalry in the post-Cold War world. But their competition will be for world markets not territory, and as such it will be "played out in boardrooms and courtrooms, not on battlefields or in command and control centers."[34] Specifically, the Big Three will be engaged in a fierce, zero-sum game to gain supremacy in seven key industries: microelectronics, biotechnology, the new materials-science industries, telecommunications, civilian aviation, robotics plus machine tools, and computers plus software. But, as Thurow argues: "No one gets killed. . . . The winner builds the world's best products and enjoys the world's highest standard of living. The loser gets to buy some of those best products—but not as many as the winner."[35]

The problem with the geoeconomic "tripolar" view is that it commits the common mistake of conferring polar status on certain states by emphasizing their strengths and ignoring their weaknesses. Japan and Germany are civilian powers that show little enthusiasm for acquiring military or political power commensurate with their economic capabilities.[36] States cannot be said to be polar powers when they have only some of the capabilities required for such exalted status. Great powers of the first rank must score high on all of the characteristic items: economic capability, military strength, population and territory, resource endowment, and political stability. As Waltz warns: "The economic, military, and other capabilities of nations cannot be sectored and separately weighed. States are not placed in the top rank because they excel in one way or another."[37]

In light of their past experiences with militaristic policies, Japan and Germany are unlikely to become first-class military powers. Indeed, they have everything to lose and nothing to gain by challenging America's military supremacy, which has served them well for more than five decades. Likewise, the United States, for its part, has no interest in promoting, directly or indirectly, the remilitarization of Japan and Germany.

The real danger to America's global predominance is not the emergence of Japan and Germany as full-fledged superpowers but rather the far more likely scenario that China and Russia will rise to polar status. Unlike Japan and Germany, China and Russia are both continental-sized, nuclear powers with enormous military and economic potential. Added to this, both have exhibited the political will—and expressed their intention—to challenge U.S. hegemony. At their April 1996 summit meeting, for instance, Boris Yeltsin and Jiang Zemin joined in denouncing American "hegemonism" in the post–Cold War world.[38] Of the two countries, China appears to be the one that will pose the more immediate challenge to a new *Pax Americana*. China is not yet a true pole or a full-blown revisionist power. But its coercive diplomacy against Taiwan, its use of force against Vietnam in the Spratly Islands, and its claims to sovereignty over the South China Sea do not inspire confidence that it will attempt to satisfy its grievances solely through peaceful means. Indeed,

China's recent behavior is consistent with a rising, dissatisfied power—one that may be preparing to launch a serious challenge to the status quo in the near future.

National security, as Bernard Brodie wrote years ago, is an extremely expansible concept, and so there is always a potential danger associated with the possession of enormous resources.[39] The distribution of capabilities, by itself, tells us only part of the story about the current nature or future course of international politics. Equally important are the goals to which those capabilities are put to use: whether power and influence is used to manage the system or to destroy it; whether power is used to threaten states or make them more secure.

For the moment, great concentrations of power reside, with the exception of China, in pro-democratic, peaceful hands. But, in contrast with capabilities, goals can change in a hurry. This is not always a bad thing, as the recent agreements in the Middle East and the demise of the Soviet Union illustrate. By the same token, we should not be surprised that many citizens in Eastern Europe and the former Soviet republics fear that the Russian bear is not dead but "simply in hibernation, waiting only for a good poke from some fire-breathing nationalist like Vladimir V. Zhirinovsky to come roaring back to expansionist life."[40] Precisely because intentions can change, history is far from over, and bold predictions of a Kantian peace are not only naively optimistic but dangerously foolish.

APPENDIX

An Assessment of the International Distribution of Power (circa 1938-1940)

The following series of tables rank the seven great powers during the 1938-1940 period. The equation used to assess the overall relative power capabilities of the seven countries is:

POWER = critical mass + economic capability + military capability

Where:

1. CRITICAL MASS = population + territory
   (The country receiving the top score gets **100** points; the other states get scores that are proportionally weighted.)

2. ECONOMIC CAPABILITY = war potential measured by capital goods production and per-capita capital goods production
   (The country receiving the top score gets **150** points; others get proportionally weighted scores.)

3. MILITARY CAPABILITY = combat power + naval and mercantile capacities + total military expenditures
   (If a country received the top score in all three categories it would receive a score of **250** points.)
   - (a) COMBAT POWER = (number of divisions + tanks + combat aircraft — all expressed in manpower equivalents) multiplied by a Combat Effectiveness Value (top score = **100**)
   - (b) NAVAL STRENGTH AND MERCANTILE CAPACITIES = aggregate displacement tonnage of battle ships, cruisers, aircraft-carriers, destroyers, and submarines + gross tonnage of mercantile shipping. (top score = **50**)
   - (c) TOTAL MILITARY EXPENDITURES = in millions of pounds sterling purchasing power, 1937-1938. (top score = **100**)

The following tables (1-9) walk you through the process. Table 9 is the final aggregated ranking of the seven countries.

TABLE A.1
Demographic Resources in 1939[1]

Country	Total Population in Million	Military Manpower: Males Age 20 to 34 in Millions	% of Total Military Manpower*	Power Weights**
USSR	170	21.6	30.5%	50
United States	132	16.2	23.0%	38
Greater Germany	80	9.4	13.3%	22
Japan	73	8.3	11.7%	19
United Kingdom	47	5.7	8.1%	13
Italy	44	5.2	7.3%	12
France	42	4.3	6.1%	10
Totals	588	70.7	100.0	164

*Individual state's percentage of total military manpower of the seven countries presented in the table.

**Power weights are obtained by arbitrarily assigning a maximum rating of 50 (in this case the USSR). The other countries' power weights are obtained by dividing their military manpower figures by 21.6 (the USSR total) and multiplying the resulting numbers by 50 (the power rating of the USSR). This process yields proportional power weights.

TABLE A.2
Territory of the Great Powers — 1938[2]
(in thousands of square miles)

Country	Area	Power Weights
USSR	8,500	50
United States	3,600	50
Greater Germany*	219	15
France*	213	15
Japan*	143	15
Italy*	116	15
United Kingdom*	94	15

*Ray Cline adds a bonus weight of ten points to these nations for occupying strategic locations on or near critical sea-lanes or ocean chokepoints and for being perceived as having some realistic capability to exercise control over these locations.

TABLE A.3
Critical Mass Assessment (population and territory)

	Power Weights		
Country	Population	Territory	Total
USSR	50	50	100
United States	38	50	88
Greater Germany	22	15	37
Japan	19	15	34
United Kingdom	13	15	28
Italy	12	15	27
France	10	15	25

TABLE A.4
Economic Capability / War Potential (1938)
(World output = 100)

Country	% of World Manufacturing	% of World Capital Goods Production*	Capital Goods Output per Head of Population	Power Weights**
United States	28.7	34.41	260	150
Greater Germany	13.2	18.22	228	90
USSR	17.6	17.15	101	65
United Kingdom	9.2	10.09	214	54
France	4.5	4.15	98	18
Japan	3.8	3.80	52	11
Italy	2.9	2.67	61	8
Totals	79.9	90.50	n.a.	396

*Computed by multiplying the first column of the table by each state's share of total manufacturing output devoted to the capital goods sector (metal goods, optical, engineering, shipbuilding, vehicles, chemical industries, and part of the heavy industries, i.e., pig-iron and crude steel.) The individual country's share of the capital goods sector in total manufacturing in 1937 was: Germany - 51%, United States - 48%, United Kingdom - 44%, Japan - 40%, France and Italy - 37%. From Hillmann, "Comparative Strengths," pp. 439, 444–446.

**Germany and the United Kingdom receive a bonus of 10 points added to their power weights because their per-capita capital goods production is almost the same as the United States. By the same token, 10 points have been subtracted from the power weight of the Soviet Union because of its far lower per-capita capital goods production. These ratios account for the greater impact that sparing industrial resources for a military buildup had on the Soviet economy compared to the impact of mobilization on the economies of the U.S., the U.K., and Greater Germany.

TABLE A.5

A Comparison of the Great Powers' Force Strengths in Manpower Equivalents (Circa January 1940)

	Army Divisions[3]	Tanks	Combat Aircraft	Manpower Equivalents* (in 1000s)	CEV**	Total Combat Power***	Power Weight
U.S.[4]	10	346	2,141	421.40	1.0	421.40	12
USSR	136	9,000	4,387	3430.96	.8	2744.77	75
Germany	123	3,862[5]	4,210	3035.48	1.2	3642.58	100
U.K.	16	100[6]	1,750	500.00	1.0	500.00	14
France****	86	4,188[7]	1,654	2094.80	1.0	2094.80	57
Italy*****	40	1,300[8]	2,448	1109.80	.9	998.82	27
Japan	45[9]	650	1,343	969.80	1.15	1115.27	31

*Each tank equals 50 men plus their share of supporting weapons. Because Russian and German tanks were inferior to those of France, Britain, and the U.S., it is assumed that German and Russian tanks were worth only 40 men plus their share of supporting weapons. All combat aircraft are assumed to be equivalent to 100 men and their supporting weapons except for those of the USSR, which are assumed to be the equivalent of only 80 men. Manpower equivalents for German and Allied tanks are taken from Col. T. N. Dupuy, *Understanding War: History and Theory of Combat* (New York: Paragon House Publishers, 1987), chap. 9.

**Greater Germany's CEV is taken from Col. Dupuy, *Understanding War*. The lower CEV of the Soviet Union is due to the Stalin Purges of the late 1930s. The Italian number indicates their lack of combat effectiveness. The slightly higher Japanese CEV adjusts for their long fighting experience (since 1931).

***In 000's of M.E.s.

****Includes French aircraft in North Africa and Levant.

*****Includes Italian aircraft in Libya, Dodencanese, East Africa, and Spain.

TABLE A.6

Naval and Mercantile Capacities (1938–1939) Converted into Power Weights in Which the Top Rating = 50

	Naval Strength*	Mercantile Strength**	Total	Power Weight
United Kingdom	1,280	15,000	16,280	50.0
Japan	906	4,100	5,006	15.4
United States	1,277	3,600	4,877	15.0
Germany	197	3,300	3,497	10.7
Italy	481	2,600	3,081	9.5
France	547	2,400	2,947	9.0
USSR	287	999	1,286	4.0

*In 000's of displacement tons.

**In 000's of gross tons.

TABLE A.7
Total Military Expenditures, 1937–1938 (in millions of pounds sterling purchasing power)

	1937	1938	Total	Power Weight
Germany	1068	1170	2238	100.0
USSR	700	924	1624	72.5
Japan	331	508	839	37.4
Britain	262	391	653	29.0
U.S.	221	231	452	20.2
France	136	207	343	15.3
Italy	147	167	314	14.0

SOURCE: Derived from data provided by Hillmann, "Comparative Strengths," p. 454.

TABLE A.8
Final Aggregation of the Great Powers' Military Capabilities (circa 1938–1939)

	Combat Power	Naval Strength & Merc. Cap.	Military Expendit.	Total Power Weight
Germany	100	10.7	100.0	210.7
USSR	75	4.7	72.5	151.5
United Kingdom	14	50.0	29.0	93.0
Japan	31	15.4	37.4	83.8
France	57	9.0	15.3	81.3
Italy	27	9.5	14.0	50.5
United States	12	15.0	20.2	47.2

TABLE A.9
Final Power Ranking of the Great Powers (circa 1938–1939)

	Critical Mass	Economic Capability	Military Capability	Total Power Weight
Greater Germany	37	90	210.7	337.7
USSR	100	65	151.5	316.5
United States	88	150	47.2	285.2
United Kingdom	28	54	93.0	175.0
Japan	34	11	83.8	128.8
France	25	18	81.3	124.3
Italy	27	8	50.5	85.5

TABLE A.10
Schweller Index: Percentage Share Distribution of Great-Power Capabilities, circa 1938–1939.

Germany	USSR	US	UK	Japan	France	Italy
23.2	21.8	19.6	12.0	8.9	8.5	5.9

COMPARE WITH:

COW Percentage Share Distribution of Great-Power Capabilities, 1938.

USSR	US	Germany	UK	Japan	France	Italy
24.9	22.5	20.1	10.5	9.3	6.9	5.3

1. Population statistics cited in H. C. Hillmann, "Comparative Strengths of the Great Powers," in Arnold Toynbee and Frank T. Ashton-Gwatkin, eds., *The World in March 1939* (Oxford: Oxford University Press, 1952), p. 373.

2. Source, except for Greater Germany: Ray S. Cline, *World Power Trends and U.S. Foreign Policy for the 1980s* (Boulder, Colorado: Westview Press, 1980), pp. 41–43.

3. Figures for divisions and combat aircraft of the USSR, U.K., France, and Italy are cited in N. H. Gibbs, *Grand Strategy: Rearmament Policy*, Volume 1 (London: Her Majesty's Stationery Office, 1976), pp. 759–760. Each division is assumed to comprise 20,000 soldiers.

4. All U.S. figures are taken from Henri Michel, *The Second World War* (New York, Praeger Publishers, 1968), pp. 428, 449. For U.S. combat aircraft figures, see also Constance Howard, "The United States of America and the European War, September 1939 to December 1941," in Arnold Toynbee and Veronica Toynbee, eds., *The Initial Triumph of the Axis* (London: Oxford University Press, 1958), p. 476 fn.2.

5. Cited in R. H. S. Stolfi, "Equipment for Victory in France in 1940," *History* Vol. 52, No. 183 (February 1970), pp. 1–20.

6. Cited in John J. Mearsheimer, *Conventional Deterrence* (Ithaca and London: Cornell University Press, 1983), p. 81.

7. Stolfi, "Equipment for Victory," pp. 1–20. The French figure does not include 500 Renault F. T. 1918 Modernized tanks, which were obsolete.

8. MacGregor Knox, *Mussolini Unleashed 1939–1941: Politics and Strategy in Fascist Italy's Last War* (Cambridge: Cambridge University Press, 1982), p. 26.

9. I have assumed that Japan had roughly 45 active army divisions by January 1940, constituting 900,000 men. Paul Kennedy puts the Japanese Army at one million men and 51 divisions by 1941. See Kennedy, *The Rise and Fall of the Great Powers*, p. 301.

Notes

Introduction

1. Hitler, as quoted in Denis Mack Smith, *Mussolini* (London: Weidenfeld and Nicolson, 1981), p. 208.

2. Chester Wilmot, *The Struggle For Europe* (New York: Harper, 1952), p. 17.

3. Gerhard L. Weinberg, *A World At Arms: A Global History of World War II* (Cambridge: Cambridge University Press, 1994), p. 2.

4. For instance, Sir Edward Grey writes of the onset of World War I: " . . . one blow to the prospects of peace followed after another . . . they were . . . like the deliberate, relentless strokes of Fate, determined on human misfortune, as they are represented in a Greek tragedy. It was as if Peace were engaged in a struggle for life, and, whenever she seemed to have a chance, some fresh and more deadly blow was struck." Viscount Edward Grey of Fallodon, *Twenty-Five Years, 1892–1916*, vol. 1 (New York: Frederick A. Stokes, 1925), pp. 314–315.

5. Meyers quoted in J. L. Richardson, "New Perspectives on Appeasement: Some Implications for International Relations," *World Politics*, vol. 40, no. 3 (April 1988), p. 305.

6. Kenneth Waltz, *Theory of International Politics* (Reading, Mass.: Addison-Wesley, 1979), pp. 175–176.

7. Emerson M. S. Niou and Peter C. Ordeshook, "Stability in Anarchic International Systems," *American Political Science Review*, vol. 84, no. 4 (December 1990), p. 1231.

8. John Mueller, "The Essential Irrelevance of Nuclear Weapons: Stability in the Postwar World," *International Security*, vol. 13, no. 2 (Fall 1988), p. 75.

9. Edward Hallett Carr, *What Is History?* (London: Macmillan, 1961), p. 81.

10. For multipolar accounts of World War II, see Waltz, *Theory of International Politics*; Barry Posen, *The Sources of Military Doctrine: France, Britain, and Germany Between the World Wars* (Ithaca and London: Cornell University Press, 1984); Thomas J. Christensen and Jack L. Snyder, "Chain Gangs and Passed Bucks: Predicting Alliance Patterns in Multipolarity," *International Organization*, vol. 44, no. 2 (Spring 1990), pp. 137–169.

11. See William Dray, *Perspectives on History* (London: Routledge and Kegan Paul, 1980), ch. 4; and Kenneth N. Waltz, *Man, the State and War: A Theoretical Analysis* (New York: Columbia University Press, 1959), pp. 232, 234, 238.

12. Kenneth N. Waltz, "Reflections on *Theory of International Politics*: A Response to My Critics," in Robert O. Keohane, ed., *Neorealism and Its Critics* (New York: Columbia University Press, 1986), p. 329.

13. A. J. P. Taylor, *The Origins of the Second World War* (New York: Atheneum, 1961, [1983 ed.]), p. 103.

14. From F. H. Hinsley's review of Taylor's *The Origins of the Second World War* in *Historical Journal*, vol. 4, no. 2 (1961), pp. 227–228, as quoted in Dray, *Perspectives on History*, p. 91.

15. See, for instance, Hugh Trevor Roper, "A. J. P. Taylor, Hitler and the War," in Wm. Roger Louis, ed., *The Origins of the Second World War: A. J. P. Taylor and His Critics* (New York: John Wiley, 1972), pp. 44–63.

16. For Hitler's ideology of race and space, see Gerhard L. Weinberg, *The Foreign Policy of Hitler's Germany: Diplomatic Revolution in Europe, 1933–1936* (Chicago: University of Chicago Press, 1970), ch. 1.

17. Robert Gilpin, *War and Change In World Politics* (Cambridge: Cambridge University Press, 1981), p. 37.

18. For the aims of "revolutionary states," see Henry A. Kissinger, *A World Restored: Castlereagh, Metternich, and the Problem of Peace, 1812–1822* (Boston: Houghton Mifflin, 1957).

19. Taylor, *The Origins of the Second World War*, p. xiii.

20. For a discussion of the "normal statesman" assumption, see Dray, *Perspectives on History*, ch. 4.

21. Taylor, *The Origins of the Second World War*, p. 71.

22. Ibid., pp. xix, 69, 86, 219.

23. Quoted in Erik Goldstein, "The Evolution of British Diplomatic Strategy for the Locarno Pact, 1924–1925," in Michael Dockrill and Brian McKercher, eds., *Diplomacy and World Power: Studies in British Foreign Policy, 1890–1950* (Cambridge: Cambridge University Press, 1996), p. 126.

24. See J. David Singer, "The Level of Analysis Problem in International Relations," *World Politics*, vol. 14, no. 1 (October 1961), pp. 77–92; Arnold Wolfers, "The Actors in International Politics," in Wolfers, *Discord and Collaboration: Essays on International Politics* (Baltimore: Johns Hopkins Press, 1962), pp. 3–24; Waltz, *Man, the State, and War*; James Rosenau, "Pre-Theories and Theories of Foreign Policy," in R. Barry Farrell, ed., *Approaches to Comparative and International Politics* (Evanston, Ill.: Northwestern University Press, 1966), pp. 29–92; and Robert Jervis, *Perception and Misperception in International Politics* (Princeton: Princeton University Press, 1976), ch. 1.

25. Dray, *Perspectives on History*, p. 91.

26. J. David Singer, "System Structure, Decision Processes, and the Incidence of International War," in Manus I. Midlarsky, ed., *Handbook of War Studies* (Boston: Unwin Hyman, 1989), p. 3.

27. Inis Claude, *Power and International Relations* (New York: Random House, 1962), p. 42.

28. Herbert Simon defines a complex system as "one made up of a large number of parts that interact in a nonsimple way. In such systems the whole is more than the sum of the parts, not in an ultimate, metaphysical sense but in the important pragmatic sense that, given the properties of the parts and the laws of their interaction, it is not a trivial matter to infer the properties of the whole." Herbert A. Simon, *The Sciences of the Artificial*, 2d. ed. (Cambridge: The MIT Press, 1969, [1981]), p. 195.

29. See Patrick Baert, "Unintended Consequences: A Typology and Examples," *International Sociology*, vol. 6, no. 2 (June 1991), pp. 201–210.

30. For nonlinear and nonadditive relationships, see Robert Jervis, "Systems and Interaction Effects," in Jack Snyder and Robert Jervis, eds., *Coping With Complexity in the International System* (Boulder, Colo.: Westview Press, 1993), pp. 25–26.

31. Ernest Nagel, *The Structure of Science: Problems in the Logic of Scientific Explanation* (Indianapolis: Hackett Publishing Company, 1979), p. 425.

32. Waltz, *Theory of International Politics*, p. 18.

33. Morton A. Kaplan, *Towards Professionalism in International Theory: Macrosystem Analysis* (New York: Free Press, 1979), pp. 8–9.

34. For the most comprehensive account of the balance of power, see Michael Sheehan, *Balance of Power: History and Theory* (London: Routledge, 1996). For the indeterminateness of predictions yielded by balance-of-power theory, see Roslyn L. Simowitz, "The Logical Consistency and Soundness of the Balance of Power Theory," in Karen Feste, ed., *Monograph Series in World Affairs* (Denver: Graduate School of International Studies, University of Denver, 1982), pp. 3–122; Claude, *Power and International Relations*; Arnold Wolfers, "The Balance of Power in Theory and Practice," in Wolfers, *Discord and Collaboration*, pp. 117–131; George Liska, *Nations in Alliance: The Limits of Interdependence* (Baltimore: Johns Hopkins University Press, 1962), pp. 26–27 passim; Ernest B. Haas, "The Balance of Power: Prescription, Concept

or Propaganda?" *World Politics*, vol. 5, no. 4 (July 1953), pp. 442–477; Edward Vose Gulick, *Europe's Classical Balance of Power* (New York: Norton, 1955); Carl Joachim Friedrich, *Foreign Policy in the Making* (New York: Norton, 1938), pp. 129–134.

35. The idea that important actors are conditioned by the system serves Waltz's theory in two ways. First, because a competitive system punishes and continually filters out unsuccessful behavior, Waltz need not assume that all units are indeed rational to predict rational behavior: "Competitive systems are regulated . . . by the 'rationality' of the more successful competitors." Waltz, *Theory of International Politics*, p. 76. For the general argument, see Ibid., pp. 75–77, 118–119.

Second, though Waltz is not explicit on this point, the socialization process may be used to explain systemic continuity and change, that is, why historically some actors rise to or maintain Great-Power status, while others never attain or fall from the first-ranking tier. Yet Waltz ignores system change almost entirely, focusing instead on how to distinguish between changes within and of systems. This theoretical weakness is partially a result of Waltz's strong association of structure with "enduring patterns" or continuity (Ibid., p. 70). Waltz argues that socialization and competition reduce variety by establishing norms, encouraging conformity, and rewarding rational (successful) behavior (Ibid., pp. 76–7).

36. Ibid., p. 165.

37. Ibid., p. 118.

38. These works include Joseph Grieco, "Anarchy and the Limits of Cooperation: A Realist Critique of the Newest Liberal Institutionalism," *International Organization*, vol. 42, no. 3 (Summer 1988), pp. 485–507; John Mearsheimer, "Back to the Future: Instability in Europe After the Cold War," *International Security*, vol. 15, no. 1 (Summer 1990), pp. 5–56; Christensen and Snyder, "Chain Gangs and Passed Bucks"; Posen, *The Sources of Military Doctrine*; Stephen Walt, *The Origins of Alliances* (Ithaca, N.Y.: Cornell University Press, 1987); and Christopher Layne, "The Unipolar Illusion: Why New Great Powers Will Rise," *International Security*, vol. 17, no. 4 (Spring 1993), pp. 5–51.

39. Helen Milner, "The Assumption of Anarchy in International Relations Theory: A Critique," *Review of International Studies*, vol. 17, no. 1 (January 1991), pp. 67–85; David Dessler, "What's At Stake in the Agent-Structure Debate?" *International Organization*, vol. 43, no. 3 (Summer 1989), pp. 441–473; Alexander Wendt, "The Agent-Structure Problem in International Relations Theory," *International Organization*, vol. 41, no. 3 (Summer 1987), pp. 335–370; Robert O. Keohane, ed., *Neorealism and Its Critics* (New York: Columbia University Press, 1986); Richard Rosecrance, "International Theory Revisited" *International Organization*, vol. 35, no. 4 (Autumn 1981), pp. 691–713; and Kaplan, *Towards Professionalism in International Theory*, pp. 1–89.

40. See Richard Ashley, "The Poverty of Neorealism," *International Organization*, vol. 38, no. 2 (Spring 1984), pp. 225–286. Glenn Snyder raises similar concerns in his

critique of Walt's *The Origins of Alliances* and Emerson M. S. Niou, Peter C. Ordeshook, and Gregory F. Rose, *The Balance of Power: Stability in International Systems* (New York: Cambridge University Press, 1989). See Glenn H. Snyder, "Alliances, Balance, and Stability," *International Organization*, vol. 45, no. 1 (Winter 1991), pp. 121–142, esp. pp. 124, 138.

41. Christensen and Snyder, "Chain Gangs and Passed Bucks," pp. 137–147; Joseph S. Nye, "Neorealism and Neoliberalism," *World Politics*, vol. 40, no. 2 (January 1988), p. 245; Robert O. Keohane, "Theory of World Politics: Structural Realism and Beyond," in Ada W. Finifter, ed., *Political Science: The State of the Discipline* (Washington, D.C.: American Political Science Association, 1983), pp. 512–527; John Gerard Ruggie, "Continuity and Transformation in the World Polity: Toward a Neorealist Synthesis," *World Politics*, vol. 35, no. 2 (January 1983), pp. 267–268.

42. See works cited in note 10.

43. Gary King, Robert O. Keohane, and Sidney Verba, *Designing Social Inquiry: Scientific Inference in Qualitative Research* (Princeton: Princeton University Press, 1994), p. 10.

44. Ibid., p. 24.

45. Ibid., pp. 49–51,

46. Hugh Trevor-Roper, "History and Imagination," in Hugh Lloyd-Jones, Valerie Pearl, and Blair Worden, eds., *History and Imagination: Essays in Honour of H. R. Trevor-Roper* (London: Duckworth, 1981), p. 358.

1: The Capabilities and Interests of the Major Powers

1. Waltz, *Theory of International Politics*, p. 93.

2. Ibid., p. 163.

3. Of this inequality, Robert Tucker writes: "The history of the international system is a history of inequality par excellence. . . . It is understandable that the natural inequalities of states should impress the observer of state relations. In their physical extent, population, natural resources, and geographic position, states are, as it were, born unequal; so much so, indeed, that by comparison the natural inequalities among individuals appear almost marginal." Robert W. Tucker, *The Inequality of Nations* (New York: Basic Books, 1977), p. 3.

4. See, for example, Mearsheimer, "Back to the Future"; Posen, *The Sources of Military Doctrine*; Walt, *The Origins of Alliances*.

5. Christensen and Snyder, "Chain Gangs and Passed Bucks," p. 138.

6. Mearsheimer, "Back to the Future," p. 18.

7. Niou, Ordeshook, and Rose, *The Balance of Power*; Niou and Ordeshook, "Stability in Anarchic International Systems"; A. F. K. Organski, *World Politics* (New York: Knopf, 1958), pp. 271–338; A. F. K. Organski and Jacek Kugler, *The War Ledger* (Chicago: University of Chicago Press, 1980), pp. 13–63; R. Harrison Wagner, "The

Theory of Games and the Balance of Power," *World Politics*, vol. 38, no. 4 (July 1986), pp. 546–576.

8. Niou and Ordeshook, "Stability in Anarchic International Systems," p. 1230.

9. Wagner, "The Theory of Games," p. 575; Niou, Ordeshook, and Rose, *The Balance of Power*.

10. Christensen and Snyder, "Chain Gangs and Passed Bucks," p. 138.

11. The Correlates of War Project, "The Capability Data-Set Printout," made available through the Inter-University Consortium for Political and Social Research at the University of Michigan, December 1987. William B. Moul has refined the COW index by substituting iron production for the demographic components of the COW index. See William B. Moul, "Measuring the 'Balances of Power': A Look at Some Numbers," *Review of International Studies*, vol. 15, no. 2 (April 1989), pp. 101–121.

12. For brief discussions of tripolar dynamics, see Ronald J. Yalem, "Tripolarity and the International System," *Orbis*, vol. 15 (1972), pp. 1051–1063; and Hsi-Sheng Chi, "The Chinese Warlord System as an International System," in Morton A. Kaplan, ed., *New Approaches to International Relations* (New York: St. Martin's Press, 1968), pp. 405–425.

13. See Kenneth N. Waltz, "The Stability of a Bipolar World," *Daedalus*, vol. 93, no. 3 (Summer 1964), pp. 881–901; Waltz, "International Structure, National Force and the Balance of World Power," *Journal of International Affairs*, vol. 21, no. 2 (1967), pp. 215–231; Karl W. Deutsch and J. David Singer, "Multipolar Power Systems and International Stability," *World Politics*, vol. 16, no. 3 (April 1964), pp. 390–406; Francis W. Hoole and Dina A. Zinnes, eds., *Quantitative International Politics: An Appraisal* (New York: Praeger, 1976); Bruce Bueno de Mesquita "Measuring Systemic Polarity," *Journal of Conflict Resolution*, vol. 19, no. 2 (June 1975), pp. 187–216; Richard Rosecrance, "Bipolarity, Multipolarity, and the Future," *Journal of Conflict Resolution*, vol. 10, no. 3 (September 1966), pp. 314–327; Frank Wayman, "Bipolarity, Multipolarity, and the Threat of War," in Alan Ned Sabrosky, ed., *Polarity and War: The Changing Structure of International Conflict* (Boulder, Colo.: Westview, 1985), pp. 115–144; and Dale C. Copeland, "Neorealism and the Myth of Bipolar Stability: Toward a New Dynamic Realist Theory of Major War," *Security Studies*, vol. 5, no. 3 (Spring 1996), pp. 29–89.

14. William C. Wohlforth, "The Perception of Power: Russia in the Pre-1914 Balance," *World Politics*, vol. 39, no. 3 (April 1987), p. 353; also see Wohlforth, *The Elusive Balance: Power and Perceptions During the Cold War* (Ithaca: Cornell University Press, 1993).

15. Waltz, *Theory of International Politics*, p. 118.

16. Ibid.

17. Or, in the words of Friedrich Gentz, to "become so strong as to be able to coerce all the rest put together." Quoted in Gulick, *Europe's Classical Balance of Power*, p. 34.

18. See Jack L. Snyder, "Introduction: New Thinking About the New International System," in Snyder and Jervis, *Coping With Complexity in the International System*, p. 9; Alexander Wendt, "Anarchy Is What States Make of It: The Social Construction of Power Politics," *International Organization*, vol. 46, No 2 (Spring 1992), p. 395.

19. Walt, *The Origins of Alliances*.

20. See Hans J. Morgenthau, *Politics Among Nations: The Struggle for Power and Peace* (New York: Knopf, 1948), esp. chaps. 2, 3, 9, 10, and p. 156; Frederick L. Schuman, *International Politics: The Destiny of the Western State System*, 4th ed. (New York: McGraw-Hill, 1948), pp. 377–380; Edward Hallett Carr, *The Twenty Years' Crisis, 1919–1939: An Introduction to the Study of International Relations* (New York: Harper, 1946); Kissinger, *A World Restored*; Johannes Mattern, *Geopolitics: Doctrine of National Self-Sufficiency and Empire* (Baltimore: Johns Hopkins University Press, 1942); Wolfers, "The Balance of Power in Theory and Practice," pp. 125–126; and Raymond Aron, *Peace and War: A Theory of International Relations*, translated by Richard Howard and Annette Baker Fox (Garden City, N.Y.: Doubleday, 1966), chap. 3.

21. For an extended discussion, see Randall L. Schweller, "Neorealism's Status-Quo Bias: What Security Dilemma?" *Security Studies*, vol. 5, no. 3 (Spring 1996), pp. 90–121.

22. Joseph M. Grieco, "Realist International Theory and the Study of World Politics," in Michael Doyle and G. John Ikenberry, eds., *New Thinking in International Relations Theory* (Boulder, Colo.: Westview Press, 1997), p. 167 (emphasis in original).

23. Waltz, *Theory of International Politics*, p. 126.

24. In this regard, Joseph M. Grieco has coined the term "defensive positionality," which essentially posits that the primary goal of states is to prevent relative losses. He argues that "it is a defensively positional concern that partners might do better—not an offensively oriented interest in doing better oneself—that drives the relative-gains problem for cooperation." Grieco, "The Relative-Gains Problem for International Cooperation," *American Political Science Review*, vol. 87, no. 3 (September 1993), p. 742, fn. 2. See also Grieco, *Cooperation Among Nations: Europe, America, and Non-Tariff Barriers to Trade* (Ithaca: Cornell University Press, 1990); and Grieco, "Anarchy and the Limits of Cooperation," p. 498. Similarly, Robert Gilpin says international competition "stimulates, and may compel, a state to increase its power; at the least, it necessitates that the prudent state prevent relative increases in the powers of competitor states." Gilpin, *War and Change*, pp. 87–88.

25. For a recent example of this status-quo bias, see Christensen and Snyder, "Chain Gangs and Passed Bucks." Their discussion of alliance patterns in Europe prior to World Wars I and II ignores the alliance choices of revisionist states: Austria-Hungary and Turkey prior to World War I; Italy and Japan prior to World War II. Likewise, they do not discuss Nazi Germany's alliance choices but focus instead on Hitler's strategy of piecemeal aggression.

26. True, Waltz admits that states may seek profit and power; but they must pursue them "safely" and only "if survival is assured." This view of state preferences is

aptly described by Arthur A. Stein: "States that place preeminent weight on security and do not gamble with it regardless of temptation to do so may, for example, act to maximize assured security rather than expected payoffs. Such states would undertake attractive gambles only when assured of survival." Stein, *Why Nations Cooperate: Circumstance and Choice in International Relations* (Ithaca: Cornell University Press, 1990), p. 90. In rational-choice terminology, this is known as lexicographic preferences: actors have a hierarchy of objectives and maximize in sequence rather than make tradeoffs. See Charles W. Ostrom, Jr., "Balance of Power and the Maintenance of 'Balance': A Rational-Choice Model With Lexical Preferences," in Dina A. Zinnes and John V. Gillespie, eds., *Mathematical Models in International Relations* (New York: Praeger, 1976), pp. 318–332.

27. Felix Gilbert, *To the Farewell Address: Ideas of Early American Foreign Policy* (Princeton, N.J.: Princeton University Press, 1961), pp. 95–96. Of contemporary Realists, Fareed Zakaria, Samuel P. Huntington, and John J. Mearsheimer come closest in their views of state interest to that of eighteenth-century power politics. See Zakaria, "Realism and Domestic Politics: A Review Essay," *International Security*, vol. 17, no. 1 (Summer 1992), pp. 177–198; Huntington, "Why International Primacy Matters," *International Security*, vol. 17, no. 4 (Spring 1993), pp. 68–83; and Mearsheimer, "Back to the Future," p. 12.

28. Arnold Wolfers recognized this when he wrote: "[Revisionist states] can accept balanced power only with utter resignation since they know that only in quite exceptional cases can the established order be seriously modified without the threat of force so preponderant that it will overcome the resistance of the opposing side." Wolfers, "The Balance of Power," p. 126.

29. Aron, *Peace and War*, p. 598.

30. Waltz, *Theory of International Politics*, p. 127. For more on balancing behavior and the goal of autonomy, see Barry R. Posen, "Nationalism, the Mass Army, and Military Power," *International Security*, vol. 18, no. 2 (Fall 1993), p. 82; Posen, *The Sources of Military Doctrine*, p. 17; Kenneth N. Waltz, "The Emerging Structure of International Politics," *International Security*, vol. 18, no. 2 (Fall 1993), p. 74. I am grateful to Michael Desch for pointing this out.

31. "Any future modifications of the Mediterranean balance of power," Hitler told Ciano in 1936, "must be in Italy's favour." Count Galeazzo Ciano, *Ciano's Diplomatic Papers*, edited by Malcolm Muggeridge (London: Odhams Press, 1948), p. 57.

32. Alan Cassels, "Switching Partners: Italy in A. J. P. Taylor's *Origins of the Second World War*," in Gordon Martel, ed., *The Origins of the Second World War Reconsidered: The A. J. P. Taylor Debate After Twenty-five Years* (Boston: Allen & Unwin, 1986), p. 82.

33. For example, in 1940, the British ambassador, Sir Stafford Cripps, was sent to Moscow to persuade Stalin that German expansion in Western Europe endangered Russia as well as Britain. " 'Therefore both countries,' he argued, 'ought to agree on a common policy of self-protection against Germany and on the re-establishment

of the European balance of power.' Stalin replied that he did not see any danger of Europe being engulfed by Germany. 'The so-called European balance of power,' he said, 'had hitherto oppressed not only Germany but also the Soviet Union. Therefore the Soviet Union would take all measures to prevent the re-establishment of the old balance of power in Europe.' " Martin Wight, *Power Politics*, edited by Hedley Bull and Carsten Holbraad (Leicester: Leicester University Press, 1978), pp. 175–176.

34. For this conceptualization, see Jervis, *Perception and Misperception*, p. 51. Jervis calls this the state's "basic intention." For a similar scheme, see Charles L. Glaser, "Political Consequences of Military Strategy: Expanding and Refining the Spiral and Deterrence Models," *World Politics*, vol. 44, no. 4 (July 1992), pp. 497–538. Glaser's two variables are myopia and greed.

35. For discussions of the terms status quo and revisionist, see Wolfers, *Discord and Collaboration*, pp. 18, 84–86; Barry Buzan, *People, States, and Fear: The National Security Problem in International Relations* (Chapel Hill: The University of North Carolina Press, 1983), pp. 175–186; and Paul Seabury, "The Idea of the Status Quo," in Seabury, ed., *Balance of Power* (San Francisco: Chandler, 1965), chap. 22.

36. Quoted in David Reynolds, *The Creation of the Anglo-American Alliance, 1937–41: A Study in Competitive Co-operation* (London: Europa Publications, 1981), p. 5.

37. My conceptualization of status-quo and revisionist interests is consistent with the logic of Fareed Zakaria's critique of "defensive-realism." See Zakaria, "Realism and Domestic Politics." While I agree with the basic thrust of Zakaria's argument, I would not replace the defensive-realist assumption with an "influence-maximizing" one as he suggests. Why choose one or the other? Both assumptions are empirically valid and, throughout history, have served to differentiate states and systems of similar structures. Zakaria roots his influence-maximizing assumption in "the urge to constantly seek survival" (Ibid., fn. 43, p. 194). In practice, states have sought to expand for reasons other than mere survival, e.g., greed, divine right, manifest destiny, and revenge, to name a few. For extremely dissatisfied states, the expansionist urge is often stronger than the wish to survive.

38. Organski and Kugler, *The War Ledger*, p. 19.

39. Buzan, *People, States, and Fear*, p. 177.

40. Schuman, *International Politics*, p. 378.

41. Wendt, "The Agent-Structure Problem."

42. For analyses of system stability and alliance dynamics based on perceived offensive/defensive advantage and geography, see Robert Jervis, "Cooperation Under the Security Dilemma," *World Politics*, vol. 30, no. 2 (January 1978), pp. 167–214; Christensen and Snyder, "Chain Gangs and Passed Bucks"; and Ted Hopf, "Polarity, the Offense-Defense Balance, and War," *American Political Science Review*, vol. 85, no. 2 (June 1991), pp. 475–493. For an analysis of the impact of actors' misperceptions

of structure on the origins of the First World War, see Wohlforth, "The Perception of Power," pp. 353–381.

43. Posen, *The Sources of Military Doctrine*, pp. 236–239. For the problems with offensive/defensive distinctions, see Jack S. Levy, "The Offensive/Defensive Balance of Military Technology: A Theoretical and Historical Analysis," *International Studies Quarterly*, vol. 28, no. 2 (June 1984), pp. 219–238; and Stephen D. Biddle, "The State of Knowledge on the Determinants of Offensiveness and Defensiveness in Conventional Ground Forces" *IDA Paper P-2295* (Alexandria, Virginia: Institute for Defense Analyses, 1989). For an intelligent argument in support of the theory, see Sean M. Lynn-Jones, "Offense-Defense Theory and Its Critics," *Security Studies*, vol. 4, no. 4 (Summer 1995), pp. 660–691.

44. See Weinberg, *A World At Arms*, pp. 13–15.

45. Arnold Wolfers, *Britain and France Between Two Wars: Conflicting Strategies of Peace Since Versailles* (New York: Harcourt, Brace, 1940), pp. 63–65.

46. Esmonde M. Robertson, "German Mobilization Preparations and the Treaties Between Germany and the Soviet Union of August and September 1939," in Robert Boyce and Esmonde M. Robertson, eds., *Paths to War: New Essays on the Origins of the Second World War* (New York: St. Martin's Press, 1989), pp. 353–354.

47. Andreas Hillgruber, *Germany and the Two World Wars*, translated by William C. Kirby (Cambridge: Harvard University Press, 1981), p. 50.

48. For the Soviet-Japanese quasi-war, see Clark W. Tinch, "Quasi-War Between Japan and The U.S.S.R., 1937–1939," *World Politics*, vol. 3, no. 2 (January 1951), pp. 172–99; James E McSherry, *Stalin, Hitler, and Europe* vol. 1, *The Origins of World War II, 1933–39* (Cleveland and New York: The World Publishing Co., 1968), ch. 1.

49. After Hitler became Reich Chancellor, Poland seriously considered a preventive war against Germany; the plan was cancelled, however, when France refused support. Disillusioned by France's unreliability and impressed by Hitler's declarations of the Reich's peaceful intentions, Poland began courting German friendship. Given the cooling of German-Soviet relations, both Poland and Germany now had a common enemy in the Soviet Union. Prior to the conclusion of the accord, the Polish ambassador to Berlin reported: "The Reich Chancellor declared that all forms of aggression were contrary to his policy and that a war wouuld be a catastrophe for everybody. Any war would simply bring Communism, which represented a fearful threat, to Europe. Poland was a bulwark against Asia." Quoted in Jeremy Noakes and Geoffrey Pridham, eds., *Nazism, 1919–1945: A History in Documents and Eyewitness Accounts* vol. 2, *Foreign Policy, War and Racial Extermination* (hereafter *Nazism*) (New York, Schocken Books, 1988), Document #493, p. 661. For Hitler, however, the main value of the Nonaggression Pact was to remove Poland from the French orbit, which, he hoped, would unravel the French security system in Eastern Europe directed against Germany.

50. Quoted in Charles L. Mowat, ed., *The New Modern Cambridge History*, vol. 12, *The Shifting Balance of World Forces, 1898–1945* (Cambridge: Cambridge University Press, 1968), p. 226.

51. For a discussion of Japan and Italy as "challengers" against the status quo, see Paul Kennedy, *The Rise and Fall of the Great Powers: Economic Change and Military Conflict from 1500 to 2000* (New York: Random House, 1987), pp. 291–343. For authoritative works on Japan's drive to achieve autarky by means of territorial expansion in East Asia, see Michael A. Barnhart, *Japan Prepares For Total War: The Search for Economic Security, 1919–1941* (Ithaca and London: Cornell University Press, 1987); James B. Crowley, *Japan's Quest for Autonomy* (Princeton: Princeton University Press, 1966); and Saburo Ienaga, *The Pacific War, 1931–1945* (New York: Pantheon Books, 1978), chap. 8.

52. Wolfers, *Britain and France Between Two Wars*, p. 5.

53. John Maynard Keynes, *The Economic Consequences of the Peace* (London: Macmillan, 1919), p. 102.

54. Martin Gilbert and Richard Gott, *The Appeasers* (London: Weidenfeld and Nicolson, 1963), p. 21.

55. The list of British appeasers includes, among others, Lloyd George, Marquess of Londonderry, Lord Lothian, T. Philip Conwell-Evans, Lord and Lady Astor, Neville Chamberlain, Stanley Baldwin, Arnold Wilson, Thomas Moore, and Sir Horace Wilson.

56. J. L. Garvin, editor of *The Observer*, as quoted in Ibid., p. 49.

57. This discussion is drawn from Wolfers, *Britain and France Between Two Wars*, chap. 1.

58. As quoted in Ibid., p. 19.

59. Edwin Borchard and William Potter Lage, *Neutrality For the United States* (New Haven: Yale University Press, 1937), pp. 313–343.

2: A Study of Tripolar Systems

1. Of course, polarity is not the only way to define the structure of the international system. For studies that define international structure in terms of its concentration of capabilities rather than its polarity, see J. David Singer, Stuart Bremer, and John Stuckey, "Capability Distribution, Uncertainty, and Major Power Wars, 1820–1965," in Bruce M. Russett, ed., *Peace, War, and Numbers* (Beverly Hills, Calif.: Sage Publications, 1972), pp. 19–48; James Lee Ray and J. David Singer, "Measuring the Concentration of Power in the International System," *Sociological Methods and Research*, vol. 1, no. 3 (May 1973), pp. 403–437; Edward D. Mansfield, "The Concentration of Capabilities and the Onset of War," *Journal of Conflict Resolution*, vol. 36, no. 1 (March 1992), pp. 3–24. For a rule-oriented definition of the international system, see Paul W. Schroeder,

The Transformation of European Politics, 1763–1848 (New York: Oxford University Press, 1994), p. x.

2. For an insightful discussion of polarity, see David P. Rapkin, "Concept (Mis)formation in International Systems Research: Polarity and Polarization," draft manuscript, University of Nebraska-Lincoln, February 16, 1993.

3. Gilpin, *War and Change*, p. 235.

4. Morton A. Kaplan, *System and Process in International Relations* (New York: Wiley, 1957), p. 34.

5. Waltz, *Theory of International Politics*, p. 163.

6. Ostrom and Aldrich, "The Relationship Between Size and Stability, p. 766.

7. David Garnham, "The Causes of War: Systemic Findings," in Alan Ned Sabrosky, ed., *Polarity and War: The Changing Structure of International Conflict* (Boulder, Colo.: Westview Press, 1985), p. 20.

8. George Simmel, "The Number of Members as Determining the Sociological Form of the Group," *American Journal of Sociology*, vol. 8, no. 1 (July 1902), pp. 45–46.

9. Claude, *Power and International Relations*, p. 13.

10. Note that this definition of system stability, which I have borrowed from R. H. Wagner, does not mean peace. Wagner writes: "I will say that an international system is stable if the independence of all the actors in it is preserved. Thus, if a theory leads to the prediction that one or more of the states in a system will be eliminated, I will say that that system is, according to the theory, unstable. Peace will be defined as the absence of war. Thus, an international system can be stable even though it is characterized by frequent wars in which many states are deprived of significant portions of their territory, so long as no state is completely eliminated." Wagner, "The Theory of Games and the Balance of Power," pp. 546–547. Niou, Ordeshook, and Rose use the same definition, and they also distinguish system stability from resource stability. See Niou, Ordeshook, and Rose, *The Balance of Power*. For an interesting critique of this work, see Snyder, "Alliances, Balance, and Stability," pp. 132–142.

11. For a description of indirect effects, see Robert Jervis, "Systems and Interaction Effects," pp. 26–29.

12. This analysis is drawn from Arthur Lee Burns, "From Balance to Deterrence: A Theoretical Analysis," *World Politics*, vol. 9, no. 4 (July 1957), pp. 494–99.

13. Ibid., p. 497.

14. For the "interaction opportunity" hypothesis, see Deutsch and Singer, "Multipolar Power Systems and International Stability."

15. The two literatures of balance of power theory and sociological theories of coalition formation seem immediately relevant to each other. As Dina Zinnes remarks, "The sociological literature contains theories which specifically predict the membership of winning coalitions as a function of the distribution of power within the group. Thus it would seem that the international relations specialist could gain insight into the balance of power theory by studying the sociological literature." Dina

A. Zinnes, "Coalition Theories and the Balance of Power," in Sven Groennings, E. W. Kelly, and Michael Leiserson, eds., *The Study of Coalition Behavior: Theoretical Perspectives and Cases From Four Continents* (New York: Holt, Rinehart & Winston, 1970), pp. 351–352.

16. Theodore Caplow, *Two Against One: Coalitions in Triads* (New Jersey: Prentice Hall, 1968); Caplow, "A Theory of Coalitions in the Triad," *American Sociological Review*, vol. 21, no. 2 (August 1956), pp. 489–493; Caplow, "Further Development of a Theory of Coalitions in the Triad," *American Journal of Sociology*, vol. 64, no. 5, (March 1959), pp. 488–493. Other important works include: Theodore Mills, "Power Relations in Three-Person Groups," *American Sociological Review*, vol. 18, no. 4, (August 1953), pp. 351–357; Mills, "The Coalition Pattern in Three-Person Groups," *American Sociological Review*, vol. 19, no. 6 (December 1954), pp. 657–667; William A. Gamson, "A Theory of Coalition Formation," *American Sociological Review*, vol. 26, no. 3 (June 1961), p. 376; Simmel, "The Number of Members as Determining the Sociological Form of the Group," pp. 1–46, 158–196; Simmel, "The Triad," in Kurt H. Wolff, (trans., ed., intro.) *The Sociology of George Simmel* (New York: Glencoe Press, 1950), pp. 145–169; Sheldon Stryker and George Psathas, "Research on Coalitions in the Triad: Findings, Problems and Strategy," *Sociometry*, vol. 23, no. 3 (September 1960), pp. 217–230; Harold Kelly and A.J. Arrowood, "Coalitions in the Triad: Critique and Experiment," *Sociometry*, vol. 23, no. 3 (September 1960), pp. 231–244; A. Paul Hare, Edgar F. Borgatta, and Robert F. Bales, eds., *Small Groups: Studies in Social Interaction* (New York: Alfred A. Knopf, 1966).

17. Caplow, *Two Against One*, p. 22; Caplow, "A Theory of Coalitions in the Triad," pp. 489–93; Mills, "Power Relations in Three-Person Groups"; Mills, "The Coalition Pattern in Three-Person Groups."

18. Caplow, *Two Against One*, pp. 21–6; idem, "A Theory of Coalitions in the Triad," pp. 489–493; idem, "Further Development of a Theory of Coalitions in the Triad," pp. 488–493.

19. Niou, Ordeshook, and Rose, *The Balance of Power*, pp. 93–97.

20. Ibid., p. 47.

21. Snyder, "Alliances, Balance, and Stability," pp. 134, 136.

22. Niou, Ordeshook, and Rose, *The Balance of Power*, p. 95.

23. Wagner, "The Theory of Games," pp. 549, 554–559.

24. Ibid., 549–550.

25. See R. Harrison Wagner, "Peace and the Balance of Power in a Three-State World," paper delivered at the Annual Meetings of the American Political Science Association. The New York Hilton, September 1–4, 1994. In this later work, Wagner makes the case for cheating by switching to the side of the victim but backs off, claiming that "incorporating such endgame moves explicitly in a model is difficult." (p. 8) Given the new rules of Wagner's game, his three-actor systems are now quite unstable.

26. For similar views of tripolar instability, see Caplow, *Two Against One*; Lowell Dittmer, "The Strategic Triangle: An Elementary Game-Theoretical Analysis," *World Politics*, vol. 33, no. 4 (July 1981), pp. 485–515; Brian Healy and Arthur Stein, "The Balance of Power in International History: Theory and Reality," *Journal of Conflict Resolution*, vol. 17, no. 1 (March 1973), pp. 33–61; Waltz, *Theory of International Politics*, p. 163; Kaplan, *System and Process*, p. 34; and Morton A. Kaplan, Arthur Lee Burns, and Richard E. Quandt, "Theoretical Analysis of the 'Balance of Power,' " *Behavioral Science*, vol. 5, no. 3 (July 1960), p. 244. For theorists who find three-actor games the most stable of all systems, see Garnham, "The Causes of War," p. 20; Ostrom and Aldrich, "The Relationship Between Size and Stability," p. 766; Niou, Ordeshook, and Rose, *The Balance of Power*, p. 95; and Wagner, "The Theory of Games," p. 575.

27. I have borrowed the terms "abettor" and "eyewitness" from Liska, *Nations In Alliance*, pp. 163–164; "*tertius gaudens*" and "the mediator" are taken from Caplow, *Two Against One*, p. 20; Caplow borrowed them from Simmel, *The Sociology of George Simmel*, pp. 148–149.

28. Glenn H. Snyder, "The Security Dilemma in Alliance Politics," *World Politics*, vol. 36, no. 4 (July 1984), pp. 461–496, esp. pp. 462–463.

29. Ibid., p. 462n.

30. This logic is drawn from James D. Fearon, "Rationalist Explanations for War," *International Organization*, vol. 49, no. 3 (Summer 1995), pp. 379–414. My argument simply extends Fearon's insightful analysis to alliances, which he does not cover.

31. See, for example, Michael Spirtas, "A House Divided: Tragedy and Evil in Realist Theory," *Security Studies*, vol. 5, no. 3 (Spring 1996), pp. 409–412.

32. Jervis, "Cooperation Under the Security Dilemma," p. 211.

33. See Schweller, "Neorealism's Status-Quo Bias," pp. 103–104.

34. For a slightly different view, see Robert Jervis, "Security Regimes," in Stephen D. Krasner, ed., *International Regimes* (Ithaca, N.Y.: Cornell University Press, 1983), p. 178.

35. Gamson, "A Theory of Coalition Formation," p. 376.

36. Ibid.

37. See Herbert Butterfield, "The Balance of Power," p. 138 and Martin Wight, "The Balance of Power," p. 159 in Butterfield and Wight, eds., *Diplomatic Investigations: Essays in the Theory of International Politics* (Cambridge: Harvard University Press, 1966).

38. Winston S. Churchill, *The Gathering Storm* (New York: Bantam, 1961), pp. 186–187.

39. Of this type of system, R. H. Wagner writes: "I conclude, then, that not only is any distribution stable which gives one player half the resources and divides the remainder unequally between the other two; but also, so long as no actor has more than half the resources in the system, any other type of distribution will be transformed into one of the former type in a three-actor game conducted according to the

rules stated above. This type of distribution can be said to represent both inequality of power (among the individual states) and equality of power (between the two sets of opposing forces); it is also the only distribution in which one state has no choice but to come to the aid of another in order to prevent an aggressor from achieving supremacy." Wagner, "Theory of Games and the Balance of Power," pp. 558–559. I disagree with this assessment, however. As I discuss below, a system in which the resources of the three actors is in a 4:3:2 ratio is equally stable, though no actor possesses half of the total resources in the system.

40. Even supposing that the stronger member promises in advance to turn over the lion's share of the spoils to its weaker partner, the latter still must reject the offer. This is because once the targeted pole has been eliminated, the stronger pole will no longer have any incentive—and it cannot be coerced—to comply with the agreement.

3: State Responses to Threats and Opportunities

1. For useful but somewhat dated overviews of alliance studies, see Michael D. Ward, *Research Gaps in Alliance Dynamics*, vol. 19, Monograph Series in World Affairs (Denver, Colo.: University of Denver, 1982); and Brian L. Job, "Grins Without Cats: In Pursuit of Knowledge of International Alliances," in P. Terrence Hopmann, Dina A. Zinnes, and J. David Singer, eds., *Cumulation in International Relations Research*, vol. 18, Monograph Series in World Affairs (Denver, Colo.: University of Denver, 1981), pp. 39–63.

2. The exceptions are Liska, *Nations In Alliance*; Walt, *The Origins of Alliances*; Harvey Starr, *War Coalitions* (Lexington, Mass.: Heath, 1972); Michael F. Altfeld and Bruce Bueno de Mesquita, "Choosing Sides in Wars," *International Studies Quarterly*, vol. 23, no. 1 (March 1979), pp. 87–112; and Ole R. Holsti, P. Terrence Hopmann, and John D. Sullivan, *Unity and Disintegration in International Alliances: Comparative Studies* (New York: John Wiley and Sons, 1973). For the alliance behavior of small states, see Robert L. Rothstein, *Alliances and Small Powers* (New York: Columbia University Press, 1968); Dan Reiter, *Crucible of Beliefs: Learning, Alliances, and World Wars* (Ithaca and London: Cornell University Press, 1996); and Steven R. David, *Choosing Sides: Alignment and Realignment in the Third World* (Baltimore, Md. The Johns Hopkins University Press, 1991).

3. For a similar proposition, see Lance E. Davis and Douglass C. North, *Institutional Change and American Economic Growth* (Cambridge: Cambridge University Press, 1971), p. 32. Davis and North focus on domestic coalitions, and so the primary benefit they see from forming a coalition is winning an election and thereby effecting or preventing change by appropriate political action.

4. William H. Riker, *The Theory of Political Coalitions* (New Haven, Conn.: Yale University Press, 1962), pp. 32–33, 47.

5. See Lloyd M. Shears, "Patterns of Coalition Formation in Two Games Played by Male Tetrads," *Behavioral Science*, vol. 12, no. 2 (March 1967), pp. 130–137; Bruce M. Russett, "Components of an Operational Theory of International Alliance Formation," *Journal of Conflict Resolution*, vol. 12, no. 3 (September 1968), p. 292.

6. Robert Rothstein's analysis of the alliance behavior of small powers supports Caplow's hypothesis: "Alliance with superior power is inherently dangerous for a Small Power. The outcome may differ very little from the effect of merely procrastinating. The Small Power may move not from insecurity to security, but from insecurity to the status of a satellite.... Small Powers, insofar as they have a choice, may prefer to gamble on a less powerful ally or on a combination of lesser states." Rothstein, *Alliances and Small Powers*, p. 61.

7. Kaplan, *Towards Professionalism in International Theory*, p. 70.

8. See Wallace J. Thies, "Alliances and Collective Goods: A Reappraisal," *Journal of Conflict Resolution*, vol. 31, no. 2 (June 1987), pp. 298–332; Todd Sandler and Jon Cauley, "On the Economic Theory of Alliances," *Journal of Conflict Resolution*, vol. 19, no. 2 (June 1975), pp. 330–348; James Murdoch and Todd Sandler, "A Theoretical and Empirical Analysis of NATO," *Journal of Conflict Resolution*, vol. 26, no. 2 (June 1982), pp. 237–265 at pp. 240–242; and John R. Oneal, "The Theory of Collective Action and Burden Sharing in NATO," *International Organization*, vol. 44, no. 3 (Summer 1990), pp. 379–402 at pp. 383–385. The seminal, and still classic, analysis of the "collective goods" problem in alliances is Mancur Olson and Richard Zeckhauser, "An Economic Theory of Alliances," *Review of Economics and Statistics*, vol. 48, no. 3 (August 1966), pp. 266–279.

9. Jervis, "Cooperation Under the Security Dilemma," pp. 204–205.

10. This is a central theme in Kennedy, *The Rise and Fall of the Great Powers*.

11. See Riker, *The Theory of Political Coalitions*, p. 160. For more on this point, see Zinnes, "Coalition Theories and the Balance of Power," pp. 356–362; and Wagner, "Theory of Games," p. 569.

12. See Stephen D. Krasner, "Global Communications and National Power: Life on the Pareto Frontier," *World Politics*, vol. 43, no. 3 (April 1991), pp. 336–366; Arthur A. Stein, "Coordination and Collaboration: Regimes in an Anarchic World," in Stephen D. Krasner, ed., *International Regimes* (Ithaca, NY: Cornell University Press, 1983), pp. 115–140.

13. *Ciano's Diary, 1937–1938*, edited by Malcolm Muggeridge, translated by Andreas Mayor (London: Methuen, 1952), p. 162.

14. Rothstein, *Alliances and Small Powers*, p. 227. For an earlier example (the Madrid Conference in 1880) of Italy following the jackal principle, see Alan J. P. Taylor, *The Struggle for Mastery in Europe, 1848–1918* (Oxford and New York: Oxford University Press, 1954), p. 286.

15. Michael Mandelbaum, *The Nuclear Revolution: International Politics Before and After Hiroshima* (New York: Cambridge University Press, 1981), ch. 6; Snyder,

"The Security Dilemma in Alliance Politics." Thomas Christensen and Jack Snyder refer to entrapment and abandonment as "chain-ganging" and "buckpassing" behavior. See Snyder and Christensen, "Chain Gangs and Passed Bucks."

16. Snyder, "The Security Dilemma in Alliance Politics," p. 467.

17. Ibid., pp. 467–471.

18. Other "b" words, "binding" and "bystanding," have recently been added to this list. But, as yet, they have not been as fully developed or used as extensively as the others. For binding, see Joseph M. Grieco, "Understanding the Problem of International Cooperation: The Limits of Neoliberal Institutionalism and the Future of Realist Theory," in David A. Baldwin, ed., *Neorealism and Neoliberalism: The Contemporary Debate* (New York: Columbia University Press, 1993). For bystanding, see John Arquilla, "Balances Without Balancing," paper presented at the annual meeting of the American Political Science Association, Chicago, Illinois, September 1992.

19. These conditions are derived from Gulick, *Europe's Classical Balance of Power*, ch. 3; and John J. Mearsheimer, "The False Promise of International Institutions," *International Security*, Vol. 19, No. 3 (Winter 1994/95), pp. 5–49. The term "alliance handicap" appears in Liska, *Nations In Alliance*, pp. 16–18.

20. The following discussion borrows heavily from Randall L. Schweller, "Bandwagoning For Profit: Bringing the Revisionist State Back In," *International Security*, vol. 19, no. 1 (Summer 1994), pp. 72–107.

21. Quincy Wright, *A Study of War*, abridged by Louise Leonard Wright (Chicago: University of Chicago, [1942], 1964), p. 136. Waltz incorrectly credits the term to Stephen Van Evera. Waltz, *Theory of International Politics*, p. 126. Actually, Arnold Wolfers mentioned the term "bandwagoning" to mean the opposite of balancing long before Waltz, but only in a passing reference. See Wolfers, "The Balance of Power," p. 124.

22. Wright, *A Study of War*, p. 136; Waltz, *Theory of International Politics*, p. 126.

23. Wright, *A Study of War*, p. 136.

24. For his other works on the subject, see Stephen M. Walt, "Alliance Formation and the Balance of World Power," *International Security*, vol. 9, no. 4 (Spring 1985), pp. 3–43; Walt, "Testing Theories of Alliance Formation: The Case of Southwest Asia," *International Organization*, vol. 43, no. 2 (Spring 1988), pp. 275–316; Walt, "The Case for Finite Containment: Analyzing U.S. Grand Strategy," *International Security*, vol. 14, no. 1 (Summer 1989), pp. 5–49; Walt, "Alliance Formation in Southwest Asia: Balancing and Bandwagoning in Cold War Competition," in Robert Jervis and Jack Snyder, eds., *Dominoes and Bandwagons: Strategic Beliefs and Great Power Competition in the Eurasian Rimland* (New York: Oxford University Press, 1991), pp. 51–84; Walt, "Alliances, Threats, and U.S. Grand Strategy: A Reply to Kaufman and Labs," *Security Studies*, vol. 1, no. 3 (Spring 1992), pp. 448–482.

25. Walt, *The Origins of Alliances*, p. 265; Walt, "Alliance Formation in Southwest Asia," p. 54.

26. Walt, *The Origins of Alliances*, p. 263.

27. Ibid., p. 264. This is a somewhat curious claim, however, since balance of power theory already has a commonly known phrase for this situation, called "holding the balance."

28. Walt, *The Origins of Alliances*, p. 17. See also Walt, "Alliance Formation and the Balance of World Power," p. 4.

29. Walt's definition of bandwagoning is used by all the authors in Jervis and Snyder, *Dominoes and Bandwagons*. Likewise, Stephen Van Evera defines balancing as aligning against the the greatest threat to a state's independence, while bandwagoning means "to give in to threats." See Stephen Van Evera, "Primed for Peace: Europe After the Cold War," *International Security*, vol. 15, no. 3 (Winter 1990/91), p. 20.

30. Walt, "Alliance Formation in Southwest Asia, p. 55. In a later passage (on p. 75), however, Walt seems to contradict himself when he states that dominoes may fall because, among other reasons, "one side's victories convince other states to shift their alignment to the winning side *voluntarily*. Strictly speaking, only the last variant should be viewed as bandwagoning." [emphasis added.]

31. David A. Baldwin, *Economic Statecraft* (Princeton, N.J.: Princeton University Press, 1985), p. 12.

32. For a discussion of "ordinary language" and conceptual definitions, see Felix E. Oppenheim, "The Language of Political Inquiry: Problems of Clarification," in Fred I. Greenstein and Nelson W. Polsby, eds., *Handbook of Political Science*, vol. 1, *Political Science: Scope and Theory* (Reading, Mass.: Addison-Wesley, 1975), pp. 283–335, especially, pp. 307–309. See, also, Baldwin, *Economic Statecraft*, ch. 3.

33. *Webster's Ninth New Collegiate Dictionary* (Springfield, Mass.: Merriam-Webster, 1986), p. 204.

34. Paul Kecskemeti, *Strategic Surrender: The Politics of Victory and Defeat* (Stanford, Calif.: Stanford University Press, 1958), chaps. 1 and 2.

35. Walt, "Alliance Formation and the Balance of World Power," pp. 7–8.

36. The Italians employed this strategy to survive the initial stage of the War of the Spanish Succession. Emperor Leopold of Austria opened the hostilities against the Franco-Spanish forces by attacking Italy, which he believed had been loyal to the Spanish regime of Louis XIV's grandson King Philip V, the seventeen-year-old Duke of Anjou. In truth, the "people of Italy had no particular love for either Bourbon or Hapsburg; they only wanted to be on the winning side." Thus, when the Imperial army led by Prince Eugene of Savoy smashed Louis's forces under the command of General Villeroi at Chiari, Italy jumped on the Austrian bandwagon. Bitter over the pro-Imperial behavior of the Italians, Louis wrote: "You should be cautious and risk nothing with people who know how to profit by everything and who entrench themselves before you." John B. Wolf, *Louis XIV* (New York: W. W. Norton, 1968), pp. 516 and 518.

37. Walt, "Alliance Formation," p. 9.

38. Paul W. Schroeder, "Alliances, 1815–1945: Weapons of Power and Tools of Management," in Klaus Knorr, ed., *Historical Dimensions of National Security Problems* (Lawrence, Kansas: University Press of Kansas, 1976), pp. 227–262.

39. Joseph M. Grieco, "The Maastricht Treaty, Economic and Monetary Union and the Neo-Realist Research Programme," *Review of International Studies*, vol. 21, no. 1 (January 1995), p. 34 (emphasis omitted).

40. The following discussion is borrowed from Alastair Iain Johnston and Robert S. Ross, "Engaging China: Managing a Rising Power," Project Proposal, Fairbank Center for East Asian Research, Harvard University, July 1996, pp. 5–6.

41. Davis and North, *Institutional Change*, p. 31.

42. See Randall L. Schweller, "Tripolarity and the Second World War," *International Studies Quarterly*, vol. 37, no. 1 (March 1993), pp. 84, 87–92. Schroeder calls this "hiding"; Arquilla introduces the term "bystanding," defined as a state's propensity to avoid conflicts for reasons of self-preservation. See Paul Schroeder, "Historical Reality vs. Neo-realist Theory," *International Security*, vol. 19, no. 1 (Summer 1994), pp. 108–148; and Arquilla, "Balances Without Balancing."

43. Rothstein, *Alliances and Small Powers*, p. 26.

44. Winston Churchill, *Blood, Sweat and Tears* (New York: G. P. Putnam's, 1941), p. 215.

45. See Christensen and Snyder, "Chain Gangs and Passed Bucks."

46. The classic realist work on engagement is Kissinger, *A World Restored*.

47. Paul Kennedy, "The Tradition of Appeasement in British Foreign Policy, 1865–1939," in Paul Kennedy, *Strategy and Diplomacy, 1870–1945* (London: George Allen and Unwin, 1983), p. 16 (emphasis omitted).

48. For the effects of differential growth in power on changes in the governance structures of the international system, see Gilpin, *War and Change*, ch. 1.

49. Johnston and Ross, "Engaging China," p. 5.

50. Wight, *Power Politics*, p. 95.

51. Anthony Downs, *An Economic Theory of Democracy* (New York: Harper and Row, 1957), pp. 64–68.

52. "Delegates wish to be on bandwagons because support of the nominee at the convention will be a basic criterion for the later distribution of Presidential favors and patronage." Gerald Pomper, *Nominating the President: The Politics of Convention Choice* (Evanston, Ill.: Northwestern University Press, 1963), p. 144.

53. See Robert Jervis, "Systems Theory and Diplomatic History," in Paul Gordon Lauren, ed., *Diplomacy: New Approaches in History, Theory, and Policy* (New York: Free Press, 1979), pp. 220–222; Jervis, "Domino Beliefs and Strategic Behavior," in Jervis and Snyder, *Dominoes and Bandwagons*, pp. 22–23; Lisa L. Martin, "Coalition Dynamics: Bandwagoning in International Politics," paper presented at the Seminar on International Political Economy, Columbia University, October, 29, 1993.

54. For this motivation for bandwagoning, see Deborah Welch Larson, "Band-wagoning Images in American Foreign Policy: Myth or Reality?" in Jervis and Snyder, *Dominoes and Bandwagons*, pp. 85–87; Jervis, "Systems Theory," p. 220; and Walt, "Alliance Formation," p. 8. None of the authors specifically refer to jackal behavior, however.

55. "In a style less grave than that of history, I should perhaps compare the emperor Alexius to the jackal, who is said to follow the steps, and to devour the leav-ings, of the lion. Whatever had been his fears and toils in the passage of the first cru-sade, they were amply recompensed by the subsequent benefits which he derived from the exploits of the Franks." Edward Gibbon, *The History of the Decline and Fall of the Roman Empire*, vol. 6 (New York: Macmillan, 1914), p. 335.

56. Roy Douglas, *New Alliances, 1940–41* (London: Macmillan, 1982), p. 40. Walt makes this point in "Alliance Formation," p. 8.

57. See Liska, *Nations in Alliance*, p. 33.

58. Norman Rich, *Hitler's War Aims: Ideology, the Nazi State, and the Course of Expansion* (London and New York: W. W. Norton, 1973), p. 184.

59. Wolf, *Louis XIV*, pp. 526–529. For similar reasons, on August 16, 1703, Sweden also acceded to the Grand Alliance. Thus, by October of 1703, "France was left with no allies except Spain, and the Electorates of Cologne and Bavaria . . . ; and when one by one the other satellites of Louis dropped off, in 1702 and 1703, Bavaria alone kept to her engagements." R. B. Mowat, *A History of European Diplomacy, 1451–1789*, (New York: Longmans, Green and Co., 1928), p. 166.

60. Gulick, *Europe's Classical Balance of Power*, p. 88.

61. The Allies were not impressed, however, and awarded Italy a loser's share at Versailles.

62. Quoted in Jervis, "Domino Beliefs," p. 33.

63. Stephen Van Evera, "Why Europe Matters, Why the Third World Doesn't: American Grand Strategy After the Cold War," *The Journal of Strategic Studies*, vol. 13, no. 2 (June 1990), p. 23. On this latest domino effect, see Harvey Starr, "Democratic Dominoes: Diffusion Approaches to the Spread of Democracy in the International System," *Journal of Conflict Resolution*, vol. 35, no. 2 (June 1991), pp. 356–381; Timur Kuran, "Now Out of Never: The Element of Surprise in the East European Revolution of 1989," *World Politics*, vol. 44, no. 1 (October 1991), pp. 7–48. Note that the current definition of bandwagoning as "giving in to threats," which Van Evera endorses, does not cover this voluntary global epidemic.

64. Ralph G. Martin, *Ballots & Bandwagons* (Chicago: Rand McNally, 1964), p. 444. Also see Steven J. Brams, *The Presidential Election Game* (New Haven and London: Yale University Press, 1978), p. 43.

65. Hosoya Chihiro, "The Tripartite Pact, 1939–1940," in James William Morley, ed., *Deterrent Diplomacy: Japan, Germany, and the USSR, 1935–1940* (New York: Columbia University Press, 1976), p. 206.

66. Sumio Hatano and Sadao Asada, "The Japanese Decision to Move South (1939–1941)," in Boyce and Robertson, *Paths to War*, p. 387; Barnhart, *Japan Prepares for Total War*, p. 158; Hosoya "The Tripartite Pact," p. 207.

67. Larry M. Bartels, *Presidential Primaries and the Dynamics of Public Choice* (Princeton, N.J.: Princeton University Press, 1988), pp. 111–112.

68. Niccolò Machiavelli, *The Prince and The Discourses* (New York: Random House, 1950), p. 12.

69. Dean Acheson, *Present at the Creation* (New York: Norton, 1969), p. 219. Also quoted in Jerome Slater, "Dominoes in Central America: Will They Fall? Does It Matter?" *International Security*, vol. 12, no. 2 (Fall 1987), p. 106.

70. Quoted in Ross Gregory, "The Domino Theory," in Alexander DeConde, ed., *Encyclopedia of American Foreign Policy*, vol. 1 (New York: Scribner's, 1978), p. 275. Also quoted in Slater, "Dominoes in Central America," p. 105.

71. Quoted in Slater, "Dominoes in Central America," p. 106. For a similar critique of the domino theory, see Robert H. Johnson, "Exaggerating America's Stakes in Third World Conflicts," *International Security*, vol. 10, no. 3 (Winter 1985/86), pp. 39–40.

72. Slater, "Dominoes in Central America," p. 107.

73. For a good overview of the empirical literature on the spread of wars through diffusion or contagion effects, see Benjamin A. Most, Harvey Starr, and Randolph M. Siverson, "The Logic and Study of the Diffusion of International Conflict," in Manus I. Midlarsky, ed., *Handbook of War Studies* (Boston: Unwin Hyman, 1989), pp. 111–139.

74. Douglas J. Macdonald, "Falling Dominoes and System Dynamics: A Risk Aversion Perspective," *Security Studies*, vol. 3, no. 2 (Winter 1993/94), p. 227.

75. Ibid., p. 228 (emphasis in original).

76. Quoted in Clyde Haberman, "Israel and Syria Reported Ready To Negotiate About Golan Heights," *New York Times*, September, 6, 1993, p. A3.

77. For Metternich's masterful use of cabinet diplomacy to maneuver Austria into the balancer/mediator role, see Kissinger, *A World Restored*, esp. chaps. 4 and 5.

78. Ibid., p. 313.

79. Ibid., p. 70.

80. Quoted in Joseph A. Mikus, *Beyond Deterrence: From Power Politics to World Public Order* (New York: Peter Lang, 1988), p. 12.

81. Machiavelli, *The Prince and The Discourses*, p. 64.

82. This argument is consistent with the power-transition model. See Organski and Kugler, *The War Ledger*, chap. 1, especially pp. 19–23; and Gilpin, *War and Change*.

83. Great-power cooperation to manage the system is often achieved by spheres of interest and informal empires. See Jan Triska, ed., *Dominant Powers and Subordinate States* (Durham, N.C.: Duke University Press, 1986).

84. See Inis L. Claude, Jr., "The Common Defense and Great-Power Responsibilities," *Political Science Quarterly*, vol. 101, no. 5 (1986), pp. 719–732, especially p. 725.

85. Walter Lippmann, *U.S. Foreign Policy: Shield of the Republic* (Boston: Little, Brown, 1943), p. 100. Quoted in Michael C. Desch, "The Keys That Lock Up the World: Identifying American Interests In the Periphery," *International Security*, vol. 14, no. 1 (Summer 1989), p. 87.

86. See Jervis, *Perception and Misperception*, chap. 3.

87. Aron, *Peace and War*, p. 83. Aron does not use the term ostrich to define great powers that act in this way.

88. Ibid.

89. See Jervis, *Perception and Misperception*, chap. 3.

90. Samuel P. Huntington, "The Clash of Civilizations?" *Foreign Affairs*, vol. 72, no. 3 (Summer 1993), p. 42. Huntington offers Turkey, Mexico, and Russia as examples of torn countries. See ibid., pp. 42–45.

91. Keith Wheelock, *Nasser's New Egypt* (New York: Praeger, 1960). I am grateful to Betsy Erickson for this quote.

92. Romania bandwagoned with the Axis for protection from Russia, Hungary, and Bulgaria, which viewed its territory as irredenta.

93. See Larson, "Bandwagon Images." The best historical works on this subject are Piotr S. Wandycz, *The Twilight of French Eastern Alliances: 1926–1936* (Princeton, N.J.: Princeton University Press, 1988); and Joseph Rothschild, *East Central Europe Between the Wars* (Seattle: University of Washington Press, 1974).

94. For an extensive discussion of prestige in international affairs, see Morgenthau, *Politics Among Nations*, chap. 6.

95. Speech by the Führer to the Commanders in Chief on August 22, 1939, *Documents on German Foreign Policy, 1918–1945*, Series D, vol. 7 (Washington, D.C.: United States Government Printing Office, 1956), p. 201.

96. This is Kissinger's description of a "revolutionary state" in *A World Restored*, p. 2.

97. Arnold Wolfers, "The Pole of Power and the Pole of Indifference," in Wolfers, *Discord and Collaboration*, p. 96.

98. Conversely, the system did not go from balance to concert after either world war this century because, in each case, some of the major powers did not view the new order as legitimate. For a different view, see Robert Jervis, "From Balance to Concert: A Study of International Security Cooperation," in Kenneth A. Oye, ed., *Cooperation Under Anarchy* (Princeton, N.J.: Princeton University Press, 1986), pp. 58–79.

99. Thus, Kupchan and Kupchan argue that, since "all major powers are coming to hold a common view of what constitutes an acceptable status quo," the current system will likely go from balance to Concert. Charles A. Kupchan and Clifford A. Kupchan, "A New Concert for Europe," in Graham Allison and Gregory F. Treverton, eds., *Rethinking America's Security: Beyond Cold War to New World Order* (New York: Norton, 1992), p. 251. Also see Kupchan and Kupchan, "Concerts, Collective Security, and the Future of Europe," *International Security*, vol. 16, no. 1 (Summer 1991), pp. 114–161.

4: Hitler's Tripolar Strategy

1. Milan Hauner, "Did Hitler Want a World Dominion?" *Journal of Contemporary History*, vol. 13, no. 1 (January 1978), p. 24.

2. Klaus Hildebrand, *The Foreign Policy of the Third Reich*, translated by Anthony Fothergill (Berkeley and Los Angeles: The University of California Press, 1970), p. 21.

3. For Hitler's view on the balance of power and the demise of Britain and France, see Conversation, Hitler-Teleki, April 29, 1939, *Documents on German Foreign Policy* (hereafter *DGFP*), Series D, vol. 6, (Washington, D.C.: United States Government Printing Office, 1956), pp. 377–378. Similarly, Joachim von Ribbentrop declared in a conversation with M. Cincar-Markovic, the Yugoslav Foreign Minister, "Let there be no doubt about it, Germany could face calmly any combination of enemies." Conversation, Ribbentrop-Cincar-Markovik, April 25, 1939, *DGFP*, Series D, vol 6, p. 326. See also Conversation, Ribbentrop-Teleki and Csaky, April 30, 1939, *DGFP*, Series D, vol 6, p. 372, wherein Ribbentrop says, "If . . . Britain and France wanted such a trial of strength, they could have it any day."

4. "The threat to the world is precisely the growth of the space-colossi and the economic giants, like the realm of the Soviets, descendant of white Czarism, and the United States, heir of British colonial tradition; viz., encompassing and transgressing as far as their economic-political claws can reach." Karl Haushofer, as quoted in Derwent Whittlesey, Charles C. Colby, and Richard Hartshorne, *German Strategy of World Conquest* (New York and Toronto: Farrar and Rinehart, 1942), p. 162. Haushofer's ideas on German foreign policy and their influence on Hitler's expansionist goals are discussed at length in Geoffrey Stoakes, *Hitler and the Quest for World Dominion* (Leamington Spa, U.K.: Berg, 1986), chap. 5.

5. Ian Buruma, "The Europeans: The risks—and promise—of the newest superpower," *The New Republic* (August 5, 1991), p. 22. In interviews with former Waffen SS soldiers recruited in Holland, one of the soldiers, now an Amsterdam bank clerk, says: "We no longer saw Holland, Germany, or France as contradictory forces, but we saw the creation of a New Europe! That's what we were fighting for! I met some Flemish Belgians in the train to Hamburg. They had the same ideas. And besides, a greater Europe would release them from the Walloons." Another former recruit exclaims: "I have sincerely believed in a united Europe through National Socialism. That didn't happen. I still believe we will have a united Europe, but not with this democracy. Democracy cannot bind us together." Still another opines: "The division of Europe in independent nations had probably come to an end. Units grew larger all the time. Only Germany was able to achieve this in Europe. Only Germany was powerful enough to ensure that Europe played the important leading role in the world." All responses quoted in Ibid.

6. Adolf Hitler, *Hitler's Secret Book*, trans. by Salvator Attanasio, intro. by Telford Taylor (New York: Grove Press, [1928] 1961), p. 103.

7. Hitler quoted in Ibid., p. 26.

8. Hitler, speech on December 10, 1919, as quoted in Stoakes, *Hitler and the Quest for World Dominion*, p. 62.

9. Adolf Hitler, *Mein Kampf* (New York: Reynal and Hitchcock, 1941), p. 180.

10. Ibid., p. 83.

11. Ibid., p. 103; see also p. 158.

12. Gerhard L. Weinberg, *World in the Balance: Behind the Scenes of World War II* (Hanover and London: University Press of New England, 1981), p. xiii.

13. Haushofer, as quoted in Robert Strausz-Hupé, *Geopolitics: The Struggle for Space and Power* (New York: Putnam, 1942), p. 67.

14. John Lukacs, "The Coming of the Second World War," *Foreign Affairs* 68, no. 4 (Fall 1989), p. 172.

15. Hitler quoted in Hugh R. Trevor-Roper, ed., *Hitler's Table Talk, 1941–1944*, translated by Norman Cameron and R. H. Stevens (London: Weidenfeld and Nicolson, 1953), p. 199.

16. For extensive discussion on Hitler's orders to the press and the Navy regarding the United States see, Saul Friedlander, *Prelude to Downfall: Hitler and the United States, 1939–1941*, trans. by Aline B. and Alexander Werth (New York: Knopf, 1967), pp. 49–65. For Hitler's attempt to avoid incidents with the U.S. in the Atlantic, see F. H. Hinsley, *Hitler's Strategy* (Cambridge: Cambridge University Press, 1951), pp. 58–59, 169–175; James V. Compton, *The Swastika and the Eagle: Hitler, the United States, and the Origins of World War II* (Boston: Houghton Mifflin, 1967), pp. 161–173.

17. Arnold A. Offner, *American Appeasement: United States Foreign Policy and Germany, 1933–1938* (Cambridge: Harvard University Press, 1969), p. 235.

18. Dieckhoff to Weizsäcker, December 7, 1937, *DGFP*, Series D, vol. I, pp. 655–656.

19. Dieckhoff to Weizsäcker, December 20, 1937, *DGFP*, Series D, vol. I, p. 659.

20. Dieckhoff to the German Foreign Ministry, January 7, 1938, "Subject: Relations between the United States and Germany and the German-American element. Are we in a position to exert political influence on the German-Americans? The German-American Bund," *DGFP*, Series D, vol 1, pp. 664–677 at pp. 672–673.

21. Mackensen to Dieckhoff, December 22, 1937, *DGFP*, Series D, vol 1, p. 662.

22. Lukacs, "The Coming of the Second World War," p. 172, fn. 2.

23. Hitler, *Hitler's Secret Book*, p. 104. See also Hillgruber, *Germany and the Two World Wars*, pp. 50 51.

24. Hillgruber, *Germany and the Two World Wars*, p. 51.

25. Conversation, Hitler-Teleki, April 29, 1939, *DGFP*, Series D, vol 6, pp. 377–378.

26. Trevor-Roper, *Hitler's Table Talk*, p. 182.

27. Hitler in Ibid., pp. 586–587. See also Ibid., p. 182.

28. William Carr, *Hitler: A Study in Personality and Politics* (London: Edward Arnold, 1978), p. 87.

29. Hitler in Trevor-Roper, *Hitler's Table Talk*, p. 24.

30. Gerhard L. Weinberg, "Hitler's Image of the United States," *The American Historical Review*, vol. 69, no. 4 (July 1964), p. 1009.

31. Hitler in Trevor-Roper, *Hitler's Table Talk*, p. 93.

32. For a good survey of the literature on this point, see Hauner, "Did Hitler Want a World Dominion?" pp. 15–32.

33. The concept of *blitzkrieg* or "lightning war" has generated a mountain of literature and a heated historical debate. See, for instance, the comments by David Kaiser, Tim Mason, and Richard Overy in "Debate: Germany, 'Domestic Crisis' and War in 1939," *Past and Present*, no. 122 (February 1989), pp. 200–240. Some historians believe that *blitzkrieg* refers to the waging of short wars and the development of an extremely flexible German war economy—one that efficiently mobilized resources to meet the needs of a specific military campaign without lowering the living standards of the working class. See Alan S. Milward, *War, Economy and Society: 1939–1945* (Berkeley and Los Angeles: University of California Press, 1977); and Martin L. Van Creveld, *Hitler's Strategy 1940–1941: The Balkan Clue* (London: Cambridge University Press, 1973), p. 235, note 170.

Critics of this "functionalist" conception of *blitzkrieg* say that it overemphasizes the degree to which domestic politics and economic circumstances drove Hitler's military and foreign policy decisions. The German economy, they charge, was never in crisis after 1935; and the German working class, "after six years of repression and party rule and propaganda," was in no condition to wage a revolution. Richard Overy, "Germany, 'Domestic Crisis' and War in 1939," *Past and Present*, no. 116 (August 1987), p. 158. Overy argues that "neither Hitler nor Goering lost sight of the perspectives of *Mein Kampf*" and that "total war, not *Blitzkrieg*, was the end product of German preparations." Richard J. Overy, *Goering: "The Iron Man"* (London: Routledge & Kegan Paul, 1984), p. 76. Because Hitler's grand strategy, I believe, is generally consistent with *Mein Kampf*, I find the intentionalists' argument more persuasive than that of the functionalists.

34. Esmonde M. Robertson, *Hitler's Pre-War Policy and Military Plans, 1933–1939* (London: Longmans, 1963), p. 7. For the law of odd and even numbers, see Lewis B. Namier, *Vanquished Supremacies* (London: Hamish Hamilton, 1958), p. 170; see also Robert Jervis, "Systems Effects," draft manuscript, October 1989, p. 25.

35. See Schweller, "Bandwagoning For Profit," p. 94.

36. Grieco, "Understanding the Problem of International Cooperation," p. 303.

37. See Robert Axelrod, *The Evolution of Cooperation* (New York: Basic Books, 1984). I am grateful to Sean M. Lynn-Jones for this insight.

38. I am grateful to Jack Snyder for pointing this out.

39. Albert O. Hirschman, *National Power and the Structure of Foreign Trade* (Berkeley, Calif.: University of California Press, [1945], 1980), pp. 30–32. Asymmetrical interdependence means that the more dependent state benefits more from the relationship than the less dependent state.

40. Hitler, *Mein Kampf*, p. 185.

41. Ibid., p. 191.

42. Ibid., pp. 190–191.

43. Ibid., p. 193.

44. For reasons why democratic states, like interwar France, do not wage preventive wars, see Randall L. Schweller, "Domestic Structure and Preventive War: Are Democracies More Pacific?" *World Politics*, vol. 44, no. 2 (January 1992), pp. 235–269.

45. "Speaking deliberately as a German National Socialist, I desire to declare in the name of the National Government, and of the whole movement of national regeneration, that we in this new Germany are filled with deep understanding for the same feelings and opinions and for the rightful claims to life of the other nations. The present generation of this new Germany which so far has only experienced the poverty, misery and distress of its own people, has suffered too deeply from the madness of our time to be able to contemplate treating others in the same way. Our boundless love for and loyalty to our own national traditions makes us respect the national claims of others and makes us desire from the bottom of our hearts to live with them in peace and friendship. We therefore have no use for the idea of Germanization." Hitler, speech delivered on May 17, 1933, quoted in *Nazism*, Document #491, p. 658.

46. Hitler, *Mein Kampf*, p. 180.

47. Adolf Hitler, Minutes of a Conference on May 23, 1939, The Führer's Study, *DGFP*, Series D, vol 6, p. 575.

48. Hitler, *Mein Kampf*, p. 181.

49. The Hossbach memorandom, *DGFP*, Series D, vol 1, pp. 29–39 at pp. 31–32.

50. Stoakes, *Hitler and the Quest for World Dominion*, pp. 59–60, 96.

51. Hitler, *Mein Kampf*, p. 183.

52. Ibid.

53. Ibid., p. 892. The Kaiser had followed a ruinous anti-British policy because they were "unpleasantly affected by the idea that now one would have to 'pull the chestnuts out of the fire' for England; as if an alliance were at all conceivable on a basis other than that of mutual business transactions! Such a business could very well have been done with England." Ibid., pp. 184–185.

54. France wanted its ally Poland to gain sole possession of this disputed province; Britain favored an equitable solution between the two claimants, Germany and Poland.

55. Hitler, private conversation in December 1922, as quoted in Stoakes, *Hitler and the Quest for World Dominion*, p. 98.

56. Hitler, *Mein Kampf*, p. 902.

57. A. Rosenberg (1922), as quoted in Stoakes, *Hitler and the Quest for World Dominion*, p. 99.

58. Hitler as quoted in John Toland, *Adolf Hitler* (New York: Doubleday, 1976), p. 693.

59. Hitler, *Hitler's Secret Book*, p. 103. For Hitler's thoughts on an Anglo-American rivalry and an eventual war between the U.S. and an Anglo-German coalition, see Conversation, Hitler-Ciano, October 25, 1941, *DGFP*, Series D, vol 13, p. 693; Trevor-Roper, *Hitler's Table Talk*, pp. 14, 26, 186, 188; Conversation, Hitler-Mussolini, June 3, 1941, *DGFP*, Series D, vol 12, p. 946.

60. K. Lüdecke, as quoted in Stoakes, *Hitler and the Quest for World Dominion*, pp. 106–107.

61. Hitler, *Mein Kampf*, p. 903.

62. Hitler, speech on November 14, 1922, as quoted in Stoakes, *Hitler and the Quest for World Dominion.*, p. 107.

63. Hitler, *Mein Kampf*, pp. 964–965. Emphasis in original.

64. Ibid., p. 908.

65. Ibid., pp. 930–931.

66. Frank William Iklé, *German-Japanese Relations, 1936–1940* (New York: Bookman Associates, 1956), p. 25.

67. Ibid., p. 21,

68. Herbert Feis, *The Road to Pearl Harbor* (Princeton: Princeton University Press, 1950), p. 112.

69. Iklé, *German-Japanese Relations*, p. 28.

70. E. L. Woodward, Rohan Butler, and Anne Orde, eds., *Documents on British Foreign Policy 1919–1939* (hereafter cited as *DBFP*) 2nd series, vol. 6 (London: Her Majesty's Stationery Office, 1946), pp. 152–153.

71. Hitler, *Mein Kampf*, pp. 930–931.

72. Hitler, as quoted in *Nazism*, p. 667.

73. Hinsley, *Hitler's Strategy*, pp. 6–7.

74. During a meeting with Hitler in Berlin in March 1935, the British Foreign Secretary noted that "the Chancellor had so expressed his thoughts that they seemed to require closer relations between Britain and Germany than between Britain and France. Britain wanted to be on good terms with Germany, but must not allow this to prejudice her friendship with France. They did not wish to substitute one friend for another. They did not wish to have special engagements with anyone; Britain was an entirely uncommitted member of the Society of Nations. It would not be 'fair' were he to allow the impression to be created that Britain was being disloyal to one friend while seeking another." Sir John Simon, in *Nazism*, Document #495, p. 666.

75. *DGFP*, Series C, vol 3, pp. 873–876; Robertson, *Hitler's Pre-War Policy*, p. 54.

76. David Calleo, *The German Problem Reconsidered: Germany and the World Order, 1870 to the Present* (London: Cambridge University Press, 1978), p. 95; Toland, *Adolf Hitler*, pp. 536–537, 614–616, 692–694; Conversation, Göring-Welles, March 4, 1940, *DGFP*, Series D, vol 8, p. 852; Sir Nevile Henderson, *Failure of a Mission: Berlin, 1937–1939* (New York: Putnam, 1940), pp. 279–280.

77. Taylor, *The Origins of the Second World War*, p. 80.

78. Interrogation of von Neurath at the *Nuremburg Trials: Nazi Conspiracy and Aggression*, Suppl. B (Washington, D.C.: United States Government Printing Office, 1948), p. 1492.

79. Wolfers, *Britain and France Between Two Wars*, p. 147. For a more detailed discussion of this complex and still-controversial issue, see Robert J. Young, *In Command of France: French Foreign Policy and Military Planning, 1933–1940* (Cambridge: Harvard University Press, 1978), chap. 4.

80. Snyder, "The Security Dilemma in Alliance Politics," p. 471.

81. According to Glenn Snyder, dependence is a function of "(1) a state's need for assistance in war as a function of the extent to which its military capability falls short of its potential adversary's capability; (2) its partner's capacity to supply the assistance (the greater the partner's strength, the more one is dependent on him, up to the point where the combined strength provides sufficient security); (3) the state's degree of conflict and tension with the adversary (the greater the conflict and tension, the more likely one will have to call on the partner for help); and (4) the state's realignment alternatives (the more numerous the alternatives, and the more satisfactory they are, the less dependence on the present partner)." p. 472.

82. See Brian J. C. McKercher, "Old Diplomacy and New: The Foreign Office and Foreign Policy, 1919–1939," in Dockrill and McKercher, *Diplomacy and World Power*, pp. 79–114.

83. Quoted in Ibid., p. 96.

84. Ibid., p. 91.

85. Quoted in Goldstein, "The Evolution of British Diplomatic Strategy," p. 117.

86. Quoted in Ibid., p. 120.

87. Quoted in Ibid.

88. Quoted in Ibid., pp. 119–120.

89. Quoted in McKercher, "Old Diplomacy and New," p. 97.

90. Ibid., p. 113.

91. Karl Bracher, quoted in Joachim C. Fest, *Hitler*, translated by Richard and Clara Winston (San Diego, New York, and London: Harcourt Brace Jovanovich, 1974), p. 492.

92. Dodd to Roosevelt, July 29, 1935, in Edgar B. Nixon, ed., *Franklin D. Roosevelt and Foreign Affairs* (hereafter *FDRFA*) vol. 2 (Cambridge: Harvard University Press, 1969), pp. 588–590 at p. 589.

93. Hitler, quoted in *Nazism*, p. 667.

5: The Path To War, 1935–1939

1. Marshal Foch, as quoted in Stephen A. Schuker, "France and the Remilitarization of the Rhineland, 1936," *French Historical Studies*, vol. 14, no. 3 (Spring 1986), 302. For the strategic significance of the Rhineland, see Jere Clemens King, *Foch*

versus Clemenceau: France and German Dismemberment, 1918–1919 (Cambridge: Harvard University Press, 1960).

2. Nicole Jordan, "The Cut Price War on the Peripheries: The French General Staff, the Rhineland and Czechoslovakia," in Boyce and Robertson, *Paths to War*, pp. 132–133.

3. Quoted in Anthony Adamthwaite, *France and the Coming of the Second World War, 1936–1939* (London: Frank Cass, 1977), p. 22.

4. Aside from the treaty with Poland, the pacts, circumscribed by the principles and procedures of the League, were not military alliances in the full sense of the term. Moreover, France was not linked by a pact of mutual assistance to the Little Entente (Czechoslovakia, Romania, and Yugoslavia); and the Entente was directed not against Germany but Hungary, the most revisionist of the small powers in East Central Europe. The best study of France's eastern alliance system is Wandycz, *The Twilight of French Eastern Alliances, 1926–1936*. For France's defensive military posture, see Judith M. Hughes, *To the Maginot Line: The Politics of French Military Preparation in the 1920's* (Cambridge: Harvard University Press, 1971); and Richard D. Challener, *The French Theory of the Nation in Arms, 1866–1939* (New York: Russell and Russell, 1955), chap. 3.

5. Robert Young "La guerre de longue durée: Some Reflections on French Strategy and Diplomacy in the 1930s," in Adrian Preston, ed., *General Staffs and Diplomacy Before the Second World War* (London: Croom Helm, 1978), pp. 43, 46.

6. Jordan, "The Cut Price War on the Peripheries," pp. 128–166. Note that Jordan's explanation of French strategy contradicts Young's discussion of the French idea of a long war, in which, he argues, France fully expected that it would bear the brunt of the initial German attack and would fight virtually without allies for the first two years of the war. See Young, "La guerre de longué durée." Gamelin's so-called "Plan D *bis*" mobilization strategy, which assumed that Germany would reoccupy the Rhineland and then attack in the east, supports Jordan's argument, which I find more compelling than Young's. To my knowledge, however, no one has yet raised the contradiction inherent in the two explanations of French strategy.

7. Joseph Paul-Boncour, as quoted in Wandycz, *The Twilight of French Eastern Alliances*, p. 245.

8. Jean-Baptiste Duroselle, as quoted in Ibid., p. 299.

9. Ibid.

10. Adamthwaite, *France and the Coming of the Second World War*, pp. 31–32; Geoffrey Warner, *Pierre Laval and the Eclipse of France* (New York: Macmillan, 1968), chaps. 2 and 3; Jordan, "The Cut Price War on the Peripheries."

11. Laval, as quoted in Warner, *Pierre Laval and the Eclipse of France*, p. 94.

12. Esmonde M. Robertson, *Mussolini as Empire-Builder: Europe and Africa, 1932–36* (London: Macmillan, 1977), pp. 149–150; Smith, *Mussolini*, p. 194; Warner, *Pierre Laval and the Eclipse of France*, p. 94.

13. Jordan, "The Cut-Price War," p. 140; also see Warner, *Laval and the Eclipse of France*, pp. 94–95.

14. *DGFP*, Series C, vol 4, pp. 113–114, 209, 337–339, 417–419.

15. The German Ambassador to Italy stated: "[T]he French sought systematically to outbid Germany's neutrality in the Abyssinian question by showing marked sympathy for Italy's action. This development received tremendous impetus from the Anglo-German Naval Agreement which caused acute dissatisfaction with Britain and redoubled fears of Germany in Paris, and thus automatically reinforced the efforts being made there to draw closer to Italy." Ulrich von Hassell, July 5, 1935, *DGFP*, Series C, vol 4, p. 418.

16. Telegram from Laval to the French ambassador in Rome, Josée de Chambrun, July 19, 1935, as quoted in Warner, *Pierre Laval and the Eclipse of France*, p. 96.

17. Robertson, *Mussolini as Empire-Builder*, p. 150.

18. Adamthwaite, *France and the Coming of the Second World War*, p. 36.

19. Albert Speer, *Inside the Third Reich*, trans. Richard and Clara Winston (New York: Macmillan, 1970), p. 72.

20. Ibid.

21. Jordan, "Cut Price War on the Peripheries," p. 145.

22. *DBFP*, 3rd Ser., vol 5, Doc. 598, "Sir P. Loraine (Rome) to Viscount Halifax, May 23, 1939," p. 655.

23. Wolfers, *Britain and France Between the Two Wars*, p. 143.

24. Mussolini at a meeting of the Grand Council on February 4, 1939, as quoted in F. W. Deakin, *The Brutal Friendship: Mussolini, Hitler and the Fall of Italian Fascism* (New York: Harper and Row, 1962), pp. 5–6.

25. Denis Mack Smith, "Appeasement as a Factor in Mussolini's Foreign Policy," in Wolfgang J. Mommsen and Lothar Kettenacker, *The Fascist Challenge and the Policy of Appeasement* (London: Allen and Unwin, 1983), p. 260.

26. In October of 1935, however, von Hassell told Mussolini that, in Hitler's judgment, "the time for the struggle between the *static* and the dynamic nations was by a long way premature." Hassell quoted in Robertson, *Hitler's Pre-War Policy*, p. 63.

27. *DGFP*, Series C, vol 3, pp. 1043–1044.

28. Hitler quoted in Robertson, *Hitler's Pre-War Policy*, p. 71.

29. Confidential briefing by Dertinger of the Propaganda Ministry to the German press regarding Hitler's views, December 2, 1936, quoted in *Nazism*, Document #500, pp. 674–675.

30. *Nazism*, p. 699.

31. For a concise summary of the Italian-German relationship during this period, see Donald Cameron Watt, "The Rome-Berlin Axis, 1936–1940: Myth and Reality," *Review of Politics*, vol. 22, no. 4 (October 1960), pp. 519–543.

32. Speer, *Inside the Third Reich*, p. 121.

33. For the full text of the Anti-Comintern Pact with the secret additional agreement see *DGFP*, Series D, vol 1, p. 734, fn.

34. In an address before the German *Wehrmacht* Academy on November 25, 1937, the German Ambassador to the Soviet Union, Schulenburg, stated: "Although the Soviet Union has at its disposal numerous submarines, a great number of tanks and planes, it ought not to be forgotten that the young Soviet industry is still unprepared for the demands of the greatly increased armed forces and that the Soviet Union has reverted to the old Russian principle of operating on the basis of *quantity* and not of *quality*." Yet, in reference to these difficulties and the "wave of murder and persecution" that "has gravely shaken the organism of the Soviet State," Schulenburg warned: "It would be unwise to assume that this downward development *must* be permanent." *DGFP*, Series D, vol 1, pp. 899–900.

35. *DGFP*, Series D, vol 1, p. 757.

36. Hassell quoted in *Ciano's Diary, 1937–1938*, October 24, 1937, p. 24. For a similar statement, see Hassell's October 20, 1937 telegram to the German Foreign Ministry, in *DGFP*, Series D, vol 1, pp. 16–18.

37. *Ciano's Diary*, November 6, 1937, p. 29. In his diary entry of November 5, 1937, Ciano noted: "The English . . . have shown the Japanese that they are very worried at the signing of the pact. They feel that the system is closing against them." Ibid., p. 28.

38. *Ciano's Diary*, November 2, 1937, p. 27. See also, Robertson, *Hitler's Pre-War Policy*, p. 102.

39. Recorded by Hassell in his November 10, 1937 Political Report on "The Effects of the Anti-Comintern Agreement" in *DGFP*, Series D, vol 1, p. 27. Ciano also said: "The alliance of three military empires the size of Italy, Germany, and Japan throws an unprecedented weight of armed strength into the balance of power. England will have to reconsider her position everywhere." *Ciano's Diary*, November 1, 1937, p. 27.

40. Iklé, *German-Japanese Relations*, p. 61.

41. Unsigned Memorandum, "Note of the Discussion held on July 3, 1935, between the Führer and Chancellor, Foreign Minister Freiherr von Neurath, Minister President Göring and Herr von Ribbentrop, for Germany, and the Polish Foreign Minister, Beck, and the Polish Ambassador in Berlin, Lipski, for Poland" in *DGFP*, Series C, vol 4, pp. 398–407 at pp. 406–407.

42. Hossbach memorandum, *DGFP*, Series D, vol 1, pp. 29–39. For a slightly condensed version, see *Nazism*, Document #503, pp. 680–687. For an insightful discussion on the November 5 conference, see Robertson, *Hitler's Pre-War Policy*, chap. 11.

43. *DGFP*, Series D, vol 1, p. 32.

44. Ibid., p. 36.

45. See Williamson Murray, *The Change in the European Balance of Power, 1938–1939: The Path to Ruin* (Princeton: Princeton University Press, 1984), esp. ch. 1 and pp. 281, 290–294.

46. Anthony Read and David Fisher, *The Deadly Embrace: Hitler, Stalin, and the Nazi-Soviet Pact, 1939–1941* (New York: Norton, 1988), p. 24.

47. *DGFP*, Series D, vol 1, pp. 573–576; Robertson, *Hitler's Pre-War Policy*, pp. 115–16; Speer, *Inside the Third Reich*, pp. 109–110.

48. *DGFP*, Series D, vol 5, pp. 361–366; also quoted in Robertson, *Hitler's Pre-War Strategy*, p. 149; Speer, *Inside the Third Reich*, p. 111.

49. From Churchill, *The Gathering Storm*, as quoted in Read and Fisher, *The Deadly Embrace*, pp. 29 and 31.

50. For von Ribbentrop's anti-British, pro-colonial foreign policy, see Hildebrand, *The Foreign Policy of the Third Reich*, pp. 48–50.

51. Haushofer, as quoted in Whittlesey et al., *German Strategy of World Conquest*, p. 86.

52. Haushofer, as quoted in Ibid., p. 166.

53. See Read and Fisher, *The Deadly Embrace*, p. 27.

54. Murray, *The Change in the European Balance of Power*, pp. 292–293. Also see Peter Liberman, *Does Conquest Pay?: The Exploitation of Occupied Industrial Societies* (Princeton: Princeton University Press, 1996).

55. Hildebrand makes this point in *The Foreign Policy of the Third Reich*, pp. 83–90.

56. Halifax to Kennedy, quoted in Read and Fisher, *The Deadly Embrace*, p. 68.

57. *DBFP*, 3rd Ser., vol 5, Doc. 589, "Foreign Office Memorandum on the Anglo-Soviet Negotiations, May 22, 1939," p. 646.

58. For this interpretation of Soviet thinking, see Gerhard L. Weinberg, *Germany and the Soviet Union, 1939–1941* (Leiden, Netherlands: E. J. Brill, 1954), p. 15.

59. Trumball Higgins, *Hitler and Russia: The Third Reich in a Two-Front War, 1937–1943* (New York: Macmillan, 1966) p. 21; Joseph W. Ballantine, "Mukden to Pearl Harbor: The Foreign Policies of Japan," *Foreign Affairs*, vol. 27, no. 4 (July 1949), pp. 651–654.

60. Harold Nicolson, *Diaries and Letters, 1930–1964*, edited and condensed by Stanley Olson (London: Collins, 1980), September 26, 1938, p. 136.

61. Weinberg, *Germany and the Soviet Union*, p. 22.

62. Read and Fisher, *The Deadly Embrace*, p. 46.

63. David Kaiser in Kaiser et al., "Debate," p. 202. See also David Kaiser, *Economic Diplomacy and the Origins of the Second World War* (Princeton: Princeton University Press, 1980), pp. 263–273.

64. Kaiser in Kaiser et al, "Debate," p. 203.

65. Quoted in McSherry, *Stalin, Hitler, and Europe*, vol 1, p. 202.

66. Weinberg, *Germany and the Soviet Union*, p. 28.

67. Hitler in a conversation with Carl J. Burckhardt, the High Commissioner of the League of Nations, in Danzig (August 11, 1939), as quoted in Hillgruber, *Germany and the Two World Wars*, p. 69.

68. Ulrich von Hassell, *The Von Hassell Diaries, 1938–1944: The Story of the Forces Against Hitler Inside Germany, as Recorded by Ambassador Ulrich von Hassell, a Leader of the Movement* (Garden City, New York: Doubleday, 1947), p. 67.

6: The Western and Polar Wars, 1939–1945

1. Hitler quoted from memory by Speer in *Inside the Third Reich*, p. 163.
2. Hitler, May 23, 1939, quoted in Wilmot, *The Struggle For Europe*, p. 21.
3. Ibid.
4. Franz Halder, *The Halder War Diary, 1939–1942*, edited by Charles Burdick and Hans-Adolf Jacobsen (Novato, Calif.: Presidio, 1988), p. 165.
5. Halder's diary entry of May 30, 1940, in Ibid., p. 172.
6. Churchill, quoted in Wilmot, *The Struggle for Europe*, p. 20.
7. Hinsley, *Hitler's Strategy*, p. 37.
8. Kecskemeti, *Strategic Surrender*, pp. 53–54.
9. Hitler quoted in Wilmot, *The Struggle for Europe*, p. 26.
10. Hitler quoted in Wilmot, Ibid., p. 28.
11. To obtain bases for the naval siege against Britain, the German Naval staff had devised the Norwegian campaign, which was also intended to secure Germany's supply of Swedish iron ore. Hitler reluctantly agreed to this plan after being persuaded that Britain might land in Norway first.
12. The U-boat arm, which Admiral Doenitz considered "the backbone of warfare against England and of political pressure on her," had only 26 U-boats suitable for Atlantic operations with only 8 or 9 continually at sea, when the required minimum was 300 U-boats, out of which 90 could be kept at sea at all times. Hinsley, *Hitler's Strategy*, pp. 6–7.
13. Quoted in Ibid., p. 29.
14. See George Quester, "Bargaining and Bombing During World War II in Europe," *World Politics*, vol. 15, no. 3 (April 1963), pp. 417–437.
15. See Posen, *The Sources of Military Doctrine*, chap. 5; Christensen and Snyder, "Chain Gangs and Passed Bucks," pp. 162–165.
16. Christensen and Snyder, "Chain Gangs and Passed Bucks."
17. Ibid., p. 165.
18. See Donald Cameron Watt, *How War Came: The Immediate Origins of the Second World War, 1938–1939* (London: Heinemann, 1989), chap. 6.
19. Wesley K. Wark, *The Ultimate Enemy: British Intelligence and Nazi Germany, 1933–1939* (Ithaca: Cornell University Press, 1985), p. 217.
20. Ibid.
21. Milward, *War, Economy and Society*, p. 47.
22. Timothy J. McKeown, "The Foreign Policy of a Declining Power," *International Organization*, vol. 45, no. 2 (Spring 1991), p. 270.

23. Douglas Johnson, "The French View," in R. Douglas, ed., *1939: A Retrospective Forty Years After* (London: MacMillan, 1983), p. 58.

24. *DBFP*, 3rd Ser., vol 3, Doc. 325, "Record of Anglo-French Conversations at the Quai d'Orsay on November 24, 1938" (London: Her Majesty's Stationery Office, 1950), pp. 288, 291–292. See also, Murray, *The Change in the European Balance of Power*, p. 275.

25. Nigel Nicolson, ed., *The Diaries and Letters of Harold Nicolson: The War Years, 1939–1945* (New York: Atheneum, 1967), p. 45 (emphasis added).

26. J. R. M. Butler, *Grand Strategy*, vol. 2: *September 1939–June 1941* (London: Her Majesty's Stationery Office, 1957), p. 267.

27. Thies, "Alliances and Collective Goods," p. 323.

28. Wark, *The Ultimate Enemy*, p. 215.

29. Butler, *Grand Strategy*, p. 172.

30. Ibid.

31. Quoted in Correlli Barnett, *The Collapse of British Power* (New York: Morrow, 1972), p. 583.

32. Richardson, "New Perspectives on Appeasement," p. 303.

33. Neville Chamberlain as quoted in Sheila Lawlor, *Churchill and the Politics of War, 1940–1941* (Cambridge: Cambridge University Press, 1994), pp. 53, 56.

34. Ibid., pp. 48–49.

35. Ibid., p. 58.

36. Eleanor M. Gates, *End of the Affair: The Collapse of the Anglo-French Alliance, 1939–40* (London: George Allen & Unwin, 1981), p. 566. For a similar reaction to the French defeat, see David Dilks, ed., *The Diaries of Sir Alexander Cadogan, O.M. 1938–1945* (London: Cassell, 1971), pp. 292–293.

37. Michael Howard, *The Continental Commitment* (London: Temple Smith, 1972), p. 117.

38. Posen, *The Sources of Military Doctrine*, p. 171.

39. Churchill quoted in Butler, *Grand Strategy*, p. 184.

40. Sidney Aster, " 'Guilty Men': The Case of Neville Chamberlain," in Boyce and Robertson, *Paths to War*, pp. 242–243 (emphasis added).

41. Christopher Thorne, *The Approach of War, 1938–1939* (London: Macmillan, 1967), pp. 14–15.

42. Aster, "Guilty Men," p. 247.

43. Chamberlain quoted in Ibid., p. 246.

44. Ribbentrop Memorandum to Hitler, January 2, 1938, "The Possibilities of Agreement With Great Britain, January 1938," *DGFP*, Series D, vol 1, pp. 163, 165 (emphasis in original).

45. Ibid., p. 167.

46. Chamberlain quoted in Aster, " 'Guilty Men," pp. 252–253.

47. Chamberlain quoted in Ibid., p. 253.

48. See Watt, *How War Came*, pp. 94, 102.

49. Hildebrand, *The Foreign Policy of the Third Reich*, p. 93.

50. William L. Langer and S. Everett Gleason, *The Undeclared War, 1940–1941* (New York: Harper, 1953), p. 27.

51. The Tripartite Pact between Japan, Italy, and Germany, September 27, 1940, as quoted in *Nazism*, Document #576, p. 796.

52. Ibid.

53. Weinberg, *A World at Arms*, p. 30.

54. Hildebrand, *The Foreign Policy of the Third Reich*, p. 102.

55. General Halder, as quoted in Rich, *Hitler's War Aims*, p. 228.

56. The record of Molotov's conversations with Hitler and Ribbentrop appear in *DGFP*, Series D, vol 11, Nos. 325, 326, 329, and 348.

57. Van Creveld, *Hitler's Strategy*, p. 70.

58. Hitler-Molotov meeting on November 13, 1940, *DGFP*, Series D, vol 11, no. 328, pp. 555–556.

59. Ibid., p. 557.

60. Ibid., p. 559.

61. Ribbentrop as quoted in Geoffrey Roberts, *The Soviet Union and the Origins of the Second World War: Russo-German Relations and the Road to War, 1933–1941* (New York: St. Martin's Press, 1995), p. 129.

62. Ibid., pp. 559–560.

63. Ibid., p. 560.

64. *DGFP*, Series D, vol 11, no. 329, pp. 567–568.

65. Hitler on November 15, 1940, quoted in Van Creveld, *Hitler's Strategy*, p. 81.

66. Anton W. DePorte, *Europe Between the Superpowers: The Enduring Balance* (New Haven and London: Yale University Press, 1979), p. 42.

67. Hitler's directive No. 24, March 5, 1941, *DGFP*, Series D, vol 12, pp. 219–220 (emphasis in original).

68. Ibid., p. 220.

69. Conversation, Ribbentrop-Matsuoka, March 31, 1941, in Ibid., p. 413.

70. Admiral Raeder, as quoted in Hinsley, *Hitler's Strategy*, p. 179.

71. Compton, *The Swastika and the Eagle*, p. 111; Boetticher telegram, October 2, 1940, *DGFP*, Series D, vol 11, p. 235.

72. Conversation, Hitler-Matsuoka, April 1, 1941, *DGFP*, Series D, vol 12, p. 386.

73. Ibid., p. 388.

74. Ibid. p. 389.

75. Ibid. p. 388.

76. Ibid.

77. Quoted in Hinsley, *Hitler's Strategy*, p. 131. Also see Hildebrand, *The Foreign Policy of the Third Reich*, p. 101.

78. Hitler, as quoted in Hinsley, *Hitler's Strategy*, p. 132.

79. Ibid.

80. Calleo, *The German Problem Reconsidered*, p. 108.

81. Stalin quoted in Isaac Deutscher, *Stalin: A Political Biography*, 2nd ed. (New York: Oxford University Press, 1949), p. 411.

82. Robert C. Tucker, *Stalin in Power: The Revolution From Above, 1928–1941* (New York: Norton, 1990), p. 345.

83. Louis Fischer, *Russia's Road From Peace to War: Soviet Foreign Relations, 1917–1941* (New York: Harper and Row, 1969), p. 322.

84. Cripps report of July 16, 1940, British Public Record Office, Foreign Office 371/24846, f. 10, N 6526/30/38. Quoted in Weinberg, *World in the Balance*, p. 7.

85. Henderson, *Failure of a Mission*, p. 259.

86. Deutscher, *Stalin*, p. 441. For Stalin's overestimation of Anglo-French strength, see Adam B. Ulam, *Expansion and Coexistence: Soviet Foreign Policy, 1917–73*, 2nd ed. (New York: Holt, Rinehart and Winston, 1974), pp. 227, 229, 264.

87. Statement by Stalin before the Eighteenth Congress of the CPSU on March 10, 1939, as quoted in Ulam, *Expansion and Coexistence*, p. 264.

88. Tucker, *Stalin in Power*, pp. 587, 592.

89. Voroshilov quoted in Ibid., p. 592.

90. Supporting this view of Soviet foreign policy, Sir Nevile Henderson wrote: " . . . I always believed that Moscow's chief aim was to embroil Germany and the Western Powers in a common ruin and to emerge as the *tertius gaudens* of the conflict between them. This was, up to August, similarly the professed view of all Germans from Hitler downward who commented on our Russian negotiations." Henderson, *Failure of a Mission*, p. 259.

Ironically, Stalin accused the Western democracies of engaging in an "abettor" strategy, which he himself would employ: "The [democracies'] policy of non-intervention reveals an eagerness, a desire . . . not to hinder Germany, say, from enmeshing herself in European affairs, from embroiling herself in a war with the Soviet Union; to allow all the belligerents to sink deeply into the mire of war, to encourage them surreptitiously in this; and then, when they have become weak enough, to appear on the scene with fresh strength, to appear, of course, 'in the interest of peace,' and to dictate conditions to the enfeebled belligerents." Quoted in McSherry, *Stalin, Hitler, and Europe*, pp. 120–121.

91. Stalin quoted in Tucker, *Stalin in Power*, pp. 597–598.

92. Though debate exists on this point, Barry Leach argues that Hitler never wavered in his belief that war with the Soviet Union was inevitable. See Barry A. Leach, *German Strategy Against Russia, 1939–1941* (Oxford: Clarendon Press, 1973), chaps. 2 and 3. For the preventive-war aspects of Hitler's strategy, see Rich, *Hitler's War Aims*, chaps. 9, 14, 15, and 18. For the propensity of authoritarian regimes to wage preventive wars, see Schweller, "Domestic Structure and Preventive War."

93. James E. McSherry, *Stalin, Hitler, and Europe*, vol. 2, *The Imbalance of Power, 1939–1941* (Arlington, VA: The Open-Door Press, 1970), p. 254.

94. Cripps to Halifax, August 2, 1940, British Foreign Office Papers, Public Records Office, 371/24845. As quoted in Douglas, *New Alliances*, p. 40.

95. Hildebrand, *The Foreign Policy of the Third Reich*, p. 115.

96. Telegram from Ribbentrop to Ott, no. 1383, August 25, 1941, *DGFP.*, Series D, vol 13, p. 377.

97. Telegram from Ribbentrop to Ott, August 25, 1941, *DGFP*, Series D, vol 13, pp. 375–376.

98. Amau quoted in a telegram from Ott to Berlin, August 29, 1941, *DGFP*, Series D, vol 13, p. 410.

99. Hildebrand, *The Foreign Policy of The Third Reich*, p. 115.

100. Most power analysts agree that "nations face a 'power gradient,' which produces a decline in national capabilities due to distance." Jacek Kugler and Marina Arbetman, "Choosing Among Measures of Power: A Review of the Empirical Record," in Richard J. Stoll and Michael D. Ward, eds., *Power in World Politics* (Boulder, CO: Lynne Rienner, 1989), p. 66 and the table on p. 76; and Bruce Bueno de Mesquita, *The War Trap* (New Haven: Yale University Press, 1981), pp. 104–109.

101. Conversation, Hitler-Matsuoka, April 4, 1941, *DGFP*, Series D, vol 12, p. 455.

102. Essentially, Hitler gambled that Germany would win the race against time. Recognizing that Germany would not be fully prepared for the final hegemonic war against the U.S. until 1943–1945, Hitler claimed that in 1941, the Axis was in far better shape than the United States. History proved him wrong in this assessment. For analysis of the many problems with Germany's war economy, see Klein, *Germany's Economic Preparations for War*; Milward, *The German Economy at War*; and Berenice A. Carroll, *Design for Total War: Arms and Economics in the Third Reich* (The Hague: Mouton, 1968); and Murray, *The Change in the European Balance of Power*.

103. For the idealist-realist debate within the administration and Roosevelt's disagreement with aspects of the isolationist creed, see Reynolds, *The Creation of the Anglo-American Alliance*, pp. 27–29.

104. Offner, *American Appeasement*, pp. 31–32.

105. Robert A. Divine, *Roosevelt and World War II*, (Baltimore: The Johns Hopkins Press, 1969), p. 8.

106. Samuel Rosenman, ed., *The Public Papers and Addresses of Franklin D. Roosevelt*, vol. 5 (New York: Macmillan, 1942), p. 217.

107. For the British interim finance crisis and the underlying mutual distrust between the British and Americans, see Warren F. Kimball, " 'Beggar My Neighbor': America and the British Interim Finance Crisis, 1940–1941," *The Journal of Economic History*, vol. 29, no. 4 (December 1969), pp. 758–772.

108. Hauner, "Did Hitler Want a World Dominion?" p. 24.

109. Mussolini speaking at the Italian Council of Ministers on December 27, 1941, as quoted in Deakin, *The Brutal Friendship*, p. 17.

110. The Malta operation was also supported by Ugo Cavallero, Chief of the Italian General Staff, and General Albert Kesselring, who commanded the German Air Force based on Sicily, both of whom warned against the Egytian campaign as too risky and ill-advised prior to solving the Mediterranean traffic problem. Rommel's swift halt at El Alamein proved the doubters correct. To stiffen the weakened Axis position at Alamein, the Italian reserves of men and shipping intended for the Malta operation were diverted to Rommel according to Mussolini's instructions.

111. For discussion of the Indian Ocean strategy, see Gerhard L. Weinberg, *Germany, Hitler, and World War II* (Cambridge: Cambridge University Press, 1996), chap. 16.

112. Rommel quoted in Deakin, *The Brutal Friendship*, p. 79.

113. Weinberg, *Germany, Hitler, and World War II*, pp. 207–211.

114. Ibid.

115. Weinberg, *A World At Arms*, p. 463; Weinberg, *Germany, Hitler, and World War II*, p. 212,

116. Quoted in Deakin, *The Brutal Friendship*, pp. 93–94.

117. Hitler as quoted in Ibid., pp. 95–96.

118. *The Von Hassell Diaries*, entry of July 20, 1943, pp. 312–313.

119. Carr, *What Is History?*, p. 91. Also see Geoffrey Hawthorn, *Plausible Worlds: Possibility and Understanding in History and the Social Sciences* (Cambridge: Cambridge University Press, 1991), ch. 1.

120. Trevor-Roper, "History and Imagination," pp. 360–361. For a brief summary of Trevor-Roper's thoughts, see Hawthorn, *Plausible Worlds*, p. 4.

121. Hildebrand, *The Foreign Policy of the Third Reich*, p. 111.

122. More than half of the Russian prisoners of war died in the camps, compounds, and extermination places. For the story of Nazi Germany's unwillingness to use woman power and abuse and misuse of foreign workers and prisoners of war, see Edward L. Homze, *Foreign Labor in Nazi Germany* (Princeton: Princeton University Press, 1967).

123. Instead, Hitler met Rommel's demands for 70,000 tons a month of supplies, an Axis force of seven divisions, and a substantial amount of military hardware (260 aircraft by early 1942). All of these supplies were wasted on Rommel's two reckless offensive advances from Libya into Egypt, which not only proved to be militarily infeasible but were also undertaken at a time when all of Germany's forces should have been used to defeat the Soviets. See Martin van Creveld, *Supplying War: Logistics from Wallenstein to Patton* (Cambridge: Cambridge University Press, 1977), ch. 6, "Sirte to Alamein."

124. Taylor, *The Origins of the Second World War*, p. 278.

125. Hugh R. Trevor-Roper, ed., *The Testament of Adolf Hitler: The Hitler-Bormann Documents, February-April 1945* (London: Cassell, 1961), p. 30.

126. Ibid., pp. 107–108.

7: Conclusions

1. Waltz, *Theory of International Politics*, p. 73.

2. For a thorough review of these studies, see Patrick James, "Structural Realism and the Causes of War," *Mershon International Studies Review*, vol. 39, Suppl. 2 (October 1995), pp. 181–208.

3. Waltz, "A Response to My Critics," p. 343.

4. Singer, "System Structure, Decision Processes, and the Incidence of International War," p. 8.

5. These points are intelligently discussed in Timothy J. McKeown, "The Limitations of 'Structural' Theories of Commercial Policy," *International Organization*, vol. 40, no. 1 (Winter 1986), pp. 43–64.

6. Waltz, *Theory of International Politics*, p. 142.

7. Ibid., p. 124.

8. Morgenthau, *Politics Among Nations*, p. 137.

9. See Glenn H. Snyder, "Process Variables in Neorealist Theory," *Security Studies*, vol. 5, no. 3 (Spring 1996), p. 180.

10. James, "Structural Realism and the Causes of War," p. 197.

11. Waltz, *Theory of International Politics*, p. 167.

12. Taylor, *The Origins of the Second World War*, pp. 113–114.

13. Keohane, "Theory of World Politics," p. 173.

14. Waltz, *Theory of International Politics*, p. 91.

15. Reinhold Neibuhr, *Moral Man and Immoral Society: A Study in Ethics and Politics* (New York: Scribner's, 1932), p. 42.

16. Grey of Fallodon, *Twenty-Five Years*, pp. 5, 8.

17. Waltz, *Theory of International Politics*, p. 168.

18. Higgins, *Hitler and Russia*, p. 278.

19. Hitler, "Memorandum by Hewel of Conversation at the Berghof Between the Führer and Mr. Pirow, South African Minister of Defense and Commerce," November 24, 1938, *DGFP*, Series D, vol 4, p. 341.

20. Ribbentrop letter to Ciano, August 15, 1940, as quoted in McSherry, *Stalin, Hitler, and Europe*, vol. 2, p. 176.

21. *The Ciano Diaries, 1939–1943*, edited by Hugh Gibson (New York: Doubleday, 1946), pp. 299–300.

22. See Sheehan, *Balance of Power*, p. 57.

23. Jervis, "Cooperation Under the Security Dilemma," p. 204.

24. Robert Strausz-Hupé and Stefan T. Possony, *International Relations: In the Age of the Conflict Between Democracy and Dictatorship* (New York: McGraw Hill, 1950), pp. 231–232.

25. For a fascinating discussion of why prediction is so difficult in world politics, see Robert Jervis, "The Future of World Politics: Will It Resemble the Past?" *International Security*, vol. 16, no. 3 (Winter 1991/92), pp. 39–73.

26. See Lester Thurow, *Head to Head: The Coming Economic Battle Among Japan, Europe, and America* (New York: Morrow, 1992); Jeffrey E. Garten, *A Cold Peace: America, Japan, Germany and the Struggle for Supremacy* (New York: Times Books, 1992); Theodore H. Moran, "An Economics Agenda for Neorealists," *International Security*, vol. 18, no. 2 (Fall 1993), pp. 211–215; Jeffrey T. Bergner, *The New Superpowers: Germany, Japan, the U.S. and the New World Order* (New York: St. Martin's Press, 1991); Leonard Silk, "Some Things Are More Vital Than Money When It Comes To Creating the World Anew," *New York Times*, September 22, 1991, Section 4, p. 2; Jeffrey A. Hart, *Rival Capitalists: International Competitiveness in the United States, Japan, and Western Europe* (Ithaca, New York: Cornell University Press, 1992).

27. President Clinton, "Address to students and faculty at Waseda University, Tokyo, Japan, July 7, 1993," *U.S. Department of State Dispatch*, vol. 4, no. 28 (July 12, 1993), p. 486.

28. Thurow, *Head to Head*, p. 14.

29. Silk, "Some Things Are More Vital Than Money," p. 2.

30. John Lewis Gaddis, "Tectonics, History, and the End of the Cold War," Paper From the Mershon Center Project (Columbus, Ohio: The Ohio State University, 1992), pp. 5,7.

31. Edward Luttwak, "Obsession," *The New Republic*, February 24, 1992, p. 13. See, also, Richard Rosecrance, *The Rise of the Trading State: Commerce and Conquest in the Modern World* (New York: Basic Books, 1986); and Theodore H. Moran, "International Economics and U.S. National Security," in Charles W. Kegley, Jr and Eugene R. Wittkopf, eds., *The Future of American Foreign Policy* (New York: St. Martin's Press, 1992), pp. 307–318.

32. See Peter Schweizer, "The Growth of Economic Espionage: America is Target Number One," *Foreign Affairs*, vol. 75, no. 1 (January/February 1996), pp. 9–14.

33. Leslie H. Gelb, "Fresh Face," *New York Times*, December 8, 1991, Section 6, p. 54.

34. James M. Goldgeier and Michael McFaul, "A Tale of Two Worlds: Core and Periphery in the Post-Cold War Era," *International Organization*, vol. 46, no. 2 (Spring 1992), p. 468.

35. Thurow, *Head to Head*, p. 23.

36. Hans W. Maull, "Germany and Japan: The New Civilian Powers," in Richard K. Betts, ed., *Conflict After the Cold War: Arguments on Causes of War and Peace* (New York: Macmillan, 1994), pp. 492–504.

37. Waltz, *Theory of International Politics*, p. 131.

38. William Kristol and Robert Kagan, "Toward a Neo-Reaganite Foreign Policy," *Foreign Affairs*, vol. 75, no. 4 (July/August 1996), p. 20.

39. Bernard Brodie, *War and Politics* (New York: Macmillan, 1973), pp. 345–349.

40. Steven Erlanger, "East Europe Watches the Bear, Warily," *New York Times*, October 21, 1994, p. A1.

Index

Abandonment, 64–65
  risk of, 117, 161
Abyssinia, 75, 128, 130
  Italian designs on, 124–125
  Italo-Ethiopian War, 35, 73,
    125–126, 127
  British and French feebleness
    toward, 127
  U.S. aloofness during, 171
Africa, 35, 81, 94, 155, 174–175, 178
  North, 124, 128, 144, 155, 158, 176,
    181, 191
  South, 32
Agent-structure problem, 25
Aldrich, John, 40–41
Alexander the Great, 89
Alliances, 45–58, 59
  composition, 64
  "dilemma" of, 50, 65
  dynamics within, 64–65, 189, 196
  formation, 42–44, 45, 51–52
  freeriders in, 62, 66
  goals, 60–61, 194
  multipolar patterns, 146, 215n25
  offense/defense advantage, 25–26,
    146, 217n42, 218n43
  role of trust, 48

situation of, 1936, 132
situation of, 1938, 133
size, 61–64, 116, 194–198
  minimum winning coalition,
    61–63, 111–112, 194–196
  applied to WWII 144, 165
unity in, 187
voice opportunities, 60, 70
Allied Powers, 79, 142, 169, 174–177, 188
  intra-alliance politics of, 65
  power relative to Axis in 1939,
    141–142, 166
Alsace, 32, 98
Alsace-Lorraine, 32
Amau, Deputy Foreign Minister, 170
Anarchy, 3, 16, 45, 47–48, 51, 61
  role in shaping state behavior,
    20–21, 103
Anschluss, 81, 100, 101, 132–134
  impediment to German-Italian
    alliance, 109–110
Anti-Comintern Pact, 78, 130, 155
  Italy joins, 131
Appeasement, 74, 87 (see also
  Engagement)
  Anglo-French, at Munich, 134
  British policy, 152